The information, research, statements and opinions expressed in this work are solely that of the authors and do not reflect the view or impinge ownership on any of the parties mentioned. Logos and studio shots shown in this publication are produced by the manufacturer and/or correlating brand and are included for publicity and promotional purposes only. This work is not associated with any of the subsequent brands, organizations or copyright holders. All other photos are either taken from the author's personal collection, submitted by owner or used with permission.

All figure photography, front, spine and back cover photos shot by Matthew Goldberg (@mbg1211)
Matthew Goldberg utilizes Extreme Sets dioramas available at extreme-sets.com.

See a mistake in any of the information provided? Let us know in an e-mail to:
FigHeel@gmail.com

Fig Heel's Wrestling Figure Encyclopedia – Modern Edition (2010 – Present). Copyright © 2024 by Fig Heel. All rights reserved. Printed in the United States of America by Amazon.com, Inc. For more information, contact FigHeel@gmail.com or on social media @FigHeel

First Edition: July 2024

10 9 8 7 6 5 4 3 2 1

TABLE OF CONTENTS

INTRODUCTION	i
ALL ELITE WRESTLING (AEW)	1
JAZWARES	2
PRO WRESTLING TEES	21
DIAMOND SELECT TOYS	25
YOUTOOS	26
ALL JAPAN PRO-WRESTLING	27
GOOD SMILE COMPANY	28
GAME CHANGER WRESTLING	29
SLAM BUDDIES	30
RINGSIDE COLLECTIBLES	30
MAJOR LEAGUE WRESTLING (MLW)	31
PRO WRESTLING TEES	32
BOSS FIGHT STUDIO	32
THE MAJOR WRESTLING FIGURE PODCAST (MWFP)	33
RINGSIDE COLLECTIBLES	34
PRO WRESTLING TEES	35
MAJOR POD NETWORK	37
SUPER7	46
RELATIVITY WORLDWIDE	46
MASKED REPUBLIC	47
SUPER7	48
BOSS FIGHT STUDIO	49
MASKED WARRIORS LUCHA LIBRE USA	51
PLAYMATES TOYS	52
NEW JAPAN PRO-WRESTLING (NJPW)	53
CHARAPRO	54
TOKI-MEKI	54
FUNKO	55
SPIKE CHUNSOFT	55
GOOD SMILE COMPANY	56
MEDICOM TOY	57
STORM COLLECTIBLES	58
SUPER7	59
MAX FACTORY	59
PRO WRESTLING TEES	60
CHELLA TOYS/EPIC TOYS	60
PRO WRESTLING NOAH	61
HAO COLLECTIBLES	62
GOOD SMILE COMPANY	62
PRO WRESTLING NOAH	62
GRAPE BRAIN	62
RING OF HONOR (ROH)	63
FIGURES TOY COMPANY	64

BROTHERS GADDOR	66
PRO WRESTLING TEES	67
JAZWARES	68
SO-CAL PRO WRESTLING	69
WRESTLE WAREHOUSE	70
TOTAL NONSTOP ACTION (TNA)/IMPACT! WRESTLING	71
JAKKS PACIFIC	72
PRO WRESTLING TEES	81
SLAM BUDDIES	83
RELATIVITY WORLDWIDE	84
UNIVERSAL WRESTLING FEDERATION	85
MEDICOM TOY	86
WORLD WRESTLING ENTERTAINMENT (WWE)	87
MATTEL	88
BASIC/MAIN EVENT SERIES	88
ELITE COLLECTION	204
ULTIMATE EDITION	285
MISCELLANEOUS SCALE & ARTICULATION	294
UNCANNY BRANDS	327
FUNKO	332
WICKED COOL TOYS	344
BRIDGE DIRECT	345
MEDICOM TOY	349
PARTY ANIMAL TOYS	351
PLAYMATES TOYS	353
BAN DAI	353
JAKKS PACIFIC	354
BEVERLY HILLS TEDDY BEAR COMPANY	355
SUPER7	355
JADA TOYS	356
LOOT CRATE	358
THE LOYAL SUBJECTS	359
GOOD SMILE COMPANY	362
WWESHOP	362
FISHER PRICE	363
BULLS I TOYS	363
KIDROBOT	363
HEAD START	364
CHARACTER TOYS	364
TOMY COMPANY, LTD	365
P.M.I. LTD	365
NSI INTERNATIONAL, INC	366
TCG TOYS	366
JUNK SHOP DOG	366
MISCELLANEOUS FIGURES, UNAFFILIATED RELEASES & INDEPENDENT BRANDS	367
FIGURES TOY COMPANY	368

STORM COLLECTIBLES	372
PRO WRESTLING TEES	373
SUPER7	384
LJN	384
MEGO	384
WRESTLE WAREHOUSE	385
JUNK SHOP DOG	387
CHELLA TOYS/EPIC TOYS	388
ZOMBIE SAILOR'S TOYS	391
FC TOYS	393
RELATIVITY WORLDWIDE	394
RUSH COLLECTIBLES	395
PROVING GROUND TOYS	395
THE ASYLUM WRESTLING STORE	396
HASTTEL TOY	397
KAYFABE WRESTLING KOLLECTOR	399
GOLDEN ERA OF WRESTLING	399
MEET THE AUTHOR – FIG HEEL	400
MEET THE PHOTOGRAPHER – MATTHEW GOLDBERG	401

INTRODUCTION

Like most things in life do, The Ultimate Wrestling Figure Checklist has evolved. What started as quite literally a page-by-page list soon turned into a full color guide with photos and even contributions from former WWE Superstar Matt Cardona. In a few short years, this simple tool climbed the Amazon Bestseller list to #1 and grew into something even bigger...

Welcome to Fig Heel's Wrestling Figure Encyclopedia!

If you are reading this, I can only assume you are a member of the incredible community of wrestling figure collecting! Whether you stick to one specific company or graze across the plane, this tool will assist in keeping track of everything you have, want and need!

The Wrestling Figure Encyclopedia has been split into two separate volumes: Modern (which focuses on releases between 2010 to present day) & Vintage (focusing on all releases pre-dating 2010 – coming soon)! With a vast array of collectors only collecting vintage or only collecting modern releases, this allowed me to include more pictures & more entries while also keeping the pricing down.

So, how do you navigate The Wrestling Figure Encyclopedia? First, each wrestling promotion has their own section in the book and each section is then divided into micro sections for each toy company that manufactured product. Each toy company is then split up by individual toy line and each toy line is split up by series & lineup to make navigating a little simpler.

On the right side of each list, you will find two "empty" boxes. The first of the two boxes is the "MOC Box" and the second is the "Loose Box". This is how you will categorize your collection. There are two ways you can fill in these boxes: you can simply "check" them off when a figure is acquired or you can use a pencil to write in the current market value of the item and periodically update it. Keeping record of value will help in maintaining an overall value of your collection for personal and insurance purposes. A new feature for WWE Elites and Ultimates is the inclusion of event date which the performer wore the gear the figure depicts. Refer to the diagram below for a visual example:

Lastly, I see this more than a checklist. Consider this a coffee table book you can leave out in your man cave as anyone who picks it up is sure to get a blast of nostalgia. Now this is where the fun begins – taking inventory and filling in what you have, want and need. Enjoy!

ALL ELITE AEW WRESTLING

UNRIVALED COLLECTION

UNRIVALED COLLECTION SERIES 1 (2020)			MOC	LOOSE	VALUE
#01	D	Cody			
#02	Y	Kenny Omega			
#03	N	Matt Jackson			
#04	A	Nick Jackson			
#05	M	Brandi Rhodes			
#06	I	Chris Jericho			
#07	T	Cody (1 of 500)			
#08	E	Chris Jericho (1 of 1,000)			

UNRIVALED COLLECTION SERIES 1 V.2 (2021)			MOC	LOOSE	VALUE
#01	D	Cody			
#02	Y	Kenny Omega			
#03	N	Matt Jackson			
#04	A	Nick Jackson			
#05	M	Brandi Rhodes			
#06	I	Chris Jericho			

UNRIVALED COLLECTION SERIES 2 (2020)			MOC	LOOSE	VALUE
#10	T	Jon Moxley			
#11	H	"Hangman" Adam Page			
#12	I	MJF			
#13	S	Rey Fenix			
#14		Pentagon Jr.			
#15	I	Dustin Rhodes			
#16	S	MJF (1 of 1,000)			
#17		Jon Moxley (1 of 500)			

		UNRIVALED COLLECTION SERIES 3 (2021)	MOC	LOOSE	VALUE
#19	A	Pac			
#20	W	Riho			
#21	E	Orange Cassidy			
#22	S	Darby Allin			
#23	O	Matt Jackson			
#24	M	Nick Jackson			
#25	E	Riho (1 of 1,000)			
#26	!	Darby Allin (1 of 500)			

		UNRIVALED COLLECTION SERIES 4 (2021)	MOC	LOOSE	VALUE
#28	D	Kenny Omega			
#29	Y	Cody			
#30	N	Sammy Guevara (w/ 5 "Hit Me Up" Signs)			
#30	N	Sammy Guevara (w/ 5 Different Signs)			
#31	A	Matt Hardy			
#32	M	Santana			
#33	I	Ortiz			
#34	T	Cody (1 of 1,000)			
#35	E	Matt Hardy (1 of 500)			

		UNRIVALED COLLECTION SERIES 5 (2021)	MOC	LOOSE	VALUE
#37	P	Jon Moxley			
#38	A	Scorpio Sky			
#39	R	Frankie Kazarian			
#40	A	"Hangman" Adam Page			
#41	D	Luchasaurus			
#42	I	Jungle Boy			
#43	M	"Hangman" Adam Page (1 of 3,000)			
#44	G	Jon Moxley (1 of 5,000)			

	UNRIVALED COLLECTION SERIES 6 (2021)		MOC	LOOSE	VALUE
#45	C	Chris Jericho			
#46	H	Jake Hager			
#47	A	MJF			
#48	M	Hikaru Shida			
#49	P	Penta El Zero M (No Outline Details on Mask)			
#49	P	Penta El Zero M (w/ Outline Details on Mask)			
#50	I	Rey Fenix (All Black Boots)			
#50	I	Rey Fenix (Black & Gold Boots)			
#51	O	Chris Jericho (1 of 5,000)			
#52	N	Jake Hager (1 of 3,000)			

	UNRIVALED COLLECTION SERIES 7 (2021)		MOC	LOOSE	VALUE
#53	T	Lance Archer			
#54	A	Dax Harwood			
#55	G	Cash Wheeler			
#56	T	Matt Jackson			
#57	E	Nick Jackson			
#58	A	Nyla Rose			
#59	M	Nyla Rose (1 of 5,000)			
#60	!	Lance Archer (1 of 3,000)			

	UNRIVALED COLLECTION SERIES 8 (2022)		MOC	LOOSE	VALUE
#63	C	Chris Jericho			
#64	H	Jon Moxley			
#65	A	Trent?			
#66	M	Chuck Taylor			
#67	P	Orange Cassidy			
#68	I	Kris Statlander			
#69	O	Jon Moxley (1 of 5,000)			
#70	N	Chris Jericho (1 of 3,000)			

UNRIVALED COLLECTION SERIES 9 (2022)			CARDS	MOC	LOOSE	VALUE
#73	R	Eddie Kingston				
#74	A	Brian Cage				
#75	M	Ricky Starks				
#76	P	Christian Cage				
#77	A	Thunder Rosa				
#78	G	Powerhouse Hobbs				
#79	E	Thunder Rosa (1 of 5,000)				
#80	!	Ricky Starks (1 of 3,000)				

UNRIVALED COLLECTION SERIES 10 (2022)			MOC	LOOSE	VALUE
#81	T	Wardlow			
#82	E	Jake Hager			
#83	A	Dr. Britt Baker			
#84	M	Taz			
#85		Miro			
#86	T	Andrade El Idolo			
#87	A	Dr. Britt Baker (1 of 5,000)			
#88	Z	Taz (1 of 3,000)			

UNRIVALED COLLECTION SERIES 11 (2022)			MOC	LOOSE	VALUE
#94	S	Penelope Ford			
#95	U	Adam Cole			
#96	P	Kip Sabian			
#97	E	Jungle Boy			
#98	R	Chris Jericho			
#99	B	Darby Allin			
#100	A	Penelope Ford (1 of 5,000)			
#101	D	Jungle Boy (1 of 3,000)			

UNRIVALED COLLECTION SERIES 12 (2023)			MOC	LOOSE	VALUE
#104	B	Dax Harwood			
#105	A	Cash Wheeler			
#106	B	Jon Moxley			
#107	Y	Isiah Kassidy			
#108	F	Marq Quen			
#109	A	Jamie Hayter			
#110	C	Jon Moxley (1 of 5,000)			
#111	E	Jamie Hayter (1 of 3,000)			

UNRIVALED COLLECTION SERIES 13 (2023)			MOC	LOOSE	VALUE
#116	V	Sting			
#117	E	Darby Allin			
#118	R	Danhausen			
#119	Y	The Butcher			
#120	E	The Blade			
#121	V	Wardlow			
#122	I	The Bunny (1 of 5,000)			
#123	L	Danhausen (1 of 3,000)			

UNRIVALED COLLECTION SERIES 14 (2024)			MOC	LOOSE	VALUE
#125	S	Keith Lee			
#126	C	Swerve Strickland			
#127	I	Ricky Starks			
#128	S	Max Caster			
#129	S	Anthony Bowens (Swerve Signature On Back)			
#129	S	Anthony Bowens (Sticker Over Swerve Signature On Back)			
#129	S	Anthony Bowens (Bowens Signature On Back)			
#130	O	Toni Storm			
#131	R	Billy Gunn (1 of 5,000)			
#132	!	Keith Lee (! Of 3,000)			

UNRIVALED COLLECTION SERIES 15 (2024)			MOC	LOOSE	VALUE
#144	T	"The Devil" MJF			
#145	H	Samoa Joe			
#146	E	Ethan Page			
#147	D	Chris Jericho			
#148	E	Daniel Garcia			
#149	V	Saraya			
#150	I	"The Devil" MJF (1 of 5,000)			
#151	L	Ethan Page (1 of 3,000)			

UNRIVALED COLLECTION SERIES 16 (2024)	MOC	LOOSE	VALUE
Orange Cassidy			
Konosuke Takeshita			
Matt Hardy			
Julia Hart			
Jeff Hardy			
Austin Gunn			
Colten Gunn			

UNRIVALED COLLECTION SERIES 17 (2024)	MOC	LOOSE	VALUE

		UNRIVALED COLLECTION SERIES 18 (2025)	MOC	LOOSE	VALUE

		UNRIVALED COLLECTION SERIES 19 (2025)	MOC	LOOSE	VALUE

		UNRIVALED COLLECTION SERIES 20 (2025)	MOC	LOOSE	VALUE

UNRIVALED COLLECTION EXCLUSIVES

UNRIVALED COLLECTION AMAZON EXCLUSIVES (2021)		MIB	LOOSE	VALUE
GEAR PACK	Chris Jericho			
TAG TEAM	"Hangman" Adam Page			
	Kenny Omega			
TAG TEAM	Frankie Kazarian			
	Scorpio Sky			
RIVALS	Jon Moxley			
	Darby Allin			

UNRIVALED COLLECTION AMAZON EXCLUSIVES (2022)		MIB	LOOSE	VALUE
TAG TEAM	Nick Jackson			
	Matt Jackson			
TAG TEAM	Sting			
	Darby Allin			
TAG TEAM	Luchasaurus			
	Jungle Boy			

UNRIVALED COLLECTION AMAZON EXCLUSIVES (2023)		MIB	LOOSE	VALUE
TAG TEAM	Jon Moxley			
	Bryan Danielson			
RIVALS	Dr. Britt Baker D.M.D.			
	Jade Cargill			
TAG TEAM	Hook			
	Danhausen			
CHAMPIONS (1 OF 3,000)	MJF			
	Orange Cassidy			
	Thunder Rosa			
	Wardlow			

UNRIVALED COLLECTION COLLECT FOREVER EXCLUSIVES		MOC	LOOSE	VALUE
#01	CM Punk (1 of 1,000)			
#02	Dr. Britt Baker, D.M.D. (1 of 1,000)			
#03	Sting (1 of 1,000)			
#04	Kenny Omega (1 of 1,000)			
#05				

UNRIVALED COLLECTION EVENT EXCLUSIVES		MOC	LOOSE	VALUE
ALL IN 2023	Jamie Hayter (1 of 1,000)			

UNRIVALED COLLECTION GAMESTOP EXCLUSIVES		MOC	LOOSE	VALUE
#01	Matt Jackson (As Ryu)			
#02	Nick Jackson (As Ken)			
#03	Kenny Omega (As Akuma)			

UNRIVALED COLLECTION JAZWARES VAULT EXCLUSIVES		MIB	LOOSE	VALUE
#141	Rey Fenix			
	Pac			
	Penta El Zero Miedo			

UNRIVALED RINGSIDE COLLECTIBLES EXCLUSIVES (2020)		MIB	LOOSE	VALUE
#09	Chris Jericho (A Little Bit Of The Bubbly)			
#18	Dustin Rhodes (Blood Brothers)			
	Cody (Blood Brothers)			

UNRIVALED RINGSIDE COLLECTIBLES EXCLUSIVES (2021)		MIB	LOOSE	VALUE
#27	Cody (TNT Champion)			
#36	Jungle Boy (Jurassic Express)			
	Luchasaurus (Jurassic Express)			
	Jurassic Express (Packaging Variant)			

UNRIVALED RINGSIDE COLLECTIBLES EXCLUSIVES (2022)		MIB	LOOSE	VALUE
#61	Dr. Britt Baker D.M.D. (Blood & Guts)			
#62	Jon Moxley (Blood & Guts)			
	Kenny Omega (Blood & Guts)			
#71	Darby Allin (Coffin Drop)			
#90	Jim Ross			
#93	CM Punk (The First Dance)			
#102	Tony Schiavone			
#102	Excalibur			

UNRIVALED RINGSIDE COLLECTIBLES EXCLUSIVES (2023)		MIB	LOOSE	VALUE
#103	Owen Hart (King Of Harts)			
#112	Thunder Rosa (Blood & Guts)			
#114	CM Punk (Blood & Guts)			
	MJF (Blood & Guts)			
#124	Hook			
#136	Danhausen (Very Nice, Very Evil)			
#137	Wheeler Yuta (Blood & Guts)			
#138	Sammy Guevara (TNT Champion)			

UNRIVALED RINGSIDE COLLECTIBLES EXCLUSIVES (2024)		MIB	LOOSE	VALUE
#139	Max Caster			
	Anthony Bowens			
	Billy Gunn			
#154	Brody King			
	Darby Allin			
#163	Jerichohausen			
#164	Jeff Jarrett			
	"Switchblade" Jay White			

UNRIVALED COLLECTION SHOPAEW EXCLUSIVES		MOC	LOOSE	VALUE
#01	Chris Jericho (1 of 3,000)			
#02	Kenny Omega (1 of 3,000)			
#03	Jon Moxley (1 of 3,000)			
#04	Hikaru Shida (1 of 3,000)			
#05	MJF (1 of 3,000)			
#06	Jade Cargill (1 of 3,000)			
#07	"Hangman" Adam Page (1 of 3,000)			
#08	Hook (1 of 3,000)			
#09	Eddie Kingston (1 of 3,000)			
#10	Sting (1 of 3,000)			

UNRIVALED COLLECTION TARGET EXCLUSIVES		MOC	LOOSE	VALUE
#91	Darby Allin			
#92	Sammy Guevara			
#115	Adam Cole			
#133	Samoa Joe			

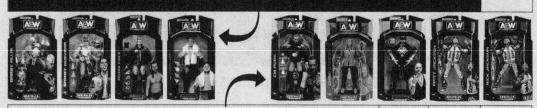

UNRIVALED COLLECTION WALMART EXCLUSIVES		MOC	LOOSE	VALUE
#89	CM Punk			
#134	Chris Jericho			
#135	Eddie Kingston			
#142	Matt Jackson			
#143	Nick Jackson			
	Brody King			
	Darby Allin			

UNMATCHED COLLECTION

UNMATCHED COLLECTION SERIES 1 (2021)			MOC	LOOSE	VALUE
#01	V	Kenny Omega			
#02	T	Darby Allin			
#03	R	Miro (Yellow Outline on Shorts)			
#03	R	Miro (Gold Outline on Shorts)			
#04	I	Dr. Britt Baker			
#05	G	Dustin Rhodes			
#06	E	Dr. Britt Baker (1 of 3,000)			
#07	G	Darby Allin (1 of 5,000)			
#08	R	Cody Rhodes (LJN)			

UNMATCHED COLLECTION SERIES 2 (2022)			MOC	LOOSE	VALUE
#09	L	Sting (Luminaries)			
#10	U	Santana			
#11	M	Ortiz			
#12	I	Wardlow			
#13	N	Tay Conti			
#14	A	MJF			
#15	R	MJF (1 of 3,000)			
#16	Y	Sting (1 of 5,000)			

UNMATCHED COLLECTION SERIES 3 (2022)			MOC	LOOSE	VALUE
#17	E	Mr. Brodie Lee			
#18	X	Stu Grayson			
#19	A	Evil Uno			
#20	L	John Silver			
#21	T	Anna Jay			
#22	E	Mr. Brodie Le (1 of 3,000)			
#23	D	Anna Jay (1 of 5,000)			

		UNMATCHED COLLECTION SERIES 4 (2022)	MOC	LOOSE	VALUE
#24	H	Corazon De Leon (Luminaries)			
#25	A	CM Punk			
#26	R	"Hangman" Adam Page			
#27	D	Cody Rhodes			
#28	C	Jade Cardgill			
#29	O	MJF			
#30	R	CM Punk (1 of 5,000)			
#31	E	Cody Rhodes (1 of 3,000)			

		UNMATCHED COLLECTION SERIES 5 (2022)	MOC	LOOSE	VALUE
#33	Y	Darby Allin (LJN)			
#34	E	Sammy Guevara			
#35	S	Shawn Spears			
#36	!	Kenny Omega			
#37	Y	Bryan Danielson			
#38	E	Red Velvet			
#39	S	Bryan Danielson (1 of 5,000)			
#40	!	Shawn Spears (1 of 3,000)			

		UNMATCHED COLLECTION SERIES 6 (2023)	MOC	LOOSE	VALUE
#41	O	Owen Hart (Luminaries)			
#42	W	Santana			
#43	E	Ortiz			
#44	N	Ruby Soho			
#45	H	Malakai Black			
#46	A	Mr. Brodie Lee			
#47	R	Owen Hart (1 of 5,000)			
#48	T	Mr. Brodie Lee (1 of 3,000)			

UNMATCHED COLLECTION SERIES 7 (2023)			MOC	LOOSE	VALUE
#51	T	CM Punk (LJN)			
#52	H	Thunder Rosa			
#53	U	Hook			
#54	N	Rey Fenix			
#55	D	Penta El Zero M			
#56	E	Pac			
#57	R	Hook (1 of 5,000)			
#58	!	Thunder Rosa (1 of 3,000)			

UNMATCHED COLLECTION SERIES 8 (2024)			MOC	LOOSE	VALUE
#59	V	CM Punk (Luminaries)			
#60	I	Malakai Black			
#61	O	Brody King			
#62	L	Buddy Matthews			
#63	E	Penta Oscuro			
#64	N	CM Punk (1 of 5,000)			
#65	T	Brody King (1 of 3,000)			

UNMATCHED COLLECTION SERIES 9 (2024)			MOC	LOOSE	VALUE
#66	B	Jeff Hardy			
#67	I	Bryan Danielson			
#68	G	Jon Moxley			
#69	S	Claudio Castagnoli			
#70	W	Wheeler Yuta			
#71	I	Jamie Hayter			
#72	N	Alex Reynolds (1 of 5,000)			
#73	G	Claudio Castagnoli (1 of 3,000)			

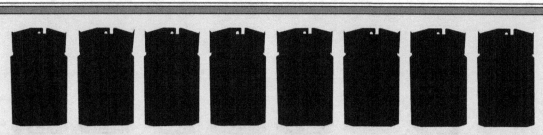

		UNMATCHED COLLECTION SERIES 10 (2024)	MOC	LOOSE	VALUE
		Adam Cole			
		Adam Copeland			
		Kenny Omega			
		Kyle O'Reilly			
		Matt Jackson			
		Nick Jackson			
		Adam Cole (1 of 5,000)			
		Brandon Cutler (1 of 3,000)			

		UNMATCHED COLLECTION SERIES 11 (2024)	MOC	LOOSE	VALUE
		Sammy Guevara			
		Tay Melo			
		Darby Allin			
		Jungle Boy			
		MJF			
		Jay White			
		Blade Runner Sting			

		UNMATCHED COLLECTION SERIES 12 (2024)	MOC	LOOSE	VALUE

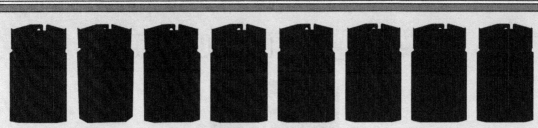

UNMATCHED COLLECTION SERIES 13 (2025)			MOC	LOOSE	VALUE

UNMATCHED COLLECTION SERIES 14 (2025)			MOC	LOOSE	VALUE

UNMATCHED COLLECTION SERIES 15 (2025)			MOC	LOOSE	VALUE

UNMATCHED COLLECTION EXCLUSIVES

UNMATCHED RINGSIDE COLLECTIBLES EXCLUSIVES		MIB	LOOSE	VALUE
N/A	Mr. Brodie Lee			
	Negative 1			

UNMATCHED COLLECTION WALMART EXCLUSIVES			MOC	LOOSE	VALUE
#08	R	Cody Rhodes (Unmatched Series 1 LJN Variant)			
#16B	Y	Sting (Unmatched Series 2 Luminaries Variant)			
#33		"Hangman" Adam Page			
#49		Wardlow			
#50		MJF			

SAN DIEGO COMIC CON EXCLUSIVES			MOC	LOOSE	VALUE
#17	2022	Mr. Brodie Lee (1 of 1,000)			
	2023	Sting (1 of 1,000)			

PAY-PER-VIEW LIMITED EDITION TARGET EXCLUSIVES		MOC	LOOSE	VALUE
#01	Bryan Danielson			
#02	Dr. Britt Baker, D.M.D.			

SUPREME COLLECTION SERIES 1 (2022)		MIB	LOOSE	VALUE
#01	Cody Rhodes			
#01B	Cody Rhodes (Walmart)			
#02	Dr. Britt Baker			

SUPREME COLLECTION SERIES 2 (2022)		MIB	LOOSE	VALUE
#03	Kenny Omega			
#03B	Kenny Omega (Walmart)			
#04	Malakai Black			

SUPREME COLLECTION SERIES 3 (2023)		MIB	LOOSE	VALUE
#05	Penta El Zero M			
#06	Rey Fenix			

SUPREME COLLECTION SERIES 4 (2023)		MIB	LOOSE	VALUE
#07	CM Punk (Walmart)			

SUPREME COLLECTION SERIES 5 (2024)		MIB	LOOSE	VALUE
#08	Sting (Walmart)			

SUPREME COLLECTION JAZWARES VAULT EXCLUSIVES	MIB	LOOSE	VALUE
Malakai Black (1 of 5,000)			

WRESTLING BUDDIES SERIES 1 (2021)	MIB	LOOSE	VALUE
Cody Rhodes			
Kenny Omega			
Darby Allin			
Luchasaurus			

WRESTLING BUDDIES EXCLUSIVES		MIB	LOOSE	VALUE
WALMART	Sting			
GAMESTOP	Kenny Omega			

RINGS, PLAYSETS & MISCELLANEOUS RELEASES		MIB	LOOSE	VALUE
ROLE PLAY	AEW World Heavyweight Championship			
	AEW Tag Team Championship			
	AEW TNT Championship			
ACCESSORIES	Barbed Wire Set			
	Barrel Set			
	Belt Pack			
	Announcer's Set			
RINGS	AEW Action Ring			
	AEW Action Ring w/ Cody (Smyths Exclusive)			
	AEW Action Ring w/ Adam Page (Smyths Exclusive)			
	AEW Authentic Scale Ring w/ Kenny Omega (RSC)			
	AEW Authentic Scale D.O.N. Ring w/ Aubrey Edwards (RSC)			
	AEW Authentic Scale Rampage Ring w/ Sting (RSC)			
PLAYSETS	AEW Pop-Up Entrance Stage			

MICRO BRAWLERS

MICRO BRAWLERS WAVE 1 (2021)	MOC	LOOSE	VALUE
Britt Baker			
Brodie Lee			
Chris Jericho			
Darby Allin			
Hikaru Shida			
Jon Moxley			
Orange Cassidy			

ALL ELITE CRATE EXCLUSIVE MICRO BRAWLERS (2019-2022)		MOC	LOOSE	VALUE
MAY 2019	MJF (Pro Wrestling Crate)			
OCT. 2021	Sting			
JAN. 2022	Nyla Rose			
APRIL 2022	Eddie Kingston			
JULY 2022	Evil Uno			
OCT. 2022	Sammy Guevara			

ALL ELITE CRATE EXCLUSIVE MICRO BRAWLERS (2023-2024)		MOC	LOOSE	VALUE
JAN. 2023	Thunder Rosa (Standard – Yellow)			
	Thunder Rosa (Chase – 1 of 100)			
APRIL 2023	Claudio Castagnoli			
JULY 2023	"Jungle Boy" Jack Perry			
	"Jungle Boy" Jack Perry (Chase)			
OCT. 2023	Billy Gunn (Daddy A$$)			
JAN. 2024	Luchasaurus			
	Luchasaurus (Chase)			
APRIL 2024	Prince Nana			
	Prince Nana (Chase)			
JULY 2024				
OCT. 2024				

	LIMITED EDITION MICRO BRAWLERS (2022)	MOC	LOOSE	VALUE
	Christian Cage			
	Sting (Retro)			
1 OF 100	Sting (Retro Chase)			
	Adam Cole			
	Malakai Black			
	Brody King			
	Anthony Bowens			
TAG TEAM	Platinum Max Caster			
	Wardlow			
	MJF (Joker)			
	Sting (Black & Red)			

	LIMITED EDITION MICRO BRAWLERS (2023)	MOC	LOOSE	VALUE
STANDARD	Bryan Danielson (White Shirt)			
1 OF 100	Bryan Danielson (Black Pool Combat Club Shirt)			
	Powerhouse Hobbs			
	Danhausen (Very Evil)			
1 OF 100	Danhausen (Very Evil Chase)			
	Negative 1			
	Kenny Omega (One-Winged Angel)			
	Matt Jacksion (Splatter Gear)			
	Nick Jackson (Splatter Gear)			
	Jeff Hardy			
	Matt Hardy			
	Cash Wheeler			
	Dax Harwood			
	CM Punk (Chicago Edition)			
1 OF 100	CM Punk (Chicago Edition Bloody Chase)			
	Sting (Retro USA)			
1 OF 100	Sting (Retro USA Chase)			
1 OF 400	Jake Hager			
	MJF (Better Than You BayBay)			
1 OF 100	MJF (Better Than You BayBay Chase)			
	Adam Cole (Better Than You BayBay)			
1 OF 100	Adam Cole (Better Than You BayBay Chase)			

	LIMITED EDITION MICRO BRAWLERS (2024)	MOC	LOOSE	VALUE
	Saraya (All In 2023)			
	Paul Wight (Captain Insano)			
	"Timeless" Toni Storm			
1 OF 400	Ethan Page			
1 OF 400	Tay Melo			
	Swerve Strickland			
	Adam Cole (The Devil)			
	"Hangman" Adam Page			
	Sting (Crow)			
	Mercedes Mone			
	Matthew Jackson			
	Nicholas Jackson			
	MJF (The Wolf Of Wrestling)			

	MICRO BRAWLER MINIS SERIES 1 (2023)	MIB	LOOSE	VALUE
	Adam Cole			
	Chris Jericho			
	Darby Allin			
	Dr. Britt Baker, D.M.D. (Black & Gold)			
CHASE	Dr. Britt Baker, D.M.D. (Black & Red)			
	Hikaru Shida			
	Jon Moxley			
	MJF			
	Orange Cassidy			
	Sting			
1 OF 1	Sting (Gold)			
	Very Evil Danhausen			
CHASE	Very Evil Danhausen (Red)			

	MICRO BRAWLER MINIS SPECIAL EDITION (2024)	MIB	LOOSE	VALUE
	Christian Cage (Orange)			
CHASE	Christian Cage (Yellow)			
CHASE	Christian Cage (Blue)			
CHASE	Christian Cage (Red)			
1 OF 1	Christian Cage (Ultra Rare Metallic Gold)			

	BRAWLER BUDDIES (2024)	MIB	LOOSE	VALUE
	Sting			

Vinimates / Minimates

4" PVC VINIMATES		MIB	LOOSE	VALUE
SDCC 2022	CM Punk			
	Sting			
HOLIDAY	Sting			
ALL OUT	Dr. Britt Baker			

2" MINIMATES SERIES 1	MIB	LOOSE	VALUE
CM Punk			
Dr. Britt Baker			
Chris Jericho			
Kenny Omega			

2" MINIMATES SERIES 2	MIB	LOOSE	VALUE
Adam Cole			
"Hangman" Adam Page			
Jon Moxley			
Orange Cassidy			

2" MINIMATES SERIES 3	MIB	LOOSE	VALUE
Darby Allin			
Sting			
Ric Flair			
Bryan Danielson			

2" MINIMATES 2-PACKS	MOC	LOOSE	VALUE
Nick Jackson			
Matt Jackson			

MISCELLANEOUS 2" MINIMATES RELEASES		MIB	LOOSE	VALUE
NYCC 2022	AEW Logo Figure			
RING SET	DLX Ring w/ Excalibur			

10" GALLERY DIORAMAS (2023)	MIB	LOOSE	VALUE
Bryan Danielson			
Chris Jericho			
CM Punk			
Jon Moxley			
Sting			

YOUTOOZ SERIES 1		MIB	LOOSE	VALUE
#0	MJF			
#1	Toni Storm			
#2	Orange Cassidy			
#3	Lionheart Chris Jericho			
#4	Toni Storm (Black & White – Ringside Collectibles)			

	16D COLLECTION	MIB	LOOSE	VALUE
019	Giant Baba (Red Robe)			
	Giant Babe (White Robe)			
023	Jumbo Tsuruta			
025	Bruiser Brody			
027	Stan Hansen			

	50th ANNIVERSARY 16D COLLECTION	MIB	LOOSE	VALUE
1	Giant Baba (Bronze)			
1	Giant Baba (Gold)			
2	Jumbo Tsuruta (Bronze)			
3	Stan Hansen (Bronze)			
4	Bruiser Brody (Bronze)			

SLAM BUDDIES	MIB	LOOSE	VALUE
Jimmy Lloyd			
Nick Gage			

BELL TO BELL COLLECTION		MIB	LOOSE	VALUE
GCW DEATH MATCH	Matt Cardona			
	Nick Gage			
GCW DEATH MATCH	Matt Cardona (Bloody)			
	Nick Gage (Bloody)			

MICRO BRAWLERS SERIES 1 (2021)	MOC	LOOSE	VALUE
Alexander Hammerstone			
LA Park			
Richard Holliday			

PREMIUM ACTION FIGURES WAVE 1 (2024)	MIB	LOOSE	VALUE
Alexander Hammerstone			
Jacob Fatu			
Killer Kross			
Mads Kruger			

FUSION ACTION FIGURES WAVE 1 (2024)	MIB	LOOSE	VALUE
EJ Nduka			
Lince Dorado			
Microman			

PLAYSETS & ACCESSORIES		MIB	LOOSE	VALUE
CHAMPIONSHIP BELT COLLECTION	MLW World Heavyweight Championship			
	MLW World Featherweight Championship			
	MLW National Openweight Championship			
	MLW World Tag Team Championship			
	MLW Opera Cup			
	Ring Playset			

THE MAJOR Wrestling Figure PODCAST

 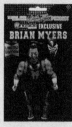  

VINTAGE REMCO-STYLE ACTION FIGURES SERIES 1		MOC	LOOSE	VALUE
1 OF 1,500	Matt Cardona			
1 OF 1,500	Brian Myers			
1 OF 1,000	Smart Mark Sterling			
1 OF 750	Referee			

VINTAGE REMCO-STYLE ACTION FIGURE 2-PACKS		MIB	LOOSE	VALUE
MWFP (1 OF 500)	Matt Cardona			
	Brian Myers			
METS (1 OF 250)	Matt Cardona			
	Brian Myers			
S.T.O.M.P. (1 OF 250)	Matt Cardona			
	Brian Myers			
NICKNAMES (1 OF 800)	Thousand Dollar Broski			
	Bare Minimum Brian			
MOMENT (1 OF 1,200)	Matt Cardona			
	Brian Myers			
BULLS (1 OF 800)	Matt Cardona			
	Brian Myers			

VINTAGE REMCO-STYLE ACTION FIGURE ACCESSORIES		MOC	LOOSE	VALUE
1 OF 300	Podcast Playset			
1 OF 300	Ultimate Ladder & Table Playset			
1 OF 500	MWFP Title & Shirt (MWFP Logo)			
1 OF 500	MWFP Title & Shirt (Scratch That Figure Itch)			

MICRO BRAWLERS

	MICRO BRAWLERS SINGLE RELEASES	MOC	LOOSE	VALUE
	Matt Cardona (Variant Card)			
	Matt Cardona (Wedding Edition)			
	Thousand Dollar Broski			
	Brian Myers (Variant Card)			
	Brian Myers (F*cked Up Edition – Black Gear)			
	Brian Myers (F*cked Up Edition – Blue Gear)			
	Brian Myers (With Mask)			
	"Smart" Mark Sterling (Red Suit)			
	"Smart" Mark Sterling (With Suit)			
	"Hot Mess" Chelsea Green			
	Chelsea Cardona (Wedding Edition)			
1 OF 450	Bob Cardona (SDCC 2021 Exclusive)			
	VSK (White)			
CHASE	VSK (Blue & Orange)			
	Rory Fox			
1 OF 400	"Indy God" Matt Cardona			
1 OF 100	"Indy God" Matt Cardona (Gold)			
	"Death Match King" Matt Cardona			

	MAJOR CRATE EXCLUSIVE MICRO BRAWLERS	MOC	LOOSE	VALUE
MAJOR CRATE 1	"Macho Man" Randy Savage			
	MWFP Referee (Standard Edtion)			
	FWF Referee (Chase)			
MAJOR CRATE 2	Major Players Matt Cardona (Standard Edition)			
	Major Players Matt Cardona (Chase – 1 of 50)			
	Major Players Brian Myers (Standard Edtion)			
	Major Players Brian Myers (Chase – 1 of 50)			
MAJOR CRATE 3	Hawkins (Black Trunks)			
	Hawkins (Yellow Trunks Chase)			
	Ryder (Black Tights)			
	Ryder (Yellow Trunks Chase)			

PRO WRESTLING CRATE EXCLUSIVE MICRO BRAWLERS		MIB	LOOSE	VALUE
MAY 2020	Matt Cardona (S.T.O.M.P. In Paradise)			
JUNE 2020	Brian Myers (S.T.O.M.P. In Paradise)			

FWF LIVE EXCLUSIVE MICRO BRAWLERS		MOC	LOOSE	VALUE
	Maven			
	Mosh (Web Shirt)			
CHASE	Mosh (FWF Shirt)			
	Thrasher (Web Shirt)			
CHASE	Thrasher (FWF Shirt)			

MICRO BRAWLER BOX SETS		MIB	LOOSE	VALUE
	Swoggle			
	"Smart" Mark Sterling			
4-PACK	Matt Cardona			
	Brian Myers			

MAJOR BUDDIES

MAJOR BUDDIES SERIES 1		MIB	LOOSE	VALUE
1 OF 250	Thousand Dollar Broski			
1 OF 250	Bare Minimum Brian			

MAJOR BUDDIES SERIES 2		MIB	LOOSE	VALUE
1 OF 225	Matt Cardona			
1 OF 225	Brian Myers			
1 OF 225	"Smart" Mark Sterling			
1 OF 225	Swoggle			

MAJOR BUDDIES SERIES 3		MIB	LOOSE	VALUE
1 OF 200	Chelsea Green			
1 OF 200	Matt Cardona			
1 OF 200	Brian Myers			
1 OF 150	Leo Sparrow			
	Steph De Lander			
	Matt Cardona (Indy God)			

	MAJOR BENDIES SERIES 1 (2021)	MOC	LOOSE	VALUE
	Brian Myers			
	Matt Cardona			
BAGGED	Matt Cardona (Super Tan Variant)			
	"Smart" Mark Sterling			
	Swoggle			

	MY WORLD PODCAST MAJOR BENDIES (2022)	MOC	LOOSE	VALUE
	Conrad Thompson			
LONG HAIR	Jeff Jarrett			
SHORT HAIR	Jeff Jarret			

	MAJOR BENDIES SERIES 2 (2022)	MOC	LOOSE	VALUE
	Brian Pillman			
	Bryan Clark (Black & Orange)			
CHASE	Bryan Clark (Blue & Yellow)			
	Danhausen			
	Nick Gage			
CHASE	Nick Gage (Bloody)			

	MAJOR BENDIES SERIES 3 (2023)	MOC	LOOSE	VALUE
	Chelsea Green			
	Colt Cabana			
	Effy			
	Gangrel			
CHASE	Gangrel (Bloody)			

	MAJOR BENDIES SERIES 4 (2023)	MOC	LOOSE	VALUE
	British Bulldog			
	Doc Gallows			
	Joey Janela			
CHASE	Joey Janela (Bloody)			
	Karl Anderson			
	Ricky Morton			

	MAJOR BENDIES SERIES 5 (2024)	MOC	LOOSE	VALUE
	Chavo Guerrero			
	Deonna Purrazzo			
	Heath			
	Konnan			

	MAJOR BENDIES SERIES 6 (2024)	MOC	LOOSE	VALUE
	Allie Katch			
CHASE	Allie Katch (Bloody)			
	Arn Anderson			
	Eddie Guerrero			
	Maven			

EXTREME

	EXTREME MAJOR BENDIES SERIES 1 (2023)	MOC	LOOSE	VALUE
	Raven			
CHASE	Raven (Bloody)			
	Sabu			
CHASE	Sabu (Bloody)			
	Sandman			
CHASE	Sandman (Bloody)			
	Tommy Dreamer			
CHASE	Tommy Dreamer (Bloody)			

	EXTREME MAJOR BENDIES SERIES 2 (2024)	MOC	LOOSE	VALUE
	Dusty Rhodes			
CHASE	Dusty Rhodes (Bloody)			
	Francine			
CHASE	Francine (Bloody)			
	Jerry Lynn			
CHASE	Jerry Lynn (Bloody)			
	Mikey Whipwreck			
CHASE	Mikey Whipwreck (Bloody)			
	Shane Douglas			
CHASE	Shane Douglas (Bloody)			

MAJOR BENDIES EXCLUSIVES

MAJOR BENDIES EXCLUSIVES & LIMITED DROPS (2022)		MOC	LOOSE	VALUE
1 OF 150	Matt Cardona (Wrestlecon/Live 12 – Major Moment Gear)			
1 OF 150	Brian Myers (Wrestlecon/Live 12 – Major Moment Gear)			
1 OF 130	Matt Cardona (WhatNot – Major Players)			
1 OF 130	Brian Myers (WhatNot – Major Players)			
	Matt Cardona (Merch Table – Death Match King Gear)			
	Brian Myers (Merch Table – Black & White Gear)			
	Matt Cardona (Predator Gear)			
	Brian Myers (Liger Tribute Gear)			
	Johnny Gargano (Carnage Gear)			
1 OF 275	Johnny Gargano (Pandora's Box - Venom Gear)			
	Johnny Gargano (Wrestling Collector Shop – Punisher Gear)			
1 OF 275	Danhausen (Pandora's Box – Black & White)			
1 OF 150	Danhausen (Highspots – Black Pants)			
	Danhausen (Comic Book)			
	Ric Flair (Starrcast's "Ric Flair's Last Match)			
	Tyrus			
1 OF 150	Nick Gage (Highspots – MDK Shirt)			
	"Smart" Mark Sterling (Gold)			
	Swoggle (Tattoos)			

	MAJOR BENDIES EXCLUSIVES & LIMITED DROPS (2023)	MOC	LOOSE	VALUE
	Matt Cardona (Pro Wrestling Tees – Ghostbusters Gear)			
	Brian Myers (Pro Wrestling Tees – Mets Gear)			
	Matt Cardona (Powercon – Indy God)			
	Brian Myers (Powercon – Green)			
	Matt Cardona (Merch Table – DMK w/ Crown)			
	Brian Myers (Merch Table – Franchise Singlet)			
1 OF 200	"Smart" Mark Sterling (WhatNot – Purple Gear)			
	"Smart" Mark Sterling (Powercon – Blue Suit)			
	"Smart" Mark Sterling (Twitch – Powder Blue Suit)			
	"Hacksaw" Jim Duggan			
CHASE	"Hacksaw" Jim Duggan (Black Trunks)			
	"Hacksaw" Jim Duggan (Wrestling Collector Shop – USA Paint)			
	"Hacksaw" Jim Duggan (4th of July)			
	Sgt. Slaughter			
	Sgt. Slaughter (Wrestling Collector Shop – G.I. Joe)			
	Chelsea Green (Wrestling Collector Shop – Pink Gear)			
	Effy (Wrestling Collector Shop – Purple Jacket)			
	Referee John			
	Referee Kanik			
	Referee TTD			
	Kanik			
	Steph De Lander			
	Steph De Lander (Omega Level Toys & Comix – Indy Goddess)			
	Ric Flair (Bloody)			
	Tyrus (Stars & Stripes)			
	Danhausen (New Year's Evil)			
	Spencer Powers (Powercon)			
	Nailz (Highspots)			
1 OF 100	Colt Cabana (FWF Live 5)			
	Raven (Omega Level Toys & Comix – Symbol Shirt)			
1 OF 300	Captain Joe Shoes			

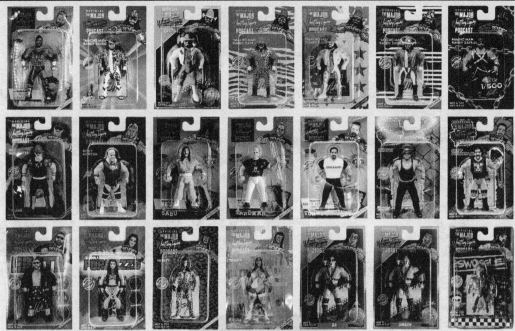

	MAJOR BENDIES EXCLUSIVES & LIMITED DROPS (2024)	MOC	LOOSE	VALUE
	Matt Cardona (Bloody Death Match King)			
	"Macho Man" Randy Savage (Unreleased Bend-Ems)			
	"Macho Man" Randy Savage (Wrestling Collector Shop – Hasbro)			
	"Macho Man" Randy Savage (Ringside – Red & Yellow)			
	"Macho Man" Randy Savage (PWTees – Pink & Yellow)			
	"Macho Man" Randy Savage (Purple & Yellow)			
1 OF 500	"Macho Man" Randy Savage (Be A Man)			
	Sgt. Slaughter (Ringside Collectibles – WWF Hasbro)			
	Ricky Morton (Live 18 – Black & Yellow)			
	Sabu (Wrestling Collector Shop – ECW OSFTM)			
	Sandman (Wrestling Collector Shop – ECW OSFTM)			
	Tommy Dreamer (Live 19 – Yellow Shirt)			
	Konnan (Mike Durband Productions – nWo Wolfpac)			
	Chavo Guerrero (Blue Gear)			
	Heath (Wrestling Collector Shop - Stars & Stripes)			
	Deonna Purrazzo (Blue)			
	Trinity			
	Trinity (Ringside Collectibles – Pink & Green Gear)			
	Demolition Ax (Wrestling Collector Shop – WWF Hasbro)			
	Demolition Smash (Wrestling Collector Shop – WWF Hasbro)			
	Swoggle (Gold)			
	Vladimir The Superfan			
	"Marvelous" Marc Mero			
	Butterbean			
	Nic Nemeth (Gold Tights)			
	Nic Nemeth (Black Tights)			
	Paul Walter Hauser			
	Steve Maclin			
	Danhausen (Muumuu)			
	Maki Itoh			
	QT Marshall (Black Trunks)			
	QT Marshall (Red, White & Blue Trunks)			

BIG RUBBER GUYS SERIES 1	MOC	LOOSE	VALUE
Matt Cardona			
Brian Myers			

	BIG RUBBER GUYS SERIES 2	MOC	LOOSE	VALUE
	Demolition Ax			
CHASE	Demolition Ax (Red Facepaint)			
	Demolition Smash			
CHASE	Demolition Smash (Red Facepaint)			

BIG RUBBER GUYS SERIES 3	MOC	LOOSE	VALUE
Marty Jannetty			
Ric Flair			
Sgt. Slaughter			

	BIG RUBBER GUYS SERIES 4	MOC	LOOSE	VALUE
	Andre The Giant (Black Singlet)			
VARIANT	Andre The Giant (Blue Singlet)			
	"Macho Man" Randy Savage (Orange Trunks)			
WRESTLECON	"Macho Man" Randy Savage (Green Trunks)			

	BIG RUBBER GUYS SERIES 5	MOC	LOOSE	VALUE
	Davey Boy Smith w/ Matilda (White)			
	Dynamite Kid (White)			
WRESTLING COLLECTOR SHOP	Davey Boy Smith (Blue)			
WRESTLING COLLECTOR SHOP	Dynamite Kid (Blue)			

BIG RUBBER GUYS SERIES 6		MOC	LOOSE	VALUE
	"Hacksaw" Jim Duggan			
VARIANT	"Hacksaw" Jim Duggan (USA Facepaint)			
	Magnum TA			

BIG RUBBER GUYS SERIES 7	MOC	LOOSE	VALUE
Barbarian			
Dusty Rhodes			
Warlord			

BIG RUBBER GUYS SERIES 8	MOC	LOOSE	VALUE
Ethan Page			
Matt Hardy			
Road Warrior Animal			
Road Warrior Hawk			

BIG RUBBER GUYS SERIES 9	MOC	LOOSE	VALUE
Jeff Hardy			

BIG RUBBER GUYS SERIES 10	MOC	LOOSE	VALUE

BIG RUBBER GUYS EXCLUSIVES & LIMITED DROPS		MOC	LOOSE	VALUE
1 OF 1,000	Ric Flair (Bloody)			

ULTIMATES!

MWFP ULTIMATES SERIES 1	MIB	LOOSE	VALUE
Matt Cardona (Entrance Vest)			
Brian Myers (Edge Tribute Gear)			

MWFP ULTIMATES SERIES 2	MIB	LOOSE	VALUE
Matt Cardona (Entrance Spikes)			
Brian Myers (Major Players)			

POWERTOWN ULTRAS 2-PACK	MIB	LOOSE	VALUE
Matt Cardona			
Brian Myers			

	LEGENDS OF LUCHA LIBRE M.U.S.C.L.E.	MOC	LOOSE	VALUE
PACK 1	Tinieblas Jr.			
	Blue Demon Jr.			
	Konnan			
PACK 2	Solar			
	Juventud Guerrera			
	Super Astro			

	LEGENDS OF LUCHA LIBRE REACTION FIGURES	MOC	LOOSE	VALUE
	Blue Demon Jr.			
SUITED	Blue Demon Jr.			
	Solar			
SUITED	Solar			
	Tinieblas Jr.			

	LEGENDS OF LUCHA LIBRE PREMIUMS	MIB	LOOSE	VALUE
SERIES 1	Penta Zero M			
	Rey Fenix			
SERIES 2	Konnan			
	Lady Maravilla			
SERIES 3	Laredo Kid			
	Taya Valkyrie			
	Tinieblas Jr.			
	Vampiro			

	LEGENDS OF LUCHA LIBRE FANATICOS	MOC	LOOSE	VALUE
SERIES 1	Juventud Guerrera			
	Penta Zero M			
	Rey Fenix			
	Taya Valkyrie			
SERIES 2	Black Taurus			
	Hijo Del Perro Aguayo			
	Ultimo Dragon			
	Vampiro			

	LEGENDS OF LUCHA LIBRE MISCELLANEOUS	MIB	LOOSE	VALUE
ACCESSORIES	Lucha De La Muerta			
	Lucha Extrema			
RINGS	14" x 14" Lucha Libre Ring			
PLAYSETS	Diorama Set			

	LUCHACITOS 3" MINI-FIGURES SERIES 1	MIB	LOOSE	VALUE
	Konnan			
CHASE	Konnan			
	Lady Maravilla			
CHASE	Lady Maravilla			
	Penta El Zero M			
CHASE	Penta El Zero M			
	Rey Fenix			
CHASE	Rey Fenix			
	Solar			
CHASE	Solar			
	Tinieblas Jr. & Alushe			
CHASE	Tinieblas Jr. & Alushe			

I AM BRILLIANCE 6" DOLLS	MIB	LOOSE	VALUE
Lady Maravilla			
Taya Valkyrie (w/ Prince Prestley)			

	MASKED WARRIORS ACTION FIGURES	MOC	LOOSE	VALUE
SERIES 1	Charly Malice			
	Lizmark Jr.			
	Marco Corleone			
	Super Nova			
	Sydistiko			
	Tinieblas Jr.			

	MASKED WARRIOR MISCELLANEOUS	MOC	LOOSE	VALUE
RINGS	Hexalateral Wrestling Ring			
MASKS	Super Nova			
	Super Nova (w/ Figure)			
	Tinieblas Jr.			
	Tinieblas Jr. (w/ Figure)			

Charapro 2011-2012

MINI BIG HEADS (2011)	MOC	LOOSE	VALUE
Manabu Nakanishi			
Tiger Mask IV			
Yuji Nagata			

PRO-KAKU HEROES (2012)	MOC	LOOSE	VALUE
Hiroshi Tanahashi (Black Pants)			
Shinsuke Nakamura (Red Pants)			
Hiroshi Tanahashi (White Pants)			
Shinsuke Nakamura (Black Pants)			

TOKI-MEKI 2015-2016

	NJPW PUROKAKU HEROES	MOC	LOOSE	VALUE
SERIES 1	Kazuchika Okada (Blonde Hair)			
	Kazuchika Okada (Black Hair)			
	Kazuchika Okada (Translucent Red)			
	Kazuchika Okada (Translucent Orange)			
	Shinsuke Nakamura (Red Pants)			
	Shinsuke Nakamura (Black Pants)			
	Shinsuke Nakamura (Translucent Red)			
	Shinsuke Nakamura (Translucent Black)			

NJPW POP! VINYLS		MIB	LOOSE	VALUE
SINGLES	Kenny Omega			
	"The American Nightmare" Cody			
2-PACKS	Matt Jackson (Red Tassels)			
	Nick Jackson (Red Tassels)			
	Matt Jackson (Yellow Tassels)			
	Nick Jackson (Yellow Tassels)			

NJPW M.U.S.C.L.E. MINI FIGURES		MIB	LOOSE	VALUE
BAGGED SINGLES	Kenny Omega			
	Hiroshi Tanahashi			
	Kazuchika Okada			
	Tetsuya Naito			

NJPW 16D COLLECTION		MIB	LOOSE	VALUE
PVC 001	Tetsuya Naito			
PVC 002	Kenny Omega (Blonde Hair)			
	Kenny Omega (Silver Hair)			
PVC 005	Kazuchika Okada			
PVC 006	Hiroshi Tanahashi (Standard Edition – White Tights)			
	Hiroshi Tanahashi (Limited Edition – Black Tights)			
PVC 009	Jushin "Thunder" Liger (Standard Edition – Red Mask)			
	Jushin "Thunder" Liger (Limited Edition – Blue Mask)			
PVC 010	Kota Ibushi (Gold Trunks)			
	Kota Ibushi (Silver Trunks)			
PVC 013	Hiromu Takahashi			
PVC 020	El Desperado (Black)			
	El Desperado (White)			
PVC 026	Bushi (Red)			
	Bushi (White)			

BE@RBRICK

	SOFUBI FIGHTING SERIES	MIB	LOOSE	VALUE
2015	Super Strong Machine			
2023	Kuniaki Kobayashi			

	BE@RBRICK 100% BLIND BOXES	MIB	LOOSE	VALUE
SERIES 34	Black Tiger (Chase)			
	Tiger Mask			
SERIES 37	Kenny Omega			
	NJPW Logo (Chase)			
SERIES 38	Hiroshi Tanahashi			

BE@RBRICK SINGLE RELEASES	MOC	LOOSE	VALUE
Kazuchika Okada			
Tetsuya Naito			

	JYUSHIN "THUNDER" LIGER ACTION FIGURES	MIB	LOOSE	VALUE
RINGSIDE EXCLUSIVES	Jyushin "Thunder" Liger (Red, White & Gold)			
	Jyushin "Thunder" Liger (Black & Gold)			
	Jyushin "Thunder" Liger (Red, White & Silver)			
	Jyushin "Thunder" Liger (Debut)			
	Jyushin "Thunder" Liger (Red)			
	Jyushin "Thunder" Liger (Green)			
	Jyushin "Thunder" Liger (Purple)			
NAUTS EX.	Jyushin "Thunder" Liger (1 of 300)			

	MINORU SUZUKI ACTION FIGURES	MIB	LOOSE	VALUE
RINGSIDE EXCLUSIVES	Minoru Suzuki (Black Trunks)			
	Minoru Suzuki (White Trunks)			

	EL DESPERADO ACTION FIGURES	MIB	LOOSE	VALUE
RINGSIDE EXCLUSIVES	El Desperado (Black Mask)			
	El Desperado (White Mask)			
	El Desperado (Red Mask)			

ULTIMATES!

NJPW ULTIMATES SERIES 1		MIB	LOOSE	VALUE
	Hiroshi Tanahashi			
	Kazuchika Okada			
	Tomohiro Ishii			
	Will Ospreay			
MISC.	Replacement Hands			

NJPW ULTIMATES SERIES 2	MIB	LOOSE	VALUE
Bushi			
Evil			
Hiromu Takahashi			
Tetusya Naito			

1:20 SCALE MODEL KITS	MIB	LOOSE	VALUE
Tetsuya Naito			

NJPW CHIBI BRAWLERS		MOC	LOOSE	VALUE
SERIES 1	Jay White			
	Tetsuya Naito			
SERIES 2	Hiromu Takahashi			
	Evil			
SERIES 3	Hiroshi Tanahashi			
	Kazuchika Okada			

NERDS CLOTHING PRESENTS NJPW		MOC	LOOSE	VALUE
RINGSIDE COLLECTIBLES	"Switchblade" Jay White (Black Tights)			
	"Switchblade" Jay White (Red Tights)			
	Hiromu Takahashi (w/ Black Cat)			
	Hiromu Takahashi (w/ Red Cat)			

PRO-WRESTLING NOAH HAO CLASSIC FIGURES		MIB	LOOSE	VALUE
Mitsuharu Misawa				

PRO-WRESTLING NOAH 16D COLLECTION		MIB	LOOSE	VALUE
PVC 024	Mitsuharu Misawa			
PVC 028	Keiji Mutoh			
PVC 028	Keiji Mutoh (Retirement)			
PVC 029	Nosawa Rongai			
PVC 029	Nosawa Rongai (Retirement)			
PVC 032	Naomichi Marufuji			

PRO-WRESTLING NOAH M.U.S.C.L.E. FIGURE	MIB	LOOSE	VALUE
Great Muta (Retirement Giveaway)			

PRO-WRESTLING NOAH X NORI-KUN SOFUBI	MIB	LOOSE	VALUE
Great Muta (Black)			
Great Muta (Blue)			
Great Muta (Green)			
Great Muta (Red)			
Great Muta (White)			

RING OF HONOR

RING OF HONOR SUPERSTARS SERIES 1	MOC	LOOSE	VALUE
Jay Briscoe			
Mark Briscoe			
Kevin Steen			
Jay Lethal			

RING OF HONOR SUPERSTARS SERIES 2	MOC	LOOSE	VALUE
Adam Cole			
Bobby Fish			
Delirious			
Kyle O'Reilly			

RING OF HONOR SUPERSTARS SERIES 3	MOC	LOOSE	VALUE
ACH			
Hanson			
Nigel McGuinness			
Raymond Rowe			

RING OF HONOR SUPERSTARS SERIES 4	MOC	LOOSE	VALUE
Dalton Castle			
Matt Taven			
Moose			
Roderick Strong			

RING OF HONOR SUPERSTARS SERIES 5	MOC	LOOSE	VALUE
Brody King			
Jay Briscoe			
Jay Lethal			

RING OF HONOR SUPERSTARS SERIES 6	MOC	LOOSE	VALUE
PCO			
Rush			

RING OF HONOR MISCELLANEOUS		MOC	LOOSE	VALUE
CHAMPIONSHIPS	Championship Belt Accessory Pack 1			
	Championship Belt Accessory Pack 2			
ACCESSORIES	ROH Chairs			
	ROH Barricades			
	ROH Wrestling Mat			
	Carrying Case			
RINGS	ROH Wrestling Ring w/ Michael Elgin			

ROH HONOR PALS SERIES 1	MIB	LOOSE	VALUE
Jay Briscoe			
Mark Briscoe			
Bandido			
Brody King			
Rush			
PCO			

ROH HONOR PALS SERIES 2	MIB	LOOSE	VALUE
Dalton Castle			
Danhausen			
Matt Taven			
Shane Taylor			
Vincent			

MICRO BRAWLERS

	ROH MICRO BRAWLERS	MOC	LOOSE	VALUE
EXCLUSIVES	Danhausen			
	Session Moth Martina			
	Angelina Love			
	Jonathan Gresham			
	Shane Taylor			
SINGLE DROPS	Samoa Joe			
	Samoa Joe (Chase – Limted to 100)			
	Jay Lethal (Black Machismo)			

ROH JAZWARES VAULT EXCLUSIVES		MIB	LOOSE	VALUE
#01	Bryan Danielson (1 of 5,000)			
#02	Kenny Omega (1 of 5,000)			
#03	Claudio Castagnoli (1 of 5,000)			
#04	Danhausen (1 of 5,000)			
#05	Nick Jackson (1 of 4,000)			
#05	Matt Jackson (1 of 4,000)			
#06	Adam Cole (1 of 4,000)			
#06	Kyle O'Reilly (1 of 4,000)			
	Jay Briscoe			
	Mark Briscoe			

JOHNNY GOODTIME

CHIMAERA

SOCAL CRAZY

JOHNNY YUMA

RICKY MANDEL

SO-CAL PRO WRESTLING ACTION FIGURES SERIES 1	MOC	LOOSE	VALUE
Chimaera			
Johnny Goodtime			
Johnny Yuma			
Ricky Mandel			
SoCal Crazy			

TNA DELUXE IMPACT! ACTION FIGURES SERIES 1	1/250	MOC	LOOSE	VALUE
AJ Styles (Clean Shaven)				
AJ Styles (Stubble)				
Jeff Jarrett (Dark Hair)				
Jeff Jarrett (Blonde Hair)				
Kurt Angle				
Samoa Joe				
Sting				
Suicide				

TNA DELUXE IMPACT! ACTION FIGURES SERIES 2	MOC	LOOSE	VALUE
AJ Styles			
Amazing Red			
Eric Young			
Hernandez			
Hulk Hogan			
Mick Foley			

TNA DELUXE IMPACT! ACTION FIGURES SERIES 3		MOC	LOOSE	VALUE
	Jay Lethal			
	Kevin Nash			
	Matt Morgan			
	Shark Boy			
	Sting			
1 OF 250	Sting (Scrifice VIP Weekend Exclusive)			
	Velvet Sky			

TNA DELUXE IMPACT! ACTION FIGURES SERIES 4		MOC	LOOSE	VALUE
Abyss				
D'Angelo Dinero				
Desmond Wolfe				
Hulk Hogan				
Jeff Hardy				
Rob Van Dam				

TNA DELUXE IMPACT! ACTION FIGURES SERIES 5		MOC	LOOSE	VALUE
	Angelina Love			
	Jeff Hardy			
	Rob Terry			
1 OF 100	Rob Terry			
	Samoa Joe			
	Raven (Legends of the Ring)			

TNA DELUXE IMPACT! ACTION FIGURES SERIES 6		MOC	LOOSE	VALUE
	Kazarian			
	Kurt Angle			
1 OF 100	Kurt Angle			
	Madison Rayne			
	Sting			
	Terry Taylor (Legends of the Ring)			

TNA DELUXE IMPACT! ACTION FIGURES SERIES 7		MOC	LOOSE	VALUE
	Bobby Roode			
	James Storm			
1 OF 100	James Storm			
	Jeff Hardy			
	Mr. Anderson			
	Velvet Sky			

TNA DELUXE IMPACT! ACTION FIGURES SERIES 8		MOC	LOOSE	VALUE
	AJ Styles			
	Hulk Hogan			
	Matt Morgan			
	Rob Van Dam			
1 OF 100	Rob Van Dam			
	Sting			

TNA DELUXE IMPACT! ACTION FIGURES SERIES 9		MOC	LOOSE	VALUE
	Austin Aries			
	Christopher Daniels			
	Magnus			
	Jeff Hardy			
1 OF 100	Jeff Hardy			
	Gail Kim			

TNA DELUXE IMPACT! ACTION FIGURES SERIES 10		MOC	LOOSE	VALUE
	Crimson			
	Kurt Angle			
1 OF 100	Kurt Angle			
	Brooke Tessmacher			
	Rob Terry			
	Rob Van Dam			

TNA DELUXE IMPACT! ACTION FIGURES SERIES 11	MOC	LOOSE	VALUE
AJ Styles			
Austin Aries			
Jeff Hardy			
Velvet Sky			

TNA DELUXE IMPACT! ACTION FIGURES SERIES 12	MOC	LOOSE	VALUE
Bully Ray			
Chris Sabin			
Hernandez			
Magnus			

TNA DELUXE IMPACT! ACTION FIGURES SERIES 13	MOC	LOOSE	VALUE
Angelina Love			
Mr. Anderson			

TNA DELUXE IMPACT! ACTION FIGURES EXCLUSIVES		MOC	LOOSE	VALUE
RINGSIDE COLLECTIBLES	Austin Aries			
	"Full Metal" Jeff Hardy			
	"Glow Paint" Jeff Hardy			
SHOPTNA	Dixie Carter			
	GITD Jeff Hardy			
	Joker Sting			

TNA DELUXE IMPACT! WRESTLING RINGS	MIB	LOOSE	VALUE
Six Sided Ring			
Hulkamania Ring w/ Hulk Hogan & Sting			

TNA DELUXE IMPACT! CROSS THE LINE 2-PACKS SERIES 1	MOC	LOOSE	VALUE
Bobby Roode			
James Storm			
Samoa Joe			
Mick Foley			
Scott Steiner			
Kevin Nash			

TNA DELUXE IMPACT! CROSS THE LINE 2-PACKS SERIES 2	MOC	LOOSE	VALUE
AJ Styles			
Jeff Jarrett			
Alex Shelley			
Chris Sabin			
Brother Ray			
Brother Devon			

TNA DELUXE IMPACT! CROSS THE LINE 2-PACKS SERIES 3	MOC	LOOSE	VALUE
AJ Styles			
Jeff Hardy			
Kurt Angle			
Mr. Anderson			
Stevie Richards			
Daphney			

TNA DELUXE IMPACT! CROSS THE LINE 2-PACKS SERIES 4	MOC	LOOSE	VALUE
Eric Young			
Kevin Nash			
Hulk Hogan			
Abyss			
Sting			
Rob Van Dam			

TNA DELUXE IMPACT! CROSS THE LINE 2-PACKS EXCLUSIVES		MOC	LOOSE	VALUE
RINGSIDE COLLECTIBLES	Matt Hardy			
	Jeff Hardy			

TNA IMPACT! ACTION FIGURES		MOC	LOOSE	VALUE
SERIES 1	Abyss			
	Jay Lethal			
	Suicide			
	Kurt Angle			
	Kevin Nash			
	Sting			
RINGS	Six Sides Of Steel			

TNA LEGENDS OF THE RING SERIES 1	MOC	LOOSE	VALUE
Hulk Hogan			
Jeff Jarrett			
Kevin Nash			
Kurt Angle			
Sting			

	TNA LEGENDS OF THE RING EXCLUSIVES	MOC	LOOSE	VALUE
SHOPTNA	AJ Styles (Hood Down)			
	AJ Styles (Hood Up)			
RINGSIDE COLLECTIBLES	Jeff Hardy			
	Earl Hebner			
	Sting			
	Hulk Hogan			
	Sting			
	Rob Van Dam			
	Jeff Hardy			

TNA IMPACT! GENESIS SERIES 1	W/ BELT	MOC	LOOSE	VALUE
AJ Styles				
Jeff Jarrett				
Kurt Angle				
Samoa Joe				
Sting				
Suicide				

TNA GENESIS MISCELLANEOUS		MIB	LOOSE	VALUE
3-PACK 1	AJ Styles, Suicide & Kurt Angle			
3-PACK 2	Sting, Jeff Jarrett & Samoa Joe			
4-PACK 1	AJ Styles, Kurt Angle, Sting & Suicide			
4-PACK 2	Jeff Jarrett, Kurt Angle, Sting & Samoa Joe			
HULKAMANIA RING SET	Hulk Hogan			
	Sting			

TNA MICRO IMPACT! 3" FIGURES SERIES 1		MOC	LOOSE	VALUE
PACK 1	AJ Styles			
	Jeff Jarrett			
	Mick Foley			
PACK 2	Christopher Daniels			
	Consequences Creed			
	Jay Lethal			
PACK 3	Kurt Angle			
	Kevin Nash			
	Sting			
PACK 4	Shark Boy			
	Abyss			
	Suicide			
TOYS 'R' US	Micro Impact 10 Pack			

TNA MICRO IMPACT! 3" FIGURES SERIES 2		MOC	LOOSE	VALUE
PACK 1	Hulk Hogan			
	Abyss			
	Jeff Hardy			
PACK 2	Kevin Nash			
	Eric Young			
	Jay Lethal			
PACK 3	Robert Roode			
	James Storm			
	Matt Morgan			
PACK 4	Sting			
	Rob Van Dam			
	Jeff Jarrett			

MICRO BRAWLERS

IMPACT! MICRO BRAWLERS SERIES 1	MOC	LOOSE	VALUE
Abyss			
Doc Gallows			
Eddie Edwards			
Jordynne Grace			
Moose			

IMPACT! MICRO BRAWLERS SERIES 2	MOC	LOOSE	VALUE
Ace Austin			
Josh Alexander			
Karl Anderson			
Rich Swann			
Scott D'Amore (Team Canada)			

IMPACT! MICRO BRAWLERS SERIES 3	MOC	LOOSE	VALUE
Eric Young			
Heath			
Deonna Purrazzo			
Willie Mack			
Gail Kim			

IMPACT! MICRO BRAWLERS SERIES 4	MOC	LOOSE	VALUE
Robert Roode			
Tasha Steelz			
Trey Miguel			
Chris Bey			

IMPACT! EXCLUSIVE MICRO BRAWLERS	MOC	LOOSE	VALUE
Madison Rayne			

IMPACT! SLAM BUDDIES SERIES 1	MIB	LOOSE	VALUE
Chris Bey			
Josh Alexander			
Santino Marella			

IMPACT! SLAM BUDDIES SERIES 2	MIB	LOOSE	VALUE
Frankie Kazarian			
Steve Maclin			
Trinity			

POWERTOWN ULTRAS SERIES 1	MIB	LOOSE	VALUE
Eddie Edwards			
Jordynne Grace			
Josh Alexander			
Moose			

BE@RBRICK

UWF SOFUBI FIGHTING SERIES	MIB	LOOSE	VALUE
Akira Maeda (Jumpsuit)			
Akira Maeda (Black Trunks)			

	UWF BE@RBRICK 100% FIGURES	MIB	LOOSE	VALUE
SERIES 44	UWF Logo			

BASIC ARTICULATION RELEASES

WWE BASIC SERIES 1 (2010)	1 OF 1,000	MOC	LOOSE	VALUE
Batista				
Big Show				
Evan Bourne				
John Cena				
Kofi Kingston				
Triple H				

WWE BASIC SERIES 2 (2010)	1 OF 1,000	MOC	LOOSE	VALUE
CM Punk				
Jack Swagger				
Kane				
Mark Henry				
Rey Mysterio (Dark Blue)				
Rey Mysterio (Light Blue)				
Vladimir Kozlov				

WWE BASIC SERIES 3 (2010)	1 OF 1,000	MOC	LOOSE	VALUE
Chris Jericho				
The Great Khali				
Mickie James				
Randy Orton				
Shelton Benjamin				
The Undertaker				

WWE BASIC SERIES 4 (2010)	1 OF 1,000	MOC	LOOSE	VALUE
Dolph Ziggler				
Goldust				
Matt Hardy				
MVP				
Shawn Michaels				
William Regal				

WWE BASIC SERIES 5 (2010)	1 OF 1,000	MOC	LOOSE	VALUE
Batista				
The Hurricane				
John Cena				
Melina				
Mike Knox				
R-Truth				

WWE BASIC SERIES 6 (2010)	1 OF 1,000	MOC	LOOSE	VALUE
Big Show				
Drew McIntyre				
Edge				
Kelly Kelly				
The Miz				
Ted Dibiase				

WWE BASIC SERIES 7 (2010)	1 OF 1,000	MOC	LOOSE	VALUE
Kofi Kingston				
Michelle McCool				
Rey Mysterio				
Sheamus				
The Undertaker				
Yoshi Tatsu				

WWE BASIC SERIES 8 (2011)	MOC	LOOSE	VALUE
Chris Masters			
Christian			
Kane			
Kofi Kingston			
Finlay			
Maryse			

WWE BASIC SERIES 9 (2011)	MOC	LOOSE	VALUE
Evan Bourne			
Jack Swagger			
JTG			
Mark Henry			
Natalya			
Rey Mysterio			

WWE BASIC SERIES 10 (2011)	MOC	LOOSE	VALUE
Dolph Ziggler			
John Cena			
Kofi Kingston			
Triple H			
Wade Barrett			
Zack Ryder			

WWE BASIC SERIES 11 (2011)	MOC	LOOSE	VALUE
Big Show			
Daniel Bryan			
Eve			
Sheamus			
Skip Sheffield			

WWE BASIC SERIES 12 (2011)	MOC	LOOSE	VALUE
Alberto Del Rio			
Evan Bourne			
John Morrison			
Randy Orton			
Rey Mysterio			
Wade Barrett			

WWE BASIC SERIES 13 (2012)		MOC	LOOSE	VALUE
#01	Rey Mysterio			
#02	Vickie Guerrero			
#03	John Morrison			
#04	R-Truth			
#05	Ezekiel Jackson			
#06	The Undertaker			

WWE BASIC SERIES 14 - ROYAL RUMBLE HERITAGE (2012)		MOC	LOOSE	VALUE
#07	Bret "Hit Man" Hart			
#08	Shawn Michaels			
#09	Goldust			
#10	Rey Mysterio			
#11	John Morrison			
#12	Alberto Del Rio			

WWE BASIC SERIES 15 (2012)		MOC	LOOSE	VALUE
#13	Layla			
#14	Kofi Kingston			
#15	John Cena			
#16	Wade Barrett			
#17	Brodus Clay			
#18	Kane			

WWE BASIC SERIES 16 - WRESTLEMANIA HERITAGE (2012)		MOC	LOOSE	VALUE
#19	Ultimate Warrior			
#20	John Cena			
#21	Eddie Guerrero			
#22	Triple H			
#23	The Undertaker			
#24	Jack Swagger			

WWE BASIC ACTION FIGURES SERIES 17		MOC	LOOSE	VALUE
#25	Rey Mysterio			
#26	Dolph Ziggler			
#27	Zack Ryder			
#28	The Miz			
#29	Alex Riley			
#30	Mark Henry			

WWE BASIC SERIES 18 - RAW SUPERSHOW (2012)		MOC	LOOSE	VALUE
#31	Kelly Kelly			
#32	Sin Cara			
#33	Hunico			
#34	CM Punk			
#35	John Cena			
#36	Cody Rhodes			

WWE BASIC SERIES 19 (2012)		MOC	LOOSE	VALUE
#37	Hornswoggle			
#38	Evan Bourne			
#39	Kofi Kingston			
#40	Justin Gabriel			
#41	Jinder Mahal			
#42	Randy Orton			

WWE BASIC SERIES 20 - GLOBAL SUPERSTARS (2012)			MOC	LOOSE	VALUE
#43	CANADA	Natalya			
#44	MEXICO	Rey Mysterio			
#45	JAPAN	Yoshi Tatsu			
#46	USA	John Cena			
#47	IRELAND	Wade Barrett			
#48	UK	Sheamus			

WWE BASIC SERIES 21 (2012)		MOC	LOOSE	VALUE
#49	Beth Pheonix			
#50	R-Truth			
#51	The Miz			
#52	Mason Ryan			
#53	Jack Swagger			
#54	Big Show			

WWE BASIC SERIES 22 (2012)		MOC	LOOSE	VALUE
#55	Booker T			
#56	Mark Henry			
#57	Chris Jericho			
#58	Christian			
#59	John Cena			
#60	Zack Ryder			

WWE BASIC SERIES 23 (2012)		MOC	LOOSE	VALUE
#61	Rey Mysterio			
#62	Alicia Fox			
#63	Hunico			
#64	Santino Marella			
#65	Triple H			
#66	Kane			

WWE BASIC SERIES 24 (2013)		MOC	LOOSE	VALUE
#01	John Cena			
#02	CM Punk			
#03	Zack Ryder			
#04	Drew McIntyre			
#05	Sheamus			
#06	AJ			

WWE BASIC SERIES 25 - RAW SUPERSHOW (2013)		MOC	LOOSE	VALUE
#07	Big Show			
#08	Brock Lesnar			
#09	Randy Orton			
#10	The Miz			
#11	Eve			
#12	David Otunga			

WWE BASIC SERIES 26 - WRESTLEMANIA HERITAGE (2013)		MOC	LOOSE	VALUE
#13	"Macho Man" Randy Savage			
#14	Shawn Michaels			
#15	The Undertaker			
#16	Kane			
#17	Mark Henry			
#18	Daniel Bryan			

WWE BASIC SERIES 27 (2013)		MOC	LOOSE	VALUE
#19	Cody Rhodes			
#20	Kofi Kingston			
#21	Wade Barrett			
#22	Ryback			
#23	Brodus Clay			
#24	Antonio Cesaro			

WWE BASIC SERIES 28 (2013)		MOC	LOOSE	VALUE
#25	Rey Mysterio			
#26	R-Truth			
#27	Heath Slater			
#28	Sin Cara			
#29	Tensai			
#30	Damien Sandow			

WWE BASIC SERIES 29 - WORLD CHAMPIONS (2013)		MOC	LOOSE	VALUE
#31	Ultimate Warrior			
#32	Eddie Guerrero			
#33	Stone Cold Steve Austin			
#34	Big Show			
#35	John Cena			
#36	CM Punk			

WWE BASIC SERIES 30 (2013)		MOC	LOOSE	VALUE
#37	The Miz			
#38	Hornswoggle			
#39	Santino Marella			
#40	Sheamus			
#41	Daniel Bryan			
#42	AJ Lee			

	WWE BASIC SERIES 31 (2013)	MOC	LOOSE	VALUE
#43	Kane			
#44	R-Truth			
#45	Zack Ryder			
#45	Zack Ryder (Alternate Head)			
#46	Rosa Mendes			
#47	Wade Barrett			
#48	Alberto Del Rio			

	WWE BASIC SERIES 32 - ROYAL RUMBLE (2013)	MOC	LOOSE	VALUE
#49	Chris Jericho			
#50	The Rock			
#51	Randy Orton			
#52	John Cena			
#53	Ryback			
#54	Antonio Cesaro			

	WWE BASIC SERIES 33 (2013)	MOC	LOOSE	VALUE
#55	Big Show			
#56	Dolph Ziggler			
#57	The Great Khali			
#58	CM Punk			
#59	Tamina Snuka			
#60	Dean Ambrose			

WWE BASIC SERIES 34 (2013)		MOC	LOOSE	VALUE
#61	John Cena			
#62	The Miz			
#63	Rey Mysterio			
#64	Sin Cara			
#65	Ricardo Rodriguez			
#66	Brodus Clay			

WWE BASIC SERIES 35 (2014)		MOC	LOOSE	VALUE
#01	Kane			
#02	Damien Sandow			
#03	Daniel Bryan			
#04	Triple H			
#05	Cody Rhodes			
#06	Jinder Mahal			

WWE BASIC SERIES 36 (2014)		MOC	LOOSE	VALUE
#07	CM Punk			
#08	Big E Langston			
#09	Christian			
#10	Jack Swagger			
#11	Fandango (Clean Shaven)			
#11	Fandango (Stubble)			
#12	Kaitlyn			

WWE BASIC SERIES 37 - WRESTLEMANIA HERITAGE (2014)		MOC	LOOSE	VALUE
#13	Mr. Perfect			
#14	Batista			
#15	Roman Reigns			
#16	Randy Orton			
#17	Zeb Colter			
#18	Ryback			

WWE BASIC SERIES 38 (2014)		MOC	LOOSE	VALUE
#19	Chris Jericho			
#20	Dolph Ziggler			
#21	Vickie Guerrero			
#22	Sheamus			
#23	The Miz			
#24	Kofi Kingston			

WWE BASIC SERIES 39 (2014)		MOC	LOOSE	VALUE
#25	Bray Wyatt			
#26	Rob Van Dam			
#27	Justin Gabriel			
#28	John Cena			
#29	Christian			
#30	Heath Slater			

WWE BASIC SERIES 40 - GLOBAL SUPERSTARS (2014)			MOC	LOOSE	VALUE
#31	CHICAGO	CM Punk			
#32	MEXICO	Alberto Del Rio			
#33	SAN DIEGO	Rey Mysterio			
#34	PUNJAB, INDIA	The Great Khali			
#35	LONG ISLAND	Zack Ryder			
#36	TORONTO	Edge			

WWE BASIC SERIES 41 (2014)		MOC	LOOSE	VALUE
#37	Daniel Bryan			
#38	Santino Marella			
#39	Cesaro			
#40	Drew McIntyre			
#41	Bray Wyatt			
#42	Fandango			

WWE BASIC SERIES 42 (2014)		MOC	LOOSE	VALUE
#43	Natalya			
#44	Batista			
#45	El Torito			
#46	Big Show			
#47	Roman Reigns			
#48	Sin Cara			

WWE BASIC SERIES 43 (2014)		MOC	LOOSE	VALUE
#49	Mark Henry			
#50	Eva Marie			
#51	Rob Van Dam			
#52	John Cena			
#54	Dolph Ziggler			
#55	Rey Mysterio			

WWE BASIC SERIES 44 (2014)		MOC	LOOSE	VALUE
#53	Kane			
#56	Big E			
#57	Randy Orton			
#58	Seth Rollins			
#59	Titus O'Neil			
#60	Goldust			

WWE BASIC SERIES 45 (2015)		MOC	LOOSE	VALUE
#01	Triple H			
#02	Chris Jericho			
#03	Mankind			
#04	The Miz			
#05	Ricky "The Dragon" Steamboat			
#06	Daniel Bryan			

WWE BASIC SERIES 46 (2015)		MOC	LOOSE	VALUE
#08	Big Show			
#09	Kofi Kingston			
#10	Bad News Barrett			
#11	Jerry "The King" Lawler			
#12	Batista			

WWE BASIC SERIES 47 (2015)		MOC	LOOSE	VALUE
#13	Alicia Fox			
#14	Rusev			
#15	Brock Lesnar			
#16	Kane			
#17	Christian			
#18	Cesaro			

WWE BASIC SERIES 48 - WRESTLEMANIA HERITAGE (2015)		MOC	LOOSE	VALUE
#19	Ric Flair			
#20	Hulk Hogan			
#21	Brie Bella			
#22	John Cena			
#23	Booker T			
#24	Randy Orton			

WWE BASIC SERIES 49 (2015)		MOC	LOOSE	VALUE
#25	Ryback			
#26	Bray Wyatt			
#27	Roman Reigns			
#28	Bret Hart			
#29	Bo Dallas			
#30	Emma (Long Legs)			
#30	Emma (Short Legs)			

WWE BASIC SERIES 50 (2015)		MOC	LOOSE	VALUE
#31	Daniel Bryan			
#32	Adam Rose			
#33	Seth Rollins			
#34	Goldust			
#35	Summer Rae			
#36	Sami Zayn			

WWE BASIC SERIES 51 (2015)		MOC	LOOSE	VALUE
#37	Dolph Ziggler			
#38	Dean Ambrose			
#39	Stardust			
#40	Stephanie McMahon			
#41	Stone Cold Steve Austin			
#42	Heath Slater			

WWE BASIC SERIES 52 (2015)		MOC	LOOSE	VALUE
#43	John Cena			
#44	Chris Jericho			
#45	The Miz			
#46	Nikki Bella			
#47	Mark Henry			
#48	Adrian Neville			

WWE BASIC SERIES 53 (2015)		MOC	LOOSE	VALUE
#49	Brock Lesnar			
#50	The Rock			
#51	Triple H			
#52	Damien Mizdow			
#53	AJ Lee			
#54	Tyler Breeze			

WWE BASIC SERIES 54 (2015)		MOC	LOOSE	VALUE
#55	Roman Reigns			
#56	The Rock			
#57	Rusev			
#58	Big Show			
#59	Dolph Ziggler			
#60	Tyson Kidd			

WWE BASIC SERIES 55 (2015)		MOC	LOOSE	VALUE
#60	Sting			
#61	John Cena			
#62	El Torito			
#63	Kane			
#64	Randy Orton			
#65	Bray Wyatt			
#66	The Undertaker			
#67	Charlotte			

WWE BASIC SERIES 56 (2016)		CHASE	MOC	LOOSE	VALUE
RAW	Dean Ambrose				
NXT	Hideo Itami				
RAW	John Cena				
DIVAS	Naomi				
LEGENDS	Ultimate Warrior				
SMACKDOWN	Xavier Woods				

WWE BASIC SERIES 57 (2016)		CHASE	MOC	LOOSE	VALUE
SMACKDOWN	Big Show				
RAW	Daniel Bryan				
SMACKDOWN	Erick Rowan				
NXT	Finn Balor				
DIVAS	Paige				
RAW	Ryback				

WWE BASIC SERIES 58 (2016)		CHASE	MOC	LOOSE	VALUE
SMACKDOWN	Bad News Barrett				
NXT	Bayley				
LEGENDS	Edge				
SMACKDOWN	Fandango				
NXT	Kevin Owens				
DIVAS	Lana				
LEGENDS	Paul Orndorff				
SMACKDOWN	Stardust				
RAW	The Undertaker				

WWE BASIC SERIES 59 (2016)		CHASE	MOC	LOOSE	VALUE
RAW	Bray Wyatt				
DIVAS	Eva Marie				
LEGENDS	Honky Tonk Man				
SMACKDOWN	R-Truth				
NXT	Sasha Banks				
SMACKDOWN	Sheamus				
LEGENDS	The Iron Sheik				
RAW	Triple H				

WWE BASIC SERIES 60 (2016)		CHASE	MOC	LOOSE	VALUE
RAW	Brock Lesnar				
RAW	John Cena				
NXT	Kalisto				
SMACKDOWN	Kofi Kingston				
SMACKDOWN	Luke Harper				
RAW	Randy Orton				
DIVAS	Renee Young				
RAW	Seth Rollins				

WWE BASIC SERIES 61 (2016)		CHASE	MOC	LOOSE	VALUE
SMACKDOWN	Big E				
RAW	Dean Ambrose				
RAW	Dolph Ziggler				
NXT	Finn Balor				
RAW	John Cena				
DIVAS	Natalya				
NXT/SD	Neville				
NXT	Sami Zayn				
SMACKDOWN	Zack Ryder				

WWE BASIC SERIES 62 (2016)		MOC	LOOSE	VALUE
DIVAS	Becky Lynch			
SMACKDOWN	Roman Reigns			
RAW	Sin Cara			
LEGENDS	Sting			
SMACKDOWN	The Miz			

WWE BASIC SERIES 63 (2016)		CHASE	MOC	LOOSE	VALUE
RAW	Alberto Del Rio				
NXT	Baron Corbin				
RAW	Paul Heyman				
SMACKDOWN	Rusev				
SMACKDOWN	Ryback				
RAW	Seth Rollins				
LEGENDS	Sid Justice				
RAW	The Undertaker				

WWE BASIC SERIES 64 (2016)		MOC	LOOSE	VALUE
NXT	Apollo Crews			
RAW	Braun Strowman			
RAW	Brock Lesnar			
SMACKDOWN	Dolph Ziggler			
RAW	John Cena			
RAW	Lana			
SMACKDOWN	Xavier Woods			

WWE BASIC SERIES 65 (2016)		MOC	LOOSE	VALUE
SMACKDOWN	Kane			
NXT	Emma			
RAW	Kevin Owens			
RAW	Roman Reigns			
NXT	Samoa Joe			
SMACKDOWN	Sheamus			
RAW	The Rock			

WWE BASIC SERIES 66 (2016)		MOC	LOOSE	VALUE
SMACKDOWN	Albertio Del Rio			
SMACKDOWN	Big Show			
RAW	Daniel Bryan			
RAW	Dean Ambrose			
RAW	Paige			
RAW	Roman Reigns			
SMACKDOWN	Tyler Breeze			

WWE BASIC SERIES 67 (2017)		CHASE	MOC	LOOSE	VALUE
SMACKDOWN	Cesaro				
SMACKDOWN	Goldust				
RAW	JBL				
RAW	John Cena				
SMACKDOWN	Luke Harper				
WOMEN'S	Naomi				
RAW	Randy Orton				
SMACKDWON	Xavier Woods				

WWE BASIC SERIES 68A (2017)		CHASE	MOC	LOOSE	VALUE
SMACKDOWN	Bo Dallas				
RAW	Braun Strowman				
RAW	Brock Lesnar				
NXT	Dana Brooke				
LEGENDS	Diamond Dallas Page				
NXT	Finn Balor				
SMACKDOWN	Kalisto				
RAW	Neville				

WWE BASIC SERIES 68B (2017)		CHASE	MOC	LOOSE	VALUE
RAW	AJ Styles				
NXT	Alexa Bliss				
RAW	Chris Jericho				
RAW	Seth Rollins				
LEGENDS	Sting				
NXT	The Rock				

	WWE BASIC SERIES 69 (2017)	CHASE	MOC	LOOSE	VALUE
SMACKDOWN	Bray Wyatt				
SMACKDOWN	Dean Ambrose				
SMACKDOWN	John Cena				
RAW	Sami Zayn				
WOMEN'S	Sasha Banks				
LEGENDS	Sgt. Slaughter				
WOMEN'S	Tamina				
RAW	Triple H				

	WWE BASIC SERIES 70 (2017)	CHASE	MOC	LOOSE	VALUE
SMACKDOWN	Apollo Crews				
WOMEN'S	Brie Bella				
NXT	Carmella				
LEGENDS	Ric Flair				
RAW	Roman Reigns				
NXT	Samoa Joe				
RAW	The Rock				
LEGENDS	Ultimate Warrior				

	WWE BASIC SERIES 71 (2017)	CHASE	MOC	LOOSE	VALUE
NXT	Austin Aries				
SMACKDOWN	Baron Corbin				
WOMEN'S	Charlotte				
RAW	Finn Balor				
SMACKDOWN	John Cena				
RAW	Seth Rollins				
LEGENDS	The Undertaker				

WWE BASIC SERIES 72 (2017)		CHASE	MOC	LOOSE	VALUE
SMACKDOWN	Dean Ambrose				
SMACKDOWN	Dolph Ziggler				
WOMEN'S	Nia Jax				
RAW	Sheamus				
NXT	Shinsuke Nakamura				
SMACKDOWN	Zack Ryder				

WWE BASIC SERIES 73 (2017)		MOC	LOOSE	VALUE
SMACKDOWN	AJ Styles			
RAW	Big E			
RAW	Cesaro			
RAW	Kevin Owens			
RAW	Seth Rollins			
RAW	Triple H			

WWE BASIC SERIES 74 (2017)		MOC	LOOSE	VALUE
WOMEN'S	Bayley			
SMACKDOWN	John Cena			
LEGENDS	Kane			
RAW	Neville			
RAW	Roman Reigns			
NXT	Samoa Joe			

WWE BASIC SERIES 75 (2017)		MOC	LOOSE	VALUE
RAW	Braun Strowman			
RAW	Brock Lesnar			
RAW	Chris Jericho			
RAW	Finn Balor			
RAW	Lana			
RAW	Randy Orton			

WWE BASIC SERIES 76 (2017)		MOC	LOOSE	VALUE
SMACKDOWN	AJ Styles			
SMACKDOWN	Dolph Ziggler			
SMACKDOWN	John Cena			
LEGENDS	"Macho King" Randy Savage			
RAW	Sami Zayn			
SMACKDOWN	The Rock			

WWE BASIC SERIES 77 (2017)		MOC	LOOSE	VALUE
RAW	Corey Graves			
RAW	Dean Ambrose			
RAW	Finn Balor			
RAW	Roman Reigns			
RAW	Seth Rollins			

WWE BASIC SERIES 78 (2018)	CHASE	MOC	LOOSE	VALUE
AJ Styles				
Braun Strowman				
Kevin Owens				
Natalya				
Shane McMahon				
The Rock				

WWE BASIC SERIES 79 (2018)	CHASE	MOC	LOOSE	VALUE
Baron Corbin				
Neville				
Nia Jax				
Samoa Joe				
Stone Cold Steve Austin				
TJP				

WWE BASIC SERIES 80 (2018)	CHASE	MOC	LOOSE	VALUE
Brock Lesnar				
Chris Jericho				
Rich Swann				
Roman Reigns				
Sasha Banks				

WWE BASIC SERIES 81 (2018)	CHASE	MOC	LOOSE	VALUE
Dana Brooke				
Kofi Kingston				
Rhyno				
Sami Zayn				
Seth Rollins				

WWE BASIC SERIES 82 (2018)	CHASE	MOC	LOOSE	VALUE
AJ Styles				
Becky Lynch				
John Cena				
Luke Harper				
Shinsuke Nakamura				

WWE BASIC SERIES 83 (2018)	CHASE	MOC	LOOSE	VALUE
Alicia Fox				
Kurt Angle				
Randy Orton				
Triple H				
Tye Dillinger				

WWE BASIC SERIES 84 (2018)	CHASE	MOC	LOOSE	VALUE
Dean Ambrose				
Finn Balor				
Kevin Owens				
Naomi				
Rusev				

WWE BASIC SERIES 85 (2018)	CHASE	MOC	LOOSE	VALUE
AJ Styles				
Alexa Bliss				
Bobby Roode				
John Cena				
Seth Rollins				

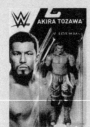

WWE BASIC SERIES 86 (2018)	MOC	LOOSE	VALUE
Akira Tozawa			
Charlotte Flair			
Dolph Ziggler			
Roman Reigns			
The Rock			

WWE BASIC SERIES 87 (2018)	MOC	LOOSE	VALUE
AJ Styles			
Bayley			
Dean Ambrose			
Jason Jordan			
The Miz			

WWE BASIC SERIES 88 (2018)	MOC	LOOSE	VALUE
Baron Corbin			
Chad Gable			
Elias			
John Cena			
Sasha Banks			

WWE BASIC SERIES 89 (2018)	MOC	LOOSE	VALUE
Carmella			
Cesaro			
Kalisto			
Kurt Angle			
Sheamus			

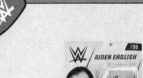     

	WWE BASIC SERIES 90 (2019)	MOC	LOOSE	VALUE
	Aiden English			
	Kane			
	Roman Reigns (Superman Punch Shirt)			
CHASE	Roman Reigns (Shield Shirt)			
	Ronda Rousey			
	The Miz			

	WWE BASIC SERIES 91 (2019)	MOC	LOOSE	VALUE
	Alexa Bliss			
	Dean Ambrose (Blank Shirt)			
CHASE	Dean Ambrose (Shield Shirt)			
	Drew Gulak			
	Finn Balor			
	Shinsuke Nakamura			

	WWE BASIC SERIES 92 (2019)	MOC	LOOSE	VALUE
	Jeff Hardy			
	John Cena			
	Mandy Rose			
	Samoa Joe			
	Seth Rollins (Kingslayer Shirt)			
CHASE	Seth Rollins (Shield Shirt)			

	WWE BASIC SERIES 93 (2019)	MOC	LOOSE	VALUE
	Bayley			
	Jinder Mahal			
	"Macho Man" Randy Savage (Yellow Lightning Bolts)			
CHASE	"Macho Man" Randy Savage (White Lightning Bolts)			
	Triple H			
	The Undertaker			

	WWE BASIC SERIES 94 (2019)	MOC	LOOSE	VALUE
	Big E			
	Kofi Kingston			
	Randy Orton			
	"Woken" Matt Hardy (Delete Shirt)			
CHASE	"Woken" Matt Hardy (Mower Of Lawn Shirt)			
	Xavier Woods			

	WWE BASIC SERIES 95 (2019)	MOC	LOOSE	VALUE
	AJ Styles			
	Bray Wyatt			
	Kurt Angle			
	Rusev			
	Sonya Deville (Red Gear)			
CHASE	Sonya Deville (Black Gear)			

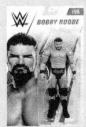     

	WWE BASIC SERIES 96 (2019)	MOC	LOOSE	VALUE
	Bobby Roode			
	Daniel Bryan			
	Kevin Owens			
	Sami Zayn (Patch Gear)			
CHASE	Sami Zayn (Black & Red Gear)			
	Sasha Banks			

	WWE BASIC SERIES 97 - SUMMERSLAM (2019)	MOC	LOOSE	VALUE
	AJ Styles			
	Bret "Hitman" Hart			
	Jeff Hardy			
	Razor Ramon			
	The Miz (White Trunks)			
CHASE	The Miz (Black Trunks)			

	WWE BASIC SERIES 98 (2019)	MOC	LOOSE	VALUE
	Elias			
	Finn Balor			
	Ruby Riott			
	Tony Nese (White Trunks)			
CHASE	Tony Nese (Silver Trunks)			
	Ultimate Warrior			

	WWE BASIC SERIES 99 (2019)	MOC	LOOSE	VALUE
	Ariya Daivari (White Trunks)			
CHASE	Ariya Daivari (Black Trunks)			
	Becky Lynch			
	Drew McIntyre			
	Rey Mysterio			
	Shinsuke Nakamura			

	WWE BASIC SERIES 100 (2019)	MOC	LOOSE	VALUE
	John Cena			
	Shawn Michaels (Red Tights)			
CHASE	Shawn Michaels (White Tights w/ Red)			
	The Rock			
	Stone Cold Steve Austin			
	The Undertaker			

    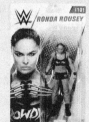 

	WWE BASIC SERIES 101 (2019)	MOC	LOOSE	VALUE
	AJ Styles			
	Ali (Grey & Purple)			
CHASE	Ali (Green & Black)			
	Bobby Lashley			
	Ronda Rousey			
	Sarah Logan			

	WWE BASIC SERIES 102 (2020)	MOC	LOOSE	VALUE
	Constable Baron Corbin			
	Drake Maverick (Green)			
CHASE	Drake Maverick (Black)			
	Jeff Hardy			
	Seth Rollins			
	The Miz			

	WWE BASIC SERIES 103 (2020)	MOC	LOOSE	VALUE
	AJ Styles			
	Becky Lynch (The Man Shirt)			
CHASE	Becky Lynch (Relent-Lass Shirt)			
	Brock Lesnar			
	Kofi Kingston			
	Matt Riddle			

	WWE BASIC SERIES 104 (2020)	MOC	LOOSE	VALUE
	Alexa Bliss			
	Daniel Bryan			
	Keith Lee (Blue)			
CHASE	Keith Lee (Black)			
	Randy Orton			
	Rey Mysterio			

	WWE BASIC SERIES 105 (2020)	MOC	LOOSE	VALUE
	John Cena			
	Lars Sullivan			
	Paige			
	Roman Reigns			
	Ronda Rousey (White Top)			
CHASE	Ronda Rousey (Black Top)			

	WWE BASIC SERIES 106 (2020)	MOC	LOOSE	VALUE
	Carmella (Blue)			
CHASE	Carmella (Red)			
	Finn Balor			
	Johnny Gargano			
	R-Truth			
	Triple H			

	WWE BASIC SERIES 107 (2020)	MOC	LOOSE	VALUE
	Bianca Belair			
	Braun Strowman			
	EC3			
	Shinsuke Nakamura (Black & Red)			
CHASE	Shinsuke Nakamura (Blue & Black)			
	The Rock			

	WWE BASIC SERIES 108 (2020)	MOC	LOOSE	VALUE
	AJ Styles (Black & Red)			
CHASE	AJ Styles (Black & Gold)			
	Aleister Black			
	Angelo Dawkins			
	Montez Ford			
	Roman Reigns			

	WWE BASIC SERIES 109 - SUMMERSLAM (2020)	MOC	LOOSE	VALUE
	Becky Lynch			
	Lana (Blue)			
CHASE	Lana (Red)			
	Ricochet			
	Seth Rollins			
	The Undertaker			

	WWE BASIC SERIES 110 (2020)	MOC	LOOSE	VALUE
	Finn Balor			
	John Cena			
	Kofi Kingston			
	Liv Morgan			
	Mike Kanellis (Rose Trunks)			
CHASE	Mike Kanellis (Kanellis Trunks)			

	WWE BASIC SERIES 111 (2020)	MOC	LOOSE	VALUE
	Bray Wyatt			
	Erick Rowan			
	Jeff Hardy			
	Kevin Owens			
	Nikki Cross (Blue & Pink Shirt)			
CHASE	Nikki Cross (Black & Blue Shirt)			

	WWE BASIC SERIES 112 (2020)	MOC	LOOSE	VALUE
	Adam Cole			
	Bobby Lashley (Tights)			
CHASE	Bobby Lashley (Trunks)			
	Braun Strowman			
	Sasha Banks			
	Seth Rollins			

	WWE BASIC SERIES 113 (2020)	MOC	LOOSE	VALUE
	Buddy Murphy			
	Drew McIntyre			
	Edge (Purple Boots)			
CHASE	Edge (Silver Boots)			
	John Cena			
	Mia Yim			

	WWE BASIC SERIES 114 (2021)	MOC	LOOSE	VALUE
	Kofi Kingston			
	Rhea Ripley			
	Ricochet (Green & Black Shorts)			
CHASE	Ricochet (Yellow & Black Shorts)			
	Shorty G			
	"The Fiend" Bray Wyatt			

	WWE BASIC SERIES 115 (2021)	MOC	LOOSE	VALUE
	Becky Lynch			
	Big E			
	Braun Strowman			
	Humberto Carrillo (Black Tights)			
CHASE	Humberto Carrillo (White Tights)			
	Tegan Nox			

	WWE BASIC SERIES 116 (2021)	MOC	LOOSE	VALUE
	Dakota Kai			
	Kevin Owens			
	Roderick Strong (Green Trunks)			
CHASE	Roderick Strong (Black Trunks)			
	Seth Rollins			
	Sheamus			

	WWE BASIC SERIES 117 (2021)	MOC	LOOSE	VALUE
	Otis			
	Roman Reigns			
	Toni Storm (Blue)			
CHASE	Toni Storm (Red)			
	Tucker			
	The Undertaker			

	WWE BASIC SERIES 118 (2021)	MOC	LOOSE	VALUE
	Austin Theory (Black Tights)			
CHASE	Austin Theory (Red Tights)			
	Erik			
	Finn Balor			
	Ivar			
	Jeff Hardy			

	WWE BASIC SERIES 119 (2021)	MOC	LOOSE	VALUE
	Dominik Dijakovic			
	John Cena			
	Lacey Evans (Black & Red)			
CHASE	Lacey Evans (Blue & Yellow)			
	Randy Orton			
	Triple H			

WWE BASIC SERIES 120 (2021)		MOC	LOOSE	VALUE
	Edge			
	Karrion Kross			
	Pete Dunne			
	Scarlett (Bodysuit)			
CHASE	Scarlett (2-Piece)			
	Shawn Michaels			

WWE BASIC SERIES 121 - SUMMERSLAM (2021)		MOC	LOOSE	VALUE
	Apollo Crews (Grey & Black Trunks)			
CHASE	Apollo Crews (Black & Blue Trunks)			
	Bayley			
	Kane			
	Rey Mysterio			
	Roman Reigns			

WWE BASIC SERIES 122 (2021)		MOC	LOOSE	VALUE
	Charlotte Flair			
	Chelsea Green (Purple)			
CHASE	Chelsea Green (Black)			
	Damian Priest			
	Drew McIntyre			

	WWE BASIC SERIES 123 (2021)	MOC	LOOSE	VALUE
	Braun Strowman			
	Bobby Lashley			
	Dexter Lumis			
	Jake Atlas (Black Shorts)			
CHASE	Jake Atlas (White Shorts)			
	Otis			

	WWE BASIC SERIES 124 (2021)	MOC	LOOSE	VALUE
	Angel Garza (Yellow)			
CHASE	Angel Garza (Green)			
	Io Shirai			
	Kyle O'Reilly			
	Rey Mysterio			
	Seth Rollins			

	WWE BASIC SERIES 125 (2022)	MOC	LOOSE	VALUE
	Elias			
	Ember Moon			
	Isaiah "Swerve" Scott (Green)			
CHASE	Isaiah "Swerve" Scott (Red)			
	Jeff Hardy			
	The Rock			

	WWE BASIC SERIES 126 (2022)	MOC	LOOSE	VALUE
	Bobby Fish			
	Drew McIntyre			
	"Macho Man" Randy Savage			
	Mandy Rose (Blue)			
CHASE	Mandy Rose (Pink)			
	Seth Rollins			

	WWE BASIC SERIES 127 (2022)	MOC	LOOSE	VALUE
	Joaquinn Wilde (Face Paint)			
CHASE	Joaquinn Wilde (Unpainted)			
	Keith Lee			
	Rey Mysterio			
	Santos Escobar			
	Shayna Baszler			

	WWE BASIC SERIES 128 (2022)	MOC	LOOSE	VALUE
	Big E			
	Edge			
	MVP			
	Raul Mendoza (Face Paint)			
CHASE	Raul Mendoza (Unpainted)			
	Sasha Banks			

	WWE BASIC SERIES 129 (2022)	MOC	LOOSE	VALUE
	Carmella			
	Dominik Mysterio			
	Noam Dar			
	The Miz			
	Roman Reigns (Black Shirt)			
CHASE	Roman Reigns (White Shirt)			

	WWE BASIC SERIES 130 (2022)	MOC	LOOSE	VALUE
	AJ Styles			
	Gran Metalik			
	John Cena			
	Johnny Gargano (The Way Gear)			
CHASE	Johnny Gargano (HBK Gear)			
	Omos			

	WWE BASIC SERIES 131 (2022)	MOC	LOOSE	VALUE
	Bianca Bel Air			
	Candice LaRae (The Way Gear)			
CHASE	Candice LaRae (1-2-3 Kid Gear)			
	Happy Corbin			
	Lince Dorado			
	Randy Orton			

	WWE BASIC SERIES 132 (2022)	MOC	LOOSE	VALUE
	Bobby Lashley			
	Kushida			
	Rey Mysterio			
	Riddle			
	Tamina (Blue)			
CHASE	Tamina (Green)			

	WWE BASIC SERIES 133 (2022)	MOC	LOOSE	VALUE
	Cedric Alexander (Red)			
CHASE	Cedric Alexander (Black)			
	Finn Balor			
	Natalya			
	Roman Reigns			
	Stone Cold Steve Austin			

	WWE BASIC SERIES 134 (2022)	MOC	LOOSE	VALUE
	Becky Lynch			
	Indi Hartwell			
	Sami Zayn			
	Seth Rollins			
	Shelton Benjamin (Gold)			
CHASE	Shelton Benjamin (Black & Bronze)			

	WWE BASIC SERIES 135 (2023)	MOC	LOOSE	VALUE
	Brock Lesnar			
	Bron Breakker			
	Damian Priest			
	Nikki A.S.H.			
	Reggie (Red Pants)			
CHASE	Reggie (White Pants)			

	WWE BASIC SERIES 136 (2023)	MOC	LOOSE	VALUE
	Bobby Roode			
	Cody Rhodes			
	Dolph Ziggler (Pink)			
CHASE	Dolph Ziggler (Blue)			
	Goldberg			
	Xia Li			

	WWE BASIC SERIES 137 (2023)	MOC	LOOSE	VALUE
	Aliyah			
	Austin Theory			
	Commander Azeez			
	Roman Reigns			
	Seth Rollins (White Kneepad On Right Knee)			
CHASE	Seth Rollins (White Kneepad On Left Knee)			

	WWE BASIC SERIES 138 (2023)	MOC	LOOSE	VALUE
	Drew McIntyre			
	Edge			
	Gigi Dolin			
	Jacy Jayne			
	Shinsuke Nakamura (Black & White Pants)			
CHASE	Shinsuke Nakamura (White & Red Pants)			

	WWE BASIC SERIES 139 (2023)	MOC	LOOSE	VALUE
	Hulk Hogan			
	John Cena			
	Liv Morgan			
	Pat McAfee (Plain Black Shirt)			
CHASE	Pat McAfee (For The Brand Shirt)			
	Riddle			

	WWE BASIC SERIES 140 (2023)	MOC	LOOSE	VALUE
	Ciampa (Tights)			
CHASE	Ciampa (Trunks)			
	Cody Rhodes			
	Randy Orton			
	Rey Mysterio			
	Ronda Rousey			

	WWE BASIC SERIES 141 (2023)	MOC	LOOSE	VALUE
	Bianca Belair			
	Brock Lesnar			
	LA Knight (Red Trunks)			
CHASE	LA Knight (Yellow Trunks)			
	Seth Rollins			
	The Rock			

	WWE BASIC SERIES 142 (2023)	MOC	LOOSE	VALUE
	Charlotte Flair			
	Honky Tonk Man (Red Tights)			
CHASE	Honky Tonk Man (Blue Tights)			
	Hulk Hogan			
	Top Dolla			
	The Undertaker			

	WWE BASIC SERIES 143 (2023)	MOC	LOOSE	VALUE
	Ashante "Thee" Adonis			
	Becky Lynch			
	Cody Rhodes			
	John Cena			
	Mr. T (Short Sleeves)			
CHASE	Mr. T (Long Sleeves)			

	WWE BASIC SERIES 144 (2024)	MOC	LOOSE	VALUE
	B-Fab			
	Dominik Mysterio			
	Karrion Kross			
	Rey Mysterio			
	Ultimate Warrior (Orange Trunks)			
CHASE	Ultimate Warrior (Yellow Trunks)			

	WWE BASIC SERIES 145 (2024)	MOC	LOOSE	VALUE
	Gunther			
	Kane			
	Ludwig Kaiser (Blue Trunks)			
CHASE	Ludwig Kaiser (Red Trunks)			
	Sami Zayn			
	Tiffany Stratton			

	WWE BASIC SERIES 146 (2024)	MOC	LOOSE	VALUE
	Bret "Hit Man" Hart (Pink Singlet)			
CHASE	Bret "Hit Man" Hart (Pink & Black Singlet)			
	Giovanni Vinci			
	Kevin Owens			
	Roman Reigns			
	Shayna Baszler			

	MAIN EVENT SERIES 147 (2024)	MOC	LOOSE	VALUE
	AJ Styles			
	Brock Lesnar			
	Katana Chance			
	"Million Dollar Man" Ted Dibiase (Black Suit)			
CHASE	"Million Dollar Man" Ted Dibiase (Green Suit)			
	Seth Rollins			

	MAIN EVENT SERIES 148 (2024)	MOC	LOOSE	VALUE
	Carmello Hayes			
	Hulk Hogan			
	John Cena (Transluscent)			
CHASE	John Cena (Green Shirt)			
	Kayden Carter			
	"Rowdy" Roddy Piper			

	MAIN EVENT SERIES 149 (2024)	MOC	LOOSE	VALUE
	Cody Rhodes			
	Eddie Guerrero (Black Tights)			
CHASE	Eddie Guerrero (Green Tights)			
	Maxxine Dupri			
	The Miz			
	Sheamus			

MAIN EVENT SERIES 150 (2024)		MOC	LOOSE	VALUE
	CM Punk (Blue Stars)			
CHASE	CM Punk (Red Stars)			
	Lita			
	Rey Mysterio			
	Stone Cold Steve Austin			
	The Rock			

MAIN EVENT SERIES 151 (2025)		MOC	LOOSE	VALUE
CHASE				

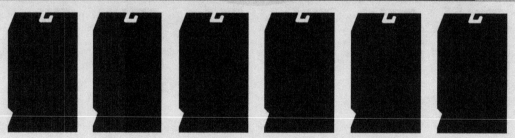

MAIN EVENT SERIES 152 (2025)		MOC	LOOSE	VALUE
CHASE				

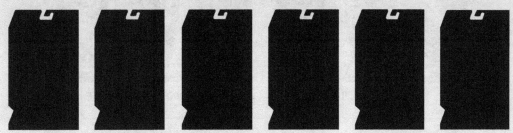

	MAIN EVENT SERIES 153 (2025)	MOC	LOOSE	VALUE
CHASE				

	MAIN EVENT SERIES 154 (2025)	MOC	LOOSE	VALUE
CHASE				

	MAIN EVENT SERIES 155 (2025)	MOC	LOOSE	VALUE
CHASE				

2010 ROYAL RUMBLE	1 OF 1,000	MOC	LOOSE	VALUE
Beth Phoenix				
Chris Jericho				
CM Punk				
Cody Rhodes				
Edge				
Triple H				

2010 ROYAL RUMBLE HERITAGE SERIES	1 OF 1,000	MOC	LOOSE	VALUE
Christian				
John Cena				
Randy Orton				
Rey Mysterio				
Sheamus				
The Undertaker				

2010 ELIMINATION CHAMBER	1 OF 1,000	MOC	LOOSE	VALUE
Batista				
Chris Jericho				
Drew McIntyre				
John Cena				
Rey Mysterio				
The Undertaker				

2010 WRESTLEMANIA HERITAGE SERIES	1 OF 1,000	MOC	LOOSE	VALUE
Batista				
Edge				
John Cena				
Randy Orton				
Stone Cold Steve Austin				
The Undertaker				

2010 WRESTLEMANIA XXVI (TOYS 'R' US)	MOC	LOOSE	VALUE
Chris Jericho			
Christian			
Drew Mcintyre			
Kane			
Matt Hardy			
Shawn Michaels			
Shelton Benjamin			

2010 OVER THE LIMIT	MOC	LOOSE	VALUE
Big Show			
CM Punk			
Jack Swagger			
John Cena			
Rey Mysterio			
R-Truth			

2010 SURVIVOR SERIES	1 OF 1,000	MOC	LOOSE	VALUE
John Cena				
John Morrison				
Kofi Kingston				
Rey Mysterio				
The Miz				
The Undertaker				

2011 WRESTLEMANIA HERITAGE SERIES	1 OF 1,000	MOC	LOOSE	VALUE
CM Punk				
John Cena				
Kane				
Melina				
Randy Orton				
Triple H				

2011 WRESTLEMANIA XXVII	MOC	LOOSE	VALUE
Alberto Del Rio			
Christian			
John Cena			
John Morrison			
Randy Orton			
Triple H			

2011 EXTREME RULES	1 OF 1,000	MOC	LOOSE	VALUE
Alberto Del Rio				
Christian				
John Cena				
Rey Mysterio				
R-Truth				
Sheamus				

2011 SUMMERSLAM	1 OF 1,000	MOC	LOOSE	VALUE
Edge				
John Cena				
Randy Orton				
Rey Mysterio				
The Great Khali				
Triple H				

2011 SURVIVOR SERIES	1 OF 1,000	MOC	LOOSE	VALUE
Big Show				
Chris Masters				
Evan Bourne				
John Cena				
Sheamus				
The Rock				

2011 TLC: TABLES, LADDERS & CHAIRS	1 OF 1,000	MOC	LOOSE	VALUE
Edge				
John Cena				
John Morrison				
Rey Mysterio				
Sheamus				
Wade Barrett				

BEST OF PAY-PER-VIEW: 2011 (TOYS 'R' US)		MOC	LOOSE	VALUE
CAPITAL PUNISHMENT	Christian			
OVER THE LIMIT	John Cena			
MONEY IN THE BANK	Mark Henry			
ROYAL RUMBLE	Rey Mysterio			

2012 WRESTLEMANIA XXVIII (TOYS 'R' US)	MOC	LOOSE	VALUE
John Cena			
Sheamus			
The Rock			
Triple H			

TRIBUTE TO THE TROOPS 2012 (K-MART)	MOC	LOOSE	VALUE
Big Show			
Rey Mysterio			
Randy Orton (Brown Vest)			
Randy Orton (Green Vest)			
John Cena			

BEST OF PAY-PER-VIEW: 2012 (TOYS 'R' US)		MOC	LOOSE	VALUE
MONEY IN THE BANK	Alberto Del Rio			
EXTREME RULES	Brock Lesnar			
NO WAY OUT	Dolph Ziggler			
OVER THE LIMIT	Randy Orton			
BUILD-A-FIGURE	Teddy Long			

2012 SURVIVOR SERIES (K-MART)	MOC	LOOSE	VALUE
CM Punk			
Ryback			

2012 TLC: TABLES, LADDERS & CHAIRS (TOYS 'R' US)	MOC	LOOSE	VALUE
Alberto Del Rio			
Kofi Kingston			
Mark Henry			
Sheamus			

BEST OF PAY-PER-VIEW: 2013 (TOYS 'R' US)		MOC	LOOSE	VALUE
WRESTLEMANIA 29	Alberto Del Rio			
WRESTLEMANIA 29	Sheamus			
WRESTLEMANIA 29	The Rock			
WRESTLEMANIA 29	The Undertaker			
BUILD-A-FIGURE	Booker T			

2014 WRESTLEMANIA XXX	MOC	LOOSE	VALUE
Brock Lesnar			
John Cena			
The Rock			
The Undertaker			

2014 SUMMERSLAM	MOC	LOOSE	VALUE
CM Punk			
Rey Mysterio			
Shawn Michaels			
Ted Dibiase			
Triple H			
The Undertaker			

BEST OF PAY-PER-VIEW: 2014 (TOYS 'R' US)		MOC	LOOSE	VALUE
MONEY IN THE BANK	Damien Sandow			
EXTREME RULES	Daniel Bryan			
PAYBACK	Dolph Ziggler			
ROYAL RUMBLE	Kofi Kingston			
BUILD-A-FIGURE	Paul Bearer			

2015 WRESTLEMANIA HERITAGE SERIES	MOC	LOOSE	VALUE
Hulk Hogan			
John Cena			
Shawn Michaels			
The Rock			

2016 WRESTLEMANIA 32	MOC	LOOSE	VALUE
Cesaro			
Eddie Guerrero			
Razor Ramon			
Roman Reigns			

2016 SUMMERSLAM		MOC	LOOSE	VALUE
2005	Batista			
1992	British Bulldog			
1989	"Hacksaw" Jim Duggan			
1998	The Undertaker			

2017 WRESTLEMANIA 33	MOC	LOOSE	VALUE
Chris Jericho			
Roman Reigns			
Stone Cold Steve Austin			
The Undertaker			

2017 SUMMERSLAM	MOC	LOOSE	VALUE
Dusty Rhodes			
Nikki Bella			
Seth Rollins			
The Rock			

2018 WRESTLEMANIA 34	MOC	LOOSE	VALUE
AJ Styles			
Bayley			
Big Show			
Dean Ambrose			
Mojo Rawley			
Seth Rollins			

WWE 2018 SUMMERSLAM BASICS	MOC	LOOSE	VALUE
John Cena			
Kurt Angle			
Ric Flair			
Roman Reigns			
Shane McMahon			
Shinsuke Nakamura			

2019 WRESTLEMANIA 35	MOC	LOOSE	VALUE
Charlotte Flair			
Elias			
John Cena			
Kevin Nash			
Trish Stratus			
"Woken" Matt Hardy			

2020 WRESTLEMANIA 36	MOC	LOOSE	VALUE
Batista			
Becky Lynch			
Seth Rollins			
Shane McMahon			
Stephanie McMahon			
The Rock			

2021 WRESTLEMANIA 37	MOC	LOOSE	VALUE
Andrade			
Drew McIntyre			
"The Fiend" Bray Wyatt			
Ricochet			
Andre The Giant (w/ Ring Cart)			
"Macho Man" Randy Savage (w/ Ring Cart)			

2022 WRESTLEMANIA 38	MOC	LOOSE	VALUE
Bianca Belair			
Hulk Hogan			
Seth Rollins			
Sheamus			

2023 WRESTLEMANIA 39	MOC	LOOSE	VALUE
Andre The Giant			
Bianca Belair			
Kane			
The Undertaker			

2024 WRESTLEMANIA 40	MOC	LOOSE	VALUE
Batista		CANCELED	
Muhammad Ali			
Roman Reigns			
Seth Rollins			

SIGNATURE SERIES 0 (2010)	MOC	LOOSE	VALUE
Batista			
Chris Jericho			
John Cena			
Shawn Michaels			

	SIGNATURE SERIES 1 (2011)	MOC	LOOSE	VALUE
BLACK	Edge			
WHITE	Edge			
	John Cena			
	Randy Orton			
	Rey Mysterio			
	Triple H			
	The Undertaker			

SIGNATURE SERIES 2 (2012)	MOC	LOOSE	VALUE
Big Show			
John Cena			
Kane			
Randy Orton			
Rey Mysterio			
The Miz			

WWE SIGNATURE SERIES 3 (2012)	MOC	LOOSE	VALUE
John Cena			
Rey Mysterio			
The Rock			

SIGNATURE SERIES 4 (2012)		MOC	LOOSE	VALUE
JORTS	John Cena			
CAMO	John Cena			
	Rey Mysterio			
	Sheamus			

SIGNATURE SERIES 5 (2013)	MOC	LOOSE	VALUE
CM Punk			
John Cena			
Kane			
Rey Mysterio			
Sin Cara			
The Rock			

SIGNATURE SERIES 6 (2014)	MOC	LOOSE	VALUE
Alberto Del Rio			
Big Show			
CM Punk			
John Cena			
Kane			
Rey Mysterio			
R-Truth			
Sin Cara			
Stone Cold Steve Austin			

SIGNATURE SERIES 7 (2015)	MOC	LOOSE	VALUE
Batista			
Bray Wyatt			
Daniel Bryan			
Dean Ambrose			
Hulk Hogan			
John Cena			
Stone Cold Steve Austin			

BEST OF 2010	CHASE	MOC	LOOSE	VALUE
Batista				
Evan Bourne				
Hornswoggle				
John Cena				
Mark Henry				
Rey Mysterio				

BEST OF 2011	MOC	LOOSE	VALUE
Big Show			
John Cena			
Kofi Kingston			
Randy Orton			
Rey Mysterio			
Santino Marella			

BEST OF 2012	MOC	LOOSE	VALUE
Alberto Del Rio			
Brodus Clay			
Daniel Bryan			
Rey Mysterio			
Sin Cara			
The Great Khali			

BEST OF 2013	MOC	LOOSE	VALUE
Brock Lesnar			
Kaitlyn			
Randy Orton			
Rey Mysterio			
Tensai			
The Undertaker			

	BEST OF 2014	MOC	LOOSE	VALUE
	Cesaro			
	El Torito			
	John Cena			
	Roman Reigns			
	Sin Cara			
	The Undertaker			

	TOP PICKS 2018	MOC	LOOSE	VALUE
	AJ Styles			
	John Cena			
	Roman Reigns			
	Seth Rollins			

	TOP PICKS 2019	MOC	LOOSE	VALUE
	AJ Styles			
	Jeff Hardy			
	John Cena			
	Seth Rollins (Black & Gold Tights)			
CHASE	Seth Rollins (Red & Black Tights)			

	TOP PICKS 2020	MOC	LOOSE	VALUE
WAVE 1	AJ Styles			
	Braun Strowman			
	Finn Balor			
	John Cena			
WAVE 2	John Cena			
	Kofi Kingston			
	Roman Reigns			
	The Rock			

	TOP PICKS 2021	MOC	LOOSE	VALUE
WAVE 1	Braun Strowman			
	John Cena			
	Roman Reigns			
	The Rock			
WAVE 2	Drew McIntyre			
	"The Fiend" Bray Wyatt			
	John Cena			
	The Rock			

	TOP PICKS 2022	MOC	LOOSE	VALUE
WAVE 1	Big E			
	Drew McIntyre			
	John Cena			
WAVE 2	Bray Wyatt			
	Roman Reigns			
	The Undertaker			
WAVE 3	Brock Lesnar			
	Seth Rollins			
	The Rock			
WAVE 4	John Cena			
	Randy Orton			
	Rey Mysterio			

	TOP PICKS 2023	MOC	LOOSE	VALUE
WAVE 1	Big E			
	Drew McIntyre			
	John Cena			
WAVE 2	AJ Styles			
	Brock Lesnar			
	The Rock			
WAVE 3	Cody Rhodes			
	Riddle			
	Roman Reigns			

	TOP PICKS 2024	MOC	LOOSE	VALUE
WAVE 1	Cody Rhodes			
	Drew McIntyre			
	Randy Orton			
WAVE 2	The Rock			
	Seth Rollins			
	The Undertaker			
WAVE 3	Cody Rhodes			
	John Cena			
	Roman Reigns			
WAVE 4	Dominik Mysterio			
	LA Knight			
	Seth Rollins			

BEST OF MAIN EVENT SERIES 1	MOC	LOOSE	VALUE
Cody Rhodes			
Gunther			
John Cena			
Roman Reigns			

ENTRANCE GREATS (2010)		MIB	LOOSE	VALUE
SERIES 1	Rey Mysterio			
	Shawn Michaels			
	Triple H			
SERIES 2	"Million Dollar Man" Ted Dibiase			
	Chris Jericho			
	"Rowdy" Roddy Piper			
SERIES 3	The Rock			
	The Undertaker			

SUPERSTAR MATCH-UPS (2010)		MIB	LOOSE	VALUE
SERIES 1	John Cena			
	Rey Mysterio (Black & Orange)			
	Rey Mysterio (Black & Green)			
	Rey Mysterio (Blue & Yellow)			
	Shawn Michaels			
	Triple H			
SERIES 2 (K-MART)	Rey Mysterio (Blue & Black)			
	Rey Mysterio (Blue & White)			
	Sin Cara			

ULTIMATE FAN PACKS		MOC	LOOSE	VALUE
SERIES 1	Finn Balor			
	John Cena			
	"Macho" Man Randy Savage			
	Roman Reigns			
SERIES 2	AJ Styles			
	Enzo Amore			
	Jeff Hardy			

RINGSIDE BATTLE SERIES 1 (2023)	MOC	LOOSE	VALUE
Rey Mysterio			
The Rock			

ZOMBIES SERIES 1 (2016)	MOC	LOOSE	VALUE
Bray Wyatt			
Dean Ambrose			
John Cena			
Paige			
Roman Reigns			
The Rock			
Triple H			
The Undertaker			

ZOMBIES SERIES 2 (2017)	MOC	LOOSE	VALUE
AJ Styles			
Brock Lesnar			
Kevin Owens			
Sasha Banks			
Seth Rollins			
Stone Cold Steve Austin			

ZOMBIES SERIES 3 (2018)	MOC	LOOSE	VALUE
Charlotte Flair			
Finn Balor			
Jeff Hardy			
Kane			
Matt Hardy			
Shinsuke Nakamura			

MUTANTS (2016)	MOC	LOOSE	VALUE
Bray Wyatt			
Brock Lesnar			
Finn Balor			
John Cena			
Stardust			
Sting			

MONSTERS (2018)	MOC	LOOSE	VALUE
Asuka (As The Phantom)			
Braun Strowman (As Frankenstein)			
Chris Jericho (As The Mummy)			
Jake "The Snake" Roberts (As The Creature)			
Roman Reigns (As The Werewolf)			
The Undertaker (As The Vampire)			

CHAMPIONS COLLECTION (K-MART)		MOC	LOOSE	VALUE
SERIES 1	Big Show			
	John Cena			
	Kane			
	Kofi Kingston			
SERIES 2	Daniel Bryan			
	The Rock			
SERIES 3	Dean Ambrose			
	John Cena			
	Randy Orton			
SERIES 4	Bad News Barrett			
	Daniel Bryan			
	Ultimate Warrior			

NXT TAKEOVER SERIES 1 (TARGET)	MOC	LOOSE	VALUE
Andrade "Cien" Almas			
Hideo Itami			
Kevin Owens			
Sami Zayn			
Samoa Joe			
Tye Dillinger			

NXT TAKEOVER SERIES 2 (TARGET)	MOC	LOOSE	VALUE
Akam			
Bobby Roode			
Eva Marie			
Johnny Gargano			
Rezar			
Tommaso Ciampa			

WWE NETWORTK SPOTLIGHT (TOYS 'R' US)	MOC	LOOSE	VALUE
Big Cass			
Brock Lesnar			
Enzo Amore			
Sting			

FAN CENTRAL SERIES 1 (K-MART)	MOC	LOOSE	VALUE
Finn Balor			
John Cena			
Ryback			
Triple H			

FAN CENTRAL SERIES 2 (TOYS 'R' US)	MOC	LOOSE	VALUE
Finn Balor			
Kevin Nash			
Randy Orton			
Rusev			

FAN CENTRAL SERIES 3 (WALMART)	MOC	LOOSE	VALUE
Bobby Roode			
Dean Ambrose			
Kevin Owens			
Ric Flair			

SUPERSTAR ENTRANCES SERIES 1 (WALMART)	MOC	LOOSE	VALUE
CM Punk			
Dolph Ziggler			
John Cena			
R-Truth			
Randy Orton			
The Miz			
Triple H			
Zack Ryder			

SUPERSTAR ENTRANCES SERIES 2 (WALMART)	MOC	LOOSE	VALUE
Daniel Bryan			
John Cena			
Ryback			
Santino Marella			
The Rock			

SUPERSTAR ENTRANCES SERIES 3 (WALMART)	MOC	LOOSE	VALUE
Brock Lesnar			
CM Punk			
Cody Rhodes			
John Cena			
"Macho Man" Randy Savage			
Sheamus			

SUPERSTAR ENTRANCES SERIES 4 (WALMART)	MOC	LOOSE	VALUE
AJ Lee			
Daniel Bryan			
Dolph Ziggler			
John Cena			
Rob Van Dam			
The Rock			

SUPERSTAR ENTRANCES SERIES 5 (WALMART)	MOC	LOOSE	VALUE
Daniel Bryan			
John Cena			
Randy Orton			
"Rowdy" Roddy Piper			
Triple H			

SUPERSTAR ENTRANCES SERIES 6 (WALMART)	MOC	LOOSE	VALUE
Bad News Barrett			
Bo Dallas			
Hulk Hogan			
John Cena			
Kofi Kingston			

THEN, NOW, FOREVER SERIES 1 (WALMART)	MOC	LOOSE	VALUE
Chris Jericho			
Seth Rollins			
Sin Cara			
The Undertaker			

THEN, NOW, FOREVER (WALMART)		MOC	LOOSE	VALUE
	Cesaro			
	Seth Rollins			
	Triple H			
	X-Pac			
BUILD-A-FIGURE	Mean Gene Okerlund			

THEN, NOW, FOREVER SERIES 2 (WALMART)	MOC	LOOSE	VALUE
Bray Wyatt			
Kevin Owens			
Seth Rollins			
Triple H			
X-Pac			

THEN, NOW, FOREVER SERIES 3 (WALMART)	MOC	LOOSE	VALUE
Neville			
Sheamus			
Stone Cold Steve Austin			
Ultimate Warrior			

BUILD-A-PAUL BEARER (WALMART)		MOC	LOOSE	VALUE
	Chris Jericho			
	Neville			
	Rusev			
	The Undertaker			
BUILD-A-FIGURE	Paul Bearer			

FLASHBACK SERIES 1 (WALMART)		MOC	LOOSE	VALUE
	"Cowboy" Bob Orton			
	"Ravishing" Rick Rude			
	Sgt. Slaughter			
	Ted Dibiase			
BUILD-A-FIGURE	Howard Finkel			

FLASHBACK SERIES 2 (WALMART)		MOC	LOOSE	VALUE
	Booker T			
	Lex Luger			
	Ric Flair			
	Sting			
BUILD-A-FIGURE	JJ Dillon			

WWE CHAMPIONS (2024)		MOC	LOOSE	VALUE
SERIES 1	Brock Lesnar (w/ WWE Championship)			
	Roman Reigns (w/ WWE Universal Championship)			
	The Rock (w/ Brahma Bull WWE Championship)			
SERIES 2	Hulk Hogan (w/ Winged Eagle WWE Championship)			
	John Cena (w/ Spinner WWE Championship)			
	Stone Cold Steve Austin (w/ Big Eagle WWE Championship)			
SERIES 3	Jey Uso (w/ Raw Tag Team Championship)			
	Jimmy Uso (w/ Raw Tag Team Championship)			
	The Undertaker (w/ WWE Championship)			

MISCELLANEOUS WWE BASIC EXCLUSIVES		MOC	LOOSE	VALUE
RINGSIDE	AJ Styles (Red Tights)			
WALGREENS	John Cena (Black Fence T-Shirt)			
TOYS 'R' US	John Cena (Make A Wish)			
WWE 2K18	John Cena (Cena Nuff)			

	BATTLE PACKS SERIES 1 (2010)	MOC	LOOSE	VALUE
UNLIKELY ALLIES	Santino Marella			
	Beth Phoenix			
ULTIMATE RIVALS	Shawn Michaels			
	Chris Jericho			
SUPREME TEAMS	Ted Dibiase			
	Cody Rhodes			

	BATTLE PACKS SERIES 2 (2010)	MOC	LOOSE	VALUE
FAMILY FURY	Carlito			
	Primo			
FAMILY FURY	Finlay			
	Hornswoggle			
SUPREME TEAMS	John Morrison			
	The Miz			

	BATTLE PACKS SERIES 3 (2010)	MOC	LOOSE	VALUE
ULTIMATE RIVALS	Edge			
	Big Show			
DUAL IMPACT	Rey Mysterio			
	Evan Bourne			
SUPREME TEAMS	Shad			
	JTG			

	BATTLE PACKS SERIES 4 (2010)	MOC	LOOSE	VALUE
ULTIMATE RIVALS	Chavo Guerrero			
	Hornswoggle			
DUAL IMPACT	Christian			
	Tommy Dreamer			
THE HART DYNASTY	DH Smith			
	Tyson Kid			

	BATTLE PACKS SERIES 5 (2010)	MOC	LOOSE	VALUE
FAMILY FURY	Carlito			
	Primo			
D-GENERATION X	Triple H			
	Shawn Michaels			
ULTIMATE RIVALS	Ricky "The Dragon" Steamboat			
	Chris Jericho			

	BATTLE PACKS SERIES 6 (2010)	MOC	LOOSE	VALUE
SUPREME TEAMS	Mark Henry			
	MVP			
ULTIMATE RIVALS	The Undertaker			
	Batista			
UNLIKELY ALLIES	Vladimir Kozlov			
	Ezekiel Jackson			

BATTLE PACKS SERIES 7 (2010)		MOC	LOOSE	VALUE
SUPREME TEAMS	CM Punk			
	Luke Gallows			
ULTIMATE RIVALS	Dolph Ziggler			
	John Morrison			
UNLIKELY ALLIES	The Miz			
	Big Show			

BATTLE PACKS SERIES 8 (2011)		MOC	LOOSE	VALUE
ULTIMATE RIVALS	John Cena			
	Randy Orton			
SUPREME TEAMS	Matt Hardy			
	The Great Khali			
SUPREME TEAMS	Ted Dibiase			
	Cody Rhodes			

BATTLE PACKS SERIES 9 (2011)		MOC	LOOSE	VALUE
DUAL IMPACT	Christian			
	Heath Slater			
ULTIMATE RIVALS	Sheamus			
	Triple H			
THE HART DYNASTY	Tyson Kidd			
	DH Smith			

	BATTLE PACKS SERIES 10 (2011)	MOC	LOOSE	VALUE
SUPREME TEAMS	Darren Young			
	Justin Gabriel			
DUAL IMPACT	David Otunga			
	Michael Tarver			
ULTIMATE RIVALS	Randy Orton			
	Edge			

	BATTLE PACKS SERIES 11 (2011)	MOC	LOOSE	VALUE
DUAL IMPACT	Drew McIntyre			
	Cody Rhodes			
FAMILY FURY	Jimmy Uso			
	Jey Uso			
FAMILY FURY	The Undertaker			
	Kane			

BATTLE PACK SERIES 12 (2012)	
Dolph Ziggler	
Kofi Kingston	
The Miz	CANCELLED
Daniel Bryan	
Santino Marella	
Vladimir Kozlov	

BATTLE PACK SERIES 13 (2012)	MOC	LOOSE	VALUE
John Cena			
R-Truth			
Rey Mysterio			
Cody Rhodes			
The Miz			
Alex Riley			

BATTLE PACK SERIES 14 (2012)	MOC	LOOSE	VALUE
Heath Slater			
Justin Gabriel			
"Macho Man" Randy Savage			
CM Punk			
Randy Orton			
Mason Ryan			

BATTLE PACK SERIES 15 (2012)	MOC	LOOSE	VALUE
Brie Bella			
Nikki Bella			
Sin Cara			
Daniel Bryan			
The Rock			
John Cena			

BATTLE PACK SERIES 16 (2012)	MOC	LOOSE	VALUE
Alberto Del Rio			
Big Show			
David Otunga			
Michael McGillicutty			
Randy Orton			
Christian			

BATTLE PACK SERIES 17 (2012)	MOC	LOOSE	VALUE
John Cena			
CM Punk			
Mark Henry			
Trent Barreta			
Rey Mysterio			
The Miz			

BATTLE PACK SERIES 18 (2012)	MOC	LOOSE	VALUE
CM Punk			
Triple H			
Randy Orton			
Wade Barrett			
Zack Ryder			
Dolph Ziggler			

BATTLE PACK SERIES 19 (2013)	MOC	LOOSE	VALUE
Daniel Bryan			
Big Show			
Epico			
Primo			
John Cena			
Kane			

BATTLE PACK SERIES 20 (2013)	MOC	LOOSE	VALUE
Brock Lesnar			
Triple H			
Brodus Clay			
Curt Hawkins			
Kofi Kingston			
R-Truth			

BATTLE PACK SERIES 21 (2013)	MOC	LOOSE	VALUE
Darren Young			
Titus O'Neil			
Kane			
Daniel Bryan			
Sheamus			
Randy Orton			

BATTLE PACK SERIES 22 (2013)	MOC	LOOSE	VALUE
Dolph Ziggler			
Vickie Guerrero			
Ryback			
Jinder Mahal			
Sin Cara			
Rey Mysterio			

BATTLE PACK SERIES 23 (2013)	MOC	LOOSE	VALUE
CM Punk			
Mr. McMahon			
Rey Mysterio			
Kofi Kingston			
Sin Cara			
Cody Rhodes			

BATTLE PACK SERIES 24 (2013)	MOC	LOOSE	VALUE
Naomi			
Cameron			
Seth Rollins			
Roman Reigns			
The Rock			
John Cena			

BATTLE PACK SERIES 25 (2014)	MOC	LOOSE	VALUE
Brock Lesnar			
Paul Heyman			
CM Punk			
The Undertaker			
Mark Henry			
Ryback			

BATTLE PACK SERIES 26 (2014)	MOC	LOOSE	VALUE
Nikki Bella			
Brie Bella			
Seth Rollins			
Dean Ambrose			
Triple H			
Curtis Axel			

BATTLE PACK SERIES 27 (2014)	MOC	LOOSE	VALUE
Big Show			
Mark Henry			
Brodus Clay			
Tensai			
Daniel Bryan			
Randy Orton			

BATTLE PACK SERIES 28 (2014)	MOC	LOOSE	VALUE
Big E			
AJ Lee			
Jimmy Uso			
Jey Uso			
Luke Harper			
Erick Rowan			

BATTLE PACK SERIES 29 (2014)	MOC	LOOSE	VALUE
CM Punk			
Ryback			
Goldust			
Cody Rhodes			
Diego			
Fernando			

BATTLE PACK SERIES 30 (2014)	MOC	LOOSE	VALUE
Brock Lesnar			
The Undertaker			
Jake "The Snake" Roberts			
Dean Ambrose			
Xavier Woods			
R-Truth			

BATTLE PACK SERIES 31 (2015)	MOC	LOOSE	VALUE
John Cena			
Ultimate Warrior			
Luke Harper			
Erick Rowan			
Sin Cara			
Alberto Del Rio			

BATTLE PACK SERIES 32 (2015)	MOC	LOOSE	VALUE
Daniel Bryan			
Triple H			
Jimmy Uso			
Jey Uso			
Road Dogg			
Billy Gunn			

BATTLE PACK SERIES 33 (2015)	MOC	LOOSE	VALUE
Andre The Giant			
Big Show			
Rey Mysterio			
Rob Van Dam			
Shawn Michaels			
The Undertaker			

BATTLE PACK SERIES 34 (2015)	MOC	LOOSE	VALUE
Animal			
Hawk			
Hornswoggle			
El Torito			
Lana			
Rusev			

BATTLE PACK SERIES 35 (2015)	MOC	LOOSE	VALUE
Kane			
Roman Reigns			
Ryback			
Curtis Axel			
Zeb Colter			
Jack Swagger			

BATTLE PACK SERIES 36 (2015)	MOC	LOOSE	VALUE
Big E			
Kofi Kingston			
Dean Ambrose			
Seth Rollins			
Kevin Nash			
Scott Hall			

	BATTLE PACK SERIES 37 (2016)	MOC	LOOSE	VALUE
SMACKDOWN	Jamie Noble			
	Joey Mercury			
RAW	Jimmy Uso			
	Jey Uso			
SMACKDOWN	Konnor			
	Viktor			

BATTLE PACK SERIES 38 (2016)		MOC	LOOSE	VALUE
SMACKDOWN	Adam Rose			
	The Bunny			
SMACKDOWN	Bray Wyatt			
	The Undertaker			
DIVAS	Nikki Bella			
	Brie Bella			

BATTLE PACK SERIES 39 (2016)		MOC	LOOSE	VALUE
SMACKDOWN	Darren Young			
	Titus O'Neil			
RAW	John Cena			
	Kevin Owens			
SMACKDOWN	Tyson Kidd			
	Cesaro			

BATTLE PACK SERIES 40 (2016)		MOC	LOOSE	VALUE
LEGENDS	Bushwhacker Luke			
	Bushwhacker Butch			
NXT	Enzo Amore			
	Big Cass			
LEGENDS	Stone Cold Steve Austin			
	Mr. McMahon			

	BATTLE PACK SERIES 41 (2016)	MOC	LOOSE	VALUE
RAW	Bubba Ray Dudley			
	D-Von Dudley			
SMACKDOWN	Charlotte			
	Ric Flair			
NXT	Simon Gotch			
	Aiden English			

	BATTLE PACK SERIES 42 (2016)	MOC	LOOSE	VALUE
LEGENDS	Edge			
	Christian			
SMACKDOWN	Sin Cara			
	Kalisto			
RAW	Tiple H			
	Stephanie McMahon			

	BATTLE PACK SERIES 43 (2017)	MOC	LOOSE	VALUE
SMACKDOWN	Big E			
	Xavier Woods			
WOMEN'S	Nikki Bella			
	Brie Bella			
RAW	The Undertaker			
	Kane			

	BATTLE PACK SERIES 43B (2017)	MOC	LOOSE	VALUE
RAW	Dean Ambrose			
	Brock Lesnar			
NXT	Finn Balor			
	Samoa Joe			
RAW	John Cena			
	Seth Rollins			
RAW	Roman Reigns			
	Sheamus			

	BATTLE PACK SERIES 44 (2017)	MOC	LOOSE	VALUE
NXT	Jason Jordan			
	Chad Gable			
RAW	Sami Zayn			
	Kevin Owens			
LEGENDS	Scott Hall			
	Kevin Nash			
SMACKDOWN	Jimmy Uso			
	Jey Uso			

	BATTLE PACK SERIES 45 (2017)	MOC	LOOSE	VALUE
RAW	AJ Styles			
	Roman Reigns			
RAW	Enzo Amore			
	Big Cass			
NXT	Scott Dawson			
	Dash Wilder			
LEGENDS	Triple H			
	Road Dogg			

BATTLE PACK SERIES 46 (2017)		MOC	LOOSE	VALUE
SMACKDOWN	Dean Ambrose			
	Shane McMahon			
RAW	Luke Gallows			
	Karl Anderson			
SMACKDOWN	The Miz			
	Maryse			
RAW	Kofi Kingston			
	Xavier Woods			

BATTLE PACK SERIES 47 (2017)		MOC	LOOSE	VALUE
SMACKDOWN	Luke Harper			
	Bray Wyatt			
RAW	Rusev			
	Roman Reigns			
WOMEN'S	Sasha Banks			
	Charlotte Flair			
LEGENDS	Bret Hart			
	Jim "The Anvil" Neidhart			

BATTLE PACK SERIES 48 (2017)		MOC	LOOSE	VALUE
SMACKDOWN	Chad Gable			
	Jason Jordan			
SMACKDOWN	Mojo Rawley			
	Zack Ryder			
LEGENDS	Shawn Michaels			
	Diesel			

BATTLE PACK SERIES 49 (2018)	MOC	LOOSE	VALUE
Daniel Bryan			
The Miz			
Sheamus			
Cesaro			
Stephanie McMahon			
Mick Foley			

BATTLE PACK SERIES 50 (2018)	MOC	LOOSE	VALUE
Konnor			
Viktor			
Luke Gallows			
Karl Anderson			
Randy Orton			
Bray Wyatt			

BATTLE PACK SERIES 51 (2018)	MOC	LOOSE	VALUE
Dash Wilder			
Scott Dawson			
The Miz			
Maryse			
Big E			
Xavier Woods			

BATTLE PACK SERIES 52 (2018)	MOC	LOOSE	VALUE
Brock Lesnar			
Roman Reigns			
Jimmy Uso			
Jey Uso			
Sheamus			
Cesaro			
Enzo Amore (Stop Release)			
Big Cass (Stop Release)			

BATTLE PACK SERIES 53 (2018)	MOC	LOOSE	VALUE
Carmella			
James Ellsworth			
Matt Hardy			
Jeff Hardy			
Shinsuke Nakamura			
Dolph Ziggler			

BATTLE PACK SERIES 54 (2018)	MOC	LOOSE	VALUE
Braun Strowman			
Roman Reigns			
Bray Wyatt			
Finn Balor			
Nia Jax			
Alexa Bliss			
Tyler Breeze			
Fandango			

BATTLE PACK SERIES 55 (2018)	MOC	LOOSE	VALUE
Becky Lynch			
Charlotte Flair			
Big Show			
Big Cass			
Dean Ambrose			
Seth Rollins			

BATTLE PACK SERIES 56 (2019)	MOC	LOOSE	VALUE
Jason Jordan			
Kurt Angle			
Bo Dallas			
Curtis Axel			
John Cena			
Roman Reigns			

BATTLE PACK SERIES 57 (2019)	MOC	LOOSE	VALUE
Braun Strowman			
Kane			
Shinsuke Nakamura			
The Miz			
Sunil Singh			
Samir Singh			

BATTLE PACK SERIES 58 (2019)	MOC	LOOSE	VALUE
Shelton Benjamin			
Chad Gable			
Triple H			
Shawn Michaels			
Kevin Owens			
Sami Zayn			

BATTLE PACK SERIES 59 (2019)	MOC	LOOSE	VALUE
Jinder Mahal			
AJ Styles			
Jeff Hardy			
Matt Hardy			
Dean Ambrose			
Seth Rollins			

BATTLE PACK SERIES 60 (2019)	MOC	LOOSE	VALUE
Sasha Banks			
Alexa Bliss			
Goldberg			
Stone Cold Steve Austin			
Sheamus			
Cesaro			

BATTLE PACK SERIES 61 (2019)	MOC	LOOSE	VALUE
Daniel Bryan			
AJ Styles			
Billie Kay			
Peyton Royce			
Jimmy Uso			
Jey Uso			

BATTLE PACK SERIES 62 (2020)	MOC	LOOSE	VALUE
Andrade			
Zelina Vega			
Akam			
Rezar			
Shinsuke Nakamura			
Rey Mysterio			

BATTLE PACK SERIES 63 (2020)	MOC	LOOSE	VALUE
Bobby Lashley			
Finn Balor			
Brock Lesnar			
Seth Rollins			
Big E			
Xavier Woods			

BATTLE PACK SERIES 64 (2020)	MOC	LOOSE	VALUE
AJ Styles			
Daniel Bryan			
Lita			
Trish Stratus			
Jimmy Uso			
Jey Uso			

BATTLE PACK SERIES 65 (2020)	MOC	LOOSE	VALUE
Kevin Owens			
Ali			
Velveteen Dream			
Ricochet			
Matt Hardy			
Jeff Hardy			

BATTLE PACK SERIES 66 (2020)	MOC	LOOSE	VALUE
Drew McIntyre			
Shane McMahon			
Seth Rollins			
Becky Lynch			
The Undertaker			
Roman Reigns			

BATTLE PACK SERIES 67 (2020)	MOC	LOOSE	VALUE
Randy Orton			
Kofi Kingston			
Stone Cold Steve Austin			
AJ Styles			
John Morrison			
The Miz			

CHAMPIONSHIP SHOWDOWN SERIES 1 (2021)	MOC	LOOSE	VALUE
Roman Reigns			
Finn Balor			
Sasha Banks			
Alexa Bliss			
The Undertaker			
Jeff Hardy			

CHAMPIONSHIP SHOWDOWN SERIES 2 (2021)	MOC	LOOSE	VALUE
Bobby Lashley			
King Booker			
Randy Orton			
John Cena			
The Rock			
Triple H			

CHAMPIONSHIP SHOWDOWN SERIES 3 (2021)	MOC	LOOSE	VALUE
Kane			
Edge			
"The Fiend" Bray Wyatt			
Daniel Bryan			
The Giant			
Ric Flair			

CHAMPIONSHIP SHOWDOWN SERIES 4 (2021)	MOC	LOOSE	VALUE
Drew McIntyre			
Seth Rollins			
John Morrison			
Kofi Kingston			
Riddle			
AJ Styles			

CHAMPIONSHIP SHOWDOWN SERIES 5 (2021)	MOC	LOOSE	VALUE
British Bulldog			
Big Boss Man			
Chyna			
Trish Stratus			
Mankind			
Stone Cold Steve Austin			

CHAMPIONSHIP SHOWDOWN SERIES 6 (2021)	MOC	LOOSE	VALUE
Shawn Michaels			
John Cena			
Montez Ford			
Angelo Dawkins			
Jimmy Uso			
Jey Uso			

CHAMPIONSHIP SHOWDOWN SERIES 7 (2022)	MOC	LOOSE	VALUE
Rhea Ripley			
Charlotte Flair			
Cesaro			
Roman Reigns			
Kane			
Stone Cold Steve Austin			

CHAMPIONSHIP SHOWDOWN SERIES 8 (2022)	MOC	LOOSE	VALUE
Drew McIntyre			
Goldberg			
Angelo Dawkins			
Montez Ford			
Bret "Hit Man" Hart			
The Undertaker			

CHAMPIONSHIP SHOWDOWN SERIES 9 (2022)	MOC	LOOSE	VALUE
The Rock			
John Cena			
Sheamus			
Ricochet			
Bayley			
Sasha Banks			

CHAMPIONSHIP SHOWDOWN SERIES 10 (2022)	MOC	LOOSE	VALUE
Andre The Giant			
Hulk Hogan			
Bobby Lashley			
The Miz			
AJ Styles			
Omos			

CHAMPIONSHIP SHOWDOWN SERIES 11 (2023)	MOC	LOOSE	VALUE
Roman Reigns			
John Cena			
Becky Lynch			
Bianca Belair			
Jimmy Uso			
Jey Uso			

CHAMPIONSHIP SHOWDOWN SERIES 12 (2023)	MOC	LOOSE	VALUE
Bobby Lashley			
Big E			
Charlotte Flair			
Alexa Bliss			
Randy Orton			
Riddle			

CHAMPIONSHIP SHOWDOWN SERIES 13 (2023)	MOC	LOOSE	VALUE
Undertaker			
Batista			
Kofi Kingston			
Xavier Woods			
Ricochet			
Gunther			

CHAMPIONSHIP SHOWDOWN SERIES 14 (2023)	MOC	LOOSE	VALUE
Austin Theory			
Cody Rhodes			
Angelo Dawkins			
Montez Ford			
Mankind			
The Rock			

CHAMPIONSHIP SHOWDOWN SERIES 15 (2023)	MOC	LOOSE	VALUE
Kevin Owens			
AJ Styles			
Roman Reigns			
Logan Paul			
Stone Cold Steve Austin			
Triple H			

CHAMPIONSHIP SHOWDOWN SERIES 16 (2023)	MOC	LOOSE	VALUE
Brock Lesnar			
Bobby Lashley			
Shawn Michaels			
British Bulldog			
Ronda Rousey			
Liv Morgan			

MAIN EVENT SHOWDOWN SERIES 17 (2024)	MOC	LOOSE	VALUE
Gunther			
Rey Mysterio			
John Cena			
Austin Theory			
Roman Reigns			
Jey Uso			

MAIN EVENT SHOWDOWN SERIES 18 (2024)	MOC	LOOSE	VALUE
Bron Breakker			
Seth "Freakin'" Rollins			
Kane			
Mankind			
Rhea Ripley			
"Dirty" Dominik Mysterio			

MAIN EVENT SHOWDOWN SERIES 19 (2024)	MOC	LOOSE	VALUE

MAIN EVENT SHOWDOWN SERIES 20 (2025)	MOC	LOOSE	VALUE

MAIN EVENT SHOWDOWN SERIES 21 (2025)	MOC	LOOSE	VALUE

MAIN EVENT SHOWDOWN SERIES 22 (2025)	MOC	LOOSE	VALUE

MAIN EVENT SHOWDOWN SERIES 23 (2025)	MOC	LOOSE	VALUE

2010 WRESTLEMANIA 26 2-PACKS	MOC	LOOSE	VALUE
Batista			
John Cena			
Big Show			
The Miz			
R-Truth			
John Morrison			

2014 WRESTLEMANIA 30 2-PACKS	MOC	LOOSE	VALUE
Brock Lesnar			
Batista			
Ultimate Warrior			
Sheamus			

2015 WRESTLEMANIA 31 2-PACKS	MOC	LOOSE	VALUE
Rey Mysterio			
Daniel Bryan			
Roman Reigns			
Triple H			

2016 WRESTLEMANIA 32 2-PACKS	MOC	LOOSE	VALUE
Ric Flair			
The Rock			
Stone Cold Steve Austin			
Bret Hart			

2016 SUMMERSLAM 2-PACKS	MOC	LOOSE	VALUE
John Cena			
Brock Lesnar			
Roman Reigns			
Dean Ambrose			

2017 WRESTLEMANIA 33 2-PACKS	MOC	LOOSE	VALUE
Andre The Giant			
Ted Dibiase			
The Rock			
John Cena			

2017 SUMMERSLAM 2-PACKS	MOC	LOOSE	VALUE
Randy Orton			
Brock Lesnar			
Ultimate Warrior			
Honky Tonk Man			

2018 WRESTLEMANIA 34 2-PACKS	MOC	LOOSE	VALUE
John Cena			
Nikki Bella			
Triple H			
Sting			
Roman Reigns			
The Undertaker			

2019 WRESTLEMANIA 35 2-PACKS	MOC	LOOSE	VALUE
Shinsuke Nakamura			
AJ Styles			
Edge			
Jeff Hardy			
Seth Rollins			
The Miz			

2020 WRESTLEMANIA 36 2-PACKS	MOC	LOOSE	VALUE
Roman Reigns			
Drew McIntyre			
Kane			
Daniel Bryan			
Randy Orton			
Rey Mysterio			

2015 THEN, NOW, FOREVER 2-PACKS (WALMART)	MOC	LOOSE	VALUE
Dean Ambrose			
Brian Pillman			
John Cena			
Stone Cold Steve Austin			
Ultimate Warrior			
Sting			

2017 FAN CENTRAL 2-PACKS (TOYS 'R' US)	MOC	LOOSE	VALUE
Seth Rollins			
Edge			
Sting			
The Undertaker			

2018 HALL OF CHAMPIONS 2-PACKS (TARGET)	MOC	LOOSE	VALUE
Dean Ambrose			
The Miz			
Batista			
John Cena			
Shawn Michaels			
Bret "Hitman" Hart			
Dash Wilder			
Scott Dawson			

MISCELLANEOUS WWE 2-PACKS		MOC	LOOSE	VALUE
WWE 2K15 (K-MART)	Triple H			
	Shawn Michaels			
SCOOBY-DOO (KMART)	John Cena			
	Scooby-Doo			
	Sin Cara			
	Scooby-Doo			

BASIC SERIES 1 COLLECTION BOX SET (TOYS 'R' US)	MIB	LOOSE	VALUE
Evan Bourne			
Big Show			
Triple H			
John Cena			
Batista			
Kofi Kingston			

ROYAL RUMBLE HERITAGE BOX SET (TOYS 'R' US)	MIB	LOOSE	VALUE
Christian			
John Cena			
Randy Orton			
Rey Mysterio			
Sheamus			
The Undertaker			

REY MYSTERIO COLLECTION BOX SET (TOYS 'R' US)		MIB	LOOSE	VALUE
JULY 1995	Rey Mysterio			
JUNE 1996	Rey Mysterio			
JULY 2002	Rey Mysterio			
JUNE 2003	Rey Mysterio			
FEB. 2005	Rey Mysterio			
DEC. 2005	Rey Mysterio			

CHAMPIONS COLLECTION BOX SET 1 (TARGET)	MIB	LOOSE	VALUE
Daniel Bryan			
John Cena			
Kane			
Dolph Ziggler			

CHAMPIONS COLLECTION BOX SET 2 (TARGET)	MIB	LOOSE	VALUE
Kofi Kingston			
John Cena			
Randy Orton			
Wade Barrett			

CHAMPIONS COLLECTION BOX SET 3 (TARGET)	MIB	LOOSE	VALUE
Rey Mysterio			
The Rock			
Stone Cold Steve Austin			
John Cena			

2012 SUPERSTAR COLLECTION BOX SET 1 (WALMART)	MIB	LOOSE	VALUE
Rey Mysterio			
The Undertaker			
The Rock			
John Cena			
Sheamus			
Alberto Del Rio			

2012 SUPERSTAR COLLECTION BOX SET 2 (WALMART)	MIB	LOOSE	VALUE
Sin Cara			
Wade Barrett			
John Cena			
Randy Orton			
Brock Lesnar			
Alberto Del Rio			

2013 SUPERSTAR COLLECTION BOX SET 3 (WALMART)	MIB	LOOSE	VALUE
Sin Cara			
Rey Mysterio			
Daniel Bryan			
John Cena			
Alberto Del Rio			
Damien Sandow			

2013 SUPERSTAR COLLECTION BOX SET 4 (WALMART)	MIB	LOOSE	VALUE
Dean Ambrose			
Roman Reigns			
Seth Rollins			
Triple H			
Randy Orton			
Batista			

2014 WRESTLEMANIA BOX SET (WALMART)	MIB	LOOSE	VALUE
Mark Henry			
Triple H			
John Cena			
Randy Orton			
The Rock			
Brock Lesnar			

2014 FAN FAVORITES BOX SET (TOYS 'R' US)	MIB	LOOSE	VALUE
"Macho Man" Randy Savage			
Ultimate Warrior			
Shawn Michaels			
The Undertaker			
John Cena			
CM Punk			
Triple H			

2015 FAN FAVORITES BOX SET (K-MART)	MIB	LOOSE	VALUE
Dean Ambrose			
Seth Rollins			
Roman Reigns			
Rusev			
Cesaro			

2015 THEN, NOW, FOREVER BOX SET (WALMART)	MIB	LOOSE	VALUE
Andre The Giant			
Ric Flair			
Bret Hart			
John Cena			
Daniel Bryan			
Brock Lesnar			

2017 NETWORK SPOTLIGHT BOX SET 1 (TOYS 'R' US)	MIB	LOOSE	VALUE
Stone Cold Steve Austin			
Mr. McMahon			
Sting			
The Rock			
Ultimate Warrior			

2017 NETWORK SPOTLIGHT BOX SET 2 (TOYS 'R' US)	MIB	LOOSE	VALUE
Batista			
John Cena			
Kevin Nash			
Scott Hall			
Brock Lesnar			

UNDERTAKER COLLECTION BOX SET (TOYS 'R' US)		MIB	LOOSE	VALUE
1990	The Undertaker			
1994	The Undertaker			
1998	The Undertaker			
2014	The Undertaker			
2016	The Undertaker			

2023 MAIN EVENT SUPERSTARS BOX SET (SAM'S CLUB)	MIB	LOOSE	VALUE
Roman Reigns			
John Cena			
The Rock			

2024 MAIN EVENT SUPERSTARS BOX SET (SAM'S CLUB)	MIB	LOOSE	VALUE
Damian Priest			
Becky Lynch			
Seth Rollins			

2024 MAIN EVENT IMPERIUM BOX SET (SAM'S CLUB)	MIB	LOOSE	VALUE
Giovanni Vinci			
Gunther			
Ludwig Kaiser			

WWE CHAMPIONSHIP COMBO PACK BOX SETS (TOYS 'R' US)		MIB	LOOSE	VALUE
WWE TITLE COMBO PACK	John Cena			
	Edge			
WORLD TITLE COMBO PACK	Randy Orton			
	Triple H			

WWE CHAMPIONSHIP RIVALS BOX SETS (SAM'S CLUB)		MIB	LOOSE	VALUE
2022	Drew McIntyre			
	Randy Orton			
2023	Roman Reigns			
	Brock Lesnar			
2024	Roman Reigns			
	LA Knight			

WWE ELITE COLLECTION

WWE ELITE COLLECTION SERIES 1 (2010)		MIB	LOOSE	VALUE
RAW – 1/19/2009	CM Punk			
ARMAGEDDON 2008	Edge			
	Jeff Hardy			
SMACKDOWN – 11/14/2008	MVP			
NO WAY OUT 2009	Rey Mysterio			
NO WAY OUT 2009	The Undertaker			

WWE ELITE COLLECTION SERIES 2 (2010)		MIB	LOOSE	VALUE
RAW – 10/13/2008	Batista			
WRESTLEMANIA 25	Matt Hardy			
ROYAL RUMBLE 2009	Randy Orton			
SMACKDOWN – 9/12/2008	R-Truth			
RAW – 6/15/2009	Ted Dibiase			
SMACKDOWN – 4/17/2009	Triple H			

WWE ELITE COLLECTION SERIES 3 (2010)		MIB	LOOSE	VALUE
WM 25/EXTREME RULES 2009	Christian			
BACKLASH 2009	Cody Rhodes			
SURVIVOR SERIES 2008	John Cena			
RAW – 2/23/2009	Santino Marella			
RAW – 9/22/2008	Shawn Michaels			
RAW – 4/13/2009	The Miz			

WWE ELITE COLLECTION SERIES 4 (2010)		MIB	LOOSE	VALUE
NIGHT OF CHAMPIONS 2009	Big Show			
UNFORGIVEN 2008	Chris Jericho (Blue Deco on Trunks)			
NO MERCY 2008	Chris Jericho (Purple Deco on Trunks)			
WRESTLEMANIA 25	Finlay			
JUDGEMENT DAY 2009	John Morrison (Maroon Coat)			
	John Morrison (Red Coat)			
RAW – 7/31/2009	Kane			
NIGHT OF CHAMPIONS 2009	Kofi Kingston			

WWE ELITE COLLECTION SERIES 5 (2010)		MIB	LOOSE	VALUE
UNFORGIVEN 2008	Chavo Guerrero			
SUMMERSLAM 2009	Dolph Ziggler			
RAW – 9/19/2009	Jack Swagger (Singlet Off)			
RAW – 7/13/2009	Jack Swagger (Singlet On)			
RAW – 8/3/2009	Mark Henry			
SMACKDOWN – 10/16/2009	Rey Mysterio			
ECW – 6/30/2009	Vladimir Kozlov (Logos On Coat)			
	Vladimir Kozlov (No Logos On Coat)			

WWE ELITE COLLECTION SERIES 6 (2010)		MIB	LOOSE	VALUE
RAW – 3/15/2009	Batista			
BREAKING POINT 2009	CM Punk			
ECW – 7/14/2009	Goldust			
SUMMERSLAM 2009	JTG			
SMACKDOWN – 10/30/2009	Matt Hardy			
RAW – 1/5/2009	Shad			

WWE ELITE COLLECTION SERIES 7 (2011)		MIB	LOOSE	VALUE
SMACKDOWN – 9/18/2009	David Hart Smith			
RAW – 12/29/2009	Hornswoggle			
SURVIVOR SERIES 2009	John Cena			
SURVIVOR SERIES 2009	Shawn Michaels			
BREAKING POINT 2009	Triple H			
SMACKDOWN – 9/18/2009	Tyson Kidd			

WWE ELITE COLLECTION SERIES 8 (2011)		MIB	LOOSE	VALUE
WRESTLEMANIA XXVI	Drew McIntyre			
WRESTLEMANIA XXVI	Edge			
RAW – 5/31/2009	Evan Bourne			
TLC 2009	Sheamus			
SURVIVOR SERIES 2009	The Undertaker			
RAW – 5/11/2009	William Regal			

WWE ELITE COLLECTION SERIES 9 (2011)		MIB	LOOSE	VALUE
ROYAL RUMBLE 2010	Kofi Kingston			
SUMMERSLAM 2010	Luke Gallows			
WRESTLEMANIA XXVI	MVP			
EXTREME RULES 2009	Randy Orton			
WRESTLEMANIA XXVI	The Miz			
SUPERSTARS – 11/19/2009	Zack Ryder			

WWE ELITE COLLECTION SERIES 10 (2011)		MIB	LOOSE	VALUE
RAW – 3/22/2010	Big Show			
SUMMERSLAM 2010	John Morrison			
MONEY IN THE BANK 2010	Kane			
OVER THE LIMIT 2010	R-Truth			
SURVIVOR SERIES 2010	Ted Dibiase (Green Trunks)			
ROYAL RUMBLE 2011	Ted Dibiase (Purple Trunks)			
ROYAL RUMBLE 2010	Yoshi Tatsu			

WWE ELITE COLLECTION SERIES 11 (2011)		MIB	LOOSE	VALUE
RAW – 4/26/2010	Christian			
NIGHT OF CHAMPIONS 2010	CM Punk			
SUMMERSLAM 2010	John Cena			
EXTREME RULES 2010	Rey Mysterio			
ELIMINATION CHAMBER 2011	The Miz			
RAW – 7/12/2010	Wade Barrett			

WWE ELITE COLLECTION SERIES 12 (2012)		MIB	LOOSE	VALUE
SMACKDOWN – 8/20/2010	Alberto Del Rio			
HELL IN A CELL 2010	Daniel Bryan			
ROYAL RUMBLE 2011	Justin Gabriel			
BADD BLOOD: IN YOUR HOUSE	Kane			
SUPERSTARS – 2/8/1992	Papa Shango			
ROYAL RUMBLE 2011	Randy Orton			

WWE ELITE COLLECTION SERIES 13 (2012)		MIB	LOOSE	VALUE
SMACKDOWN – 9/8/2010	Big Show			
WRESTLEMANIA XXVII	Cody Rhodes (Jacket Off)			
	Cody Rhodes (Jacket On)			
RAW – 5/30/2011	Dolph Ziggler			
RAW IS WAR – 5/24/1999	Edge			
SMACKDOWN – 1/7/2011	Rey Mysterio			
TLC 2010	Sheamus			

WWE ELITE COLLECTION SERIES 14 (2012)		MIB	LOOSE	VALUE
SUMMERSLAM 2011	Alberto Del Rio			
SURVIVOR SERIES 1988	Big Boss Man			
SMACKDOWN – 6/30/2006	Booker T			
SUMMERSLAM 2011	John Cena			
RAW – 4/4/2011	The Rock			
WRESTLEMANIA XXVI	The Undertaker			

WWE ELITE COLLECTION SERIES 15 (2012)		MIB	LOOSE	VALUE
NIGHT OF CHAMPIONS 2011	Evan Bourne			
NIGHT OF CHAMPIONS 2011	Mark Henry			
RAW – 10/10/2011	R-Truth			
SUMMERSLAM 2009	Rey Mysterio			
SMACKDOWN – 8/12/2011	Sin Cara (Gold)			
	Sin Cara (Yellow)			
KING OF THE RING 1993	Yokozuna			

WWE ELITE COLLECTION SERIES 16 (2012)		MIB	LOOSE	VALUE
MONEY IN THE BANK 2011	CM Punk			
IN YOUR HOUSE 1 1995	Diesel			
SMACKDOWN – 12/9/2011	Ezekiel Jackson			
MONEY IN THE BANK 2011	Heath Slater			
SPRING STAMPEDE 1999	Kevin Nash			
SMACKDOWN – 5/6/2011	Randy Orton			
RAW – 11/14/2011	The Rock			

WWE ELITE COLLECTION SERIES 17 (2012)		MIB	LOOSE	VALUE
VENGEANCE 2011	John Cena			
NIGHT OF CHAMPIONS 2011	Kelly Kelly			
NIGHT OF CHAMPIONS 2011	Kofi Kingston			
RAW – 4/12/1999	Mankind			
WRESTLEMANIA XXVII	Sheamus			
VENGEANCE 2011	Zack Ryder			

WWE ELITE COLLECTION SERIES 18 (2013)		MIB	LOOSE	VALUE
RAW – 1/9/2012	Brodus Clay			
WRESTLEMANIA XXVII	Jerry "The King" Lawler			
NO MERCY 2007	Rey Mysterio			
MONEY IN THE BANK 2011	Sin Cara			
JUDGEMENT DAY 2002	The Undertaker			
SMACKDOWN 2/17/2012	Wade Barrett			

WWE ELITE COLLECTION SERIES 19 (2013)		MIB	LOOSE	VALUE
EXTREME RULES 2012	Brock Lesnar			
RAW SUPERSHOW – 5/21/2012	Daniel Bryan			
ELIMINATION CHAMBER 2012	Dolph Ziggler			
RAW – 12/12/2011	Kane			
WRESTLEMANIA IV	Miss Elizabeth			
BADD BLOOD: IN YOUR HOUSE	Shawn Michaels			

WWE ELITE COLLECTION SERIES 20 (2013)		MIB	LOOSE	VALUE
WRESTLEMANIA XXVIII	Chris Jericho			
WRESTLEMANIA X7	Christian			
CAPITOL PUNISHMENT 2011	CM Punk			
WRESTLEMANIA XXVIII	Cody Rhodes			
MONEY IN THE BANK 2012	John Cena			
SMACKDOWN – 3/5/2012	Santino Marella			

WWE ELITE COLLECTION SERIES 21 (2013)		MIB	LOOSE	VALUE
SMACKDOWN 9/16/2011	AJ Lee			
SUMMERSLAM 2012	Alberto Del Rio			
SUMMERSLAM 1989	Honky Tonk Man			
SMACKDOWN – 3/16/2012	Randy Orton			
RAW 1000	Rey Mysterio			
NO WAY OUT 2012	Ryback			

WWE ELITE COLLECTION SERIES 22 (2013)		MIB	LOOSE	VALUE
HELL IN A CELL 2012	Big Show			
SMACKDOWN – 5/25/2012	Damien Sandow			
THE GREAT AMERICAN BASH 1998	The Giant			
NIGHT OF CHAMPIONS 2012	Kane			
RAW SUPERSHOW – 4/2/2012	Tensai			
ELIMINATION CHAMBER 2013	The Rock			

WWE ELITE COLLECTION SERIES 23 (2013)		MIB	LOOSE	VALUE
HELL IN A CELL 2012	Antonio Cesaro			
WRESTLEMANIA 21	JBL			
SURVIVOR SERIES 2012	John Cena			
WRESTLEMANIA VIII	"Macho Man" Randy Savage			
WRESTLEMANIA XV	Triple H			
SURVIVOR SERIES 1995	The Undertaker			

WWE ELITE COLLECTION SERIES 24 (2013)		MIB	LOOSE	VALUE
RAW – 4/8/2013	Dolph Ziggler			
RAW – 10/29/2012	Rey Mysterio			
HELL IN A CELL 2012	Ryback			
TLC 2012	The Miz			
SURVIVOR SERIES 2005	Trish Stratus			
RAW – 12/20/2012	Wade Barrett			

WWE ELITE COLLECTION SERIES 25 (2014)		MIB	LOOSE	VALUE
RAW – 1/14/2013	Brodus Clay			
CIRCA 1970	Bruno Sammartino			
ELIMINATION CHAMBER 2013	Dean Ambrose			
TLC 2012	Seth Rollins			
SURVIVOR SERIES 2012	Sheamus			
RAW – 2/18/2013	Sin Cara			

WWE ELITE COLLECTION SERIES 26 (2014)		MIB	LOOSE	VALUE
RAW SUPERSHOW – 1/28/2013	Big E Langston			
WRESTLEMANIA 29	Jack Swagger			
WRESTLEMANIA 29	Mark Henry			
RAW – 4/9/1999	Road Dogg			
RAW – 4/1/2013	Roman Reigns			
SUMMERSLAM 1992	Ultimate Warrior			

WWE ELITE COLLECTION SERIES 27 (2014)		MIB	LOOSE	VALUE
RAW – 7/27/1998	Billy Gunn			
EXTREME RULES 2013	Fandango			
SMACKDOWN – 10/4/2013	Kofi Kingston			
SMACKDOWN – 10/10/2002	Rikishi (Sarong On)			
WRESTLEMANIA 2000	Rikishi (Sarong Off)			
RAW – 7/13/2013	Rob Van Dam			
WRESTLEMANIA XXVIII	The Undertaker			

WWE ELITE COLLECTION SERIES 28 (2014)		MIB	LOOSE	VALUE
RAW – 8/19/2013	Big Show			
SMACKDOWN – 9/27/2013	Bray Wyatt			
ROYAL RUMBLE 2013	Daniel Bryan			
SUMMERSLAM 1990	Demolition Crush			
ROYAL RUMBLE 2014	John Cena			
EXTREME RULES 2013	Triple H			

WWE ELITE COLLECTION SERIES 29 (2014)		MIB	LOOSE	VALUE
WRESTLEMANIA III	Andre The Giant			
RAW – 8/26/2013	CM Punk			
MONEY IN THE BANK 2013	Damien Sandow			
SMACKDOWN – 7/26/2013	Erick Rowan			
SMACKDOWN – 11/3/2013	Goldust			
SMACKDOWN – 8/16/2013	Luke Harper			

WWE ELITE COLLECTION SERIES 30 (2014)		MIB	LOOSE	VALUE
BATTLE ROYAL AT THE ALBERT HALL	Animal			
ROYAL RUMBLE 2014	Batista (Facing Backward)			
ROYAL RUMBLE 2014	Batista (Facing Forward)			
RAW – 2/24/2014	Brock Lesnar			
BATTLE ROYAL AT THE ALBERT HALL	Hawk			
RAW – 6/27/1994	Lex Luger			
RAW – 9/16/2013	Ryback			

WWE ELITE COLLECTION SERIES 31 (2014)		MIB	LOOSE	VALUE
WRESTLEMANIA XXX	Dean Ambrose			
RAW – 9/16/2013	Jey Uso			
RAW – 9/16/2013	Jimmy Uso			
RAW – 10/28/2013	Kane			
RAW – 3/24/2003 & BACKLASH 2003	The Rock			
SUMMERSLAM 1996	Vader			

WWE ELITE COLLECTION SERIES 32 (2015)		MIB	LOOSE	VALUE
WRESTLEMANIA 29	Big E			
ROYAL RUMBLE 2014	Cody Rhodes			
ROYAL RUMBLE 2014	Daniel Bryan			
RAW – 2/10/2014	Mark Henry			
STARRCADE 1996	Rey Mysterio			
MAIN EVENT – 4/8/2014	Sin Cara			

WWE ELITE COLLECTION SERIES 33 (2015)		MIB	LOOSE	VALUE
PAYBACK 2014	Batista			
RAW – 4/1/2014	Cesaro			
WRESTLEMANIA III	Junkyard Dog			
WRESTLEMANIA XXX	Roman Reigns			
WRESTLEMANIA XXX	Seth Rollins			
WRESTLEMANIA 2000	X-Pac			

WWE ELITE COLLECTION SERIES 34 (2015)		MIB	LOOSE	VALUE
RAW – 4/7/2014	Bad News Barrett			
WRESTLEMANIA IX	Doink The Clown			
RAW – 2/24/2014	Hulk Hogan			
SMACKDOWN – 4/11/2014	John Cena			
RAW – 4/7/2014	Paige			
PAYBACK 2014	Rusev			

WWE ELITE COLLECTION SERIES 35 (2015)		MIB	LOOSE	VALUE
SMACKDOWN – 5/9/2014	Diego			
ROYAL RUMBLE 1991	Earthquake			
SMACKDOWN – 5/9/2014	Fernando			
WRESTLEMANIA XXX	Luke Harper			
BATTLEGROUND 2014	Randy Orton			
WRESTLEMANIA XXX	Triple H			

WWE ELITE COLLECTION SERIES 36 (2015)		MIB	LOOSE	VALUE
RAW – 6/23/2014	Bo Dallas			
SUMMERSLAM 2014	Bray Wyatt			
RAW – 7/21/2014	Dean Ambrose			
NITRO – 2/24/1997	Diamond Dallas Page			
HELL IN A CELL 2014	Goldust			
HELL IN A CELL 2014	Stardust			

WWE ELITE COLLECTION SERIES 37 (2015)		MIB	LOOSE	VALUE
NIGHT OF CHAMPIONS 2014	Brock Lesnar			
NITRO – 6/5/1996	Dean Malenko			
NIGHT OF CHAMPIONS 2014	John Cena			
SMACKDOWN – 8/29/2014	Seth Rollins			
SUMMERSLAM 2014	Stephanie McMahon			
TLC 2014	The Miz			

WWE ELITE COLLECTION SERIES 38 (2015)		MIB	LOOSE	VALUE
SMACKDOWN – 6/20/2014	Adam Rose			
RAW – 4/10/2000	Bradshaw (Sleeves)			
RAW – 4/10/2000	Bradshaw (No Sleeves)			
EXTREME RULES 2014	Daniel Bryan			
RAW – 4/10/2000	Faarooq (Sleeves)			
RAW – 4/10/2000	Faarooq (No Sleeves)			
BASH AT THE BEACH 1995	"Macho Man" Randy Savage			
RAW – 4/7/14 & HELL IN A CELL 2014	Roman Reigns			

WWE ELITE COLLECTION SERIES 39 (2016)		MIB	LOOSE	VALUE
WWF ON TELECINCO – 10/10/1991	British Bulldog			
TLC 2014	Damien Mizdow			
RAW – 12/29/2014	Dolph Ziggler			
RAW – 1/19/2015	Sting			
SURVIVOR SERIES 1996	Sycho Sid			
ROCK BOTTOM: IN YOUR HOUSE	The Godfather			

WWE ELITE COLLECTION SERIES 40 (2016)		MIB	LOOSE	VALUE
SURVIVOR SERIES 1992	Irwin R. Schyster			
WRESTLEMANIA 31	John Cena			
WRESTLEMANIA IV	"Ravishing" Rick Rude			
NXT TAKEOVER: REVIVAL	Sami Zayn			
FASTLANE 2015	Tyson Kidd			
THE GREAT AMERICAN BASH 2007	Umaga			

WWE ELITE COLLECTION SERIES 41 (2016)		MIB	LOOSE	VALUE
RAW – 1/10/1994	1-2-3 Kid			
RAW – 5/25/2015	Dean Ambrose			
NXT TAKEOVER: REVIVAL	Finn Bálor			
RAW – 10/30/2000	Lita			
WRESTLEMANIA 31	Ryback			
ECW BARELY LEGAL 1997	Terry Funk			

WWE ELITE COLLECTION SERIES 42 (2016)		MIB	LOOSE	VALUE
RAW – 5/28/2015	Kalisto			
RAW – 3/15/1993	Brian Knobbs			
RAW – 3/15/1993	Jerry Sags			
RAW – 3/30/2015	Neville			
WRESTLEMANIA 31	Triple H			
ELIMINATION CHAMBER 2015	Xavier Woods			

WWE ELITE COLLECTION SERIES 43 (2016)		MIB	LOOSE	VALUE
HELL IN A CELL 2015	Alberto Del Rio			
SUMMERSLAM 1990	Bret "Hit Man" Hart			
SUMMERSLAM 1990	Jim "The Anvil" Neidhart			
RAW – 6/8/2015	Kevin Owens			
ELIMINATION CHAMBER 2015	Kofi Kingston			
NXT – 6/10/2015	Samoa Joe			

WWE ELITE COLLECTION SERIES 44 (2016)		MIB	LOOSE	VALUE
ELIMINATION CHAMBER 2015	Big E			
RAW – 8/24/2015	Braun Strowman			
SAT. NIGHT MAIN EVENT – 11/14/1992	"Macho Man" Randy Savage			
BATTLEGROUND 2015	Sasha Banks			
SMACKDOWN – 5/28/2015	Sin Cara			
SUPERSTARS – 1/27/1990	Tugboat			

WWE ELITE COLLECTION SERIES 45 (2016)		MIB	LOOSE	VALUE
RAW – 8/31/2015	Bubba Ray Dudley			
RAW – 8/31/2015	D-Von Dudley			
NITRO – 11/26/1996	Lord Steven Regal			
ROYAL RUMBLE 1993	Lex Luger			
HELL IN A CELL 2015	Roman Reigns			
SUMMERSLAM 2015	Seth Rollins			

WWE ELITE COLLECTION SERIES 46 (2017)		MIB	LOOSE	VALUE
NITRO – 7/15/1996	Booker T			
THE BEAST IN THE EAST	Finn Bálor			
SUMMERSLAM 2015	John Cena			
RAW – 11/30/2015	Rusev			
RAW – 3/30/2015	Sheamus			
NITRO – 7/15/1996	Stevie Ray			

WWE ELITE COLLECTION SERIES 47A (2017)		MIB	LOOSE	VALUE
ROYAL RUMBLE 2016	AJ Styles			
NXT TAKEOVER: RESPECT	Asuka			
RAW – 10/12/1998	Big Boss Man			
SMACKDOWN – 10/29/2015	Cesaro			
RAW – 10/19/2015	Kevin Owens			
SUPERSTARS – 6/27/1992	Tatanka			

WWE ELITE COLLECTION SERIES 47B (2017)		MIB	LOOSE	VALUE
HALLOWEEN HAVOC 1991	Brian Pillman			
IN YOUR HOUSE 4: GREAT WHITE NORTH	Goldust			
HELL IN A CELL 2015	Kane			
ROYAL RUMBLE 2016	Konnor			
UNFORGIVEN 2000	The Rock			
ROYAL RUMBLE 2016	Viktor			

WWE ELITE COLLECTION SERIES 48 (2017)		MIB	LOOSE	VALUE
SMACKDOWN – 11/10/2006	The Boogeyman			
IWA KAWASAKI DREAM – 8/20/1995	Cactus Jack			
EXTREME RULES 2016	Dean Ambrose			
SURVIVOR SERIES 2015	Dolph Ziggler			
ROYAL RUMBLE 2016	Erick Rowan			
FASTLANE 2016	Kalisto			

WWE ELITE COLLECTION SERIES 49 (2017)		MIB	LOOSE	VALUE
NXT TAKEOVER LONDON	Apollo Crews			
ROYAL RUMBLE 2016	Becky Lynch			
RAW – 4/4/2016	Big Cass			
WRESTLING CHALLENGE – 2/5/1989	Brutus "The Barber" Beefcake			
ROADBLOCK 2016	Enzo Amore			
WRESTLEMANIA 21	Randy Orton			

WWE ELITE COLLECTION SERIES 50 (2017)		MIB	LOOSE	VALUE
NXT TAKEOVER DALLAS	Baron Corbin			
SUMMERSLAM 2016	John Cena			
SMACKDOWN – 8/30/2016	Rhyno			
WRESTLEMANIA 32	Shane McMahon			
WRESTLEMANIA 32	Stephanie McMahon			
WRESTLEMANIA VII	Warlord			

WWE ELITE COLLECTION SERIES 51 (2017)		MIB	LOOSE	VALUE
BACKLASH 2016	AJ Styles			
WRESTLING CHALLENGE – 2/16/1991	Berzerker			
SUMMERSLAM 1997	Mankind			
SUMMERSLAM 2016	Roman Reigns			
RAW – 11/21/2016	Sami Zayn			
BASH AT THE BEACH 1996	Scott Hall			

WWE ELITE COLLECTION SERIES 52 (2017)		MIB	LOOSE	VALUE
RAW – 11/21/2016	Braun Strowman			
RAW – 7/6/1998	D'Lo Brown			
IN YOUR HOUSE 15: A COLD DAY IN HELL	Ken Shamrock			
CLASH OF CHAMPIONS 2016	Kofi Kingston			
SUMMERSLAM 2016	Seth Rollins			
CLASH OF CHAMPIONS 2016	Xavier Woods			

WWE ELITE COLLECTION SERIES 53 (2017)		MIB	LOOSE	VALUE
BACKLASH 2016	Alexa Bliss			
CLASH OF CHAMPIONS 2016	Big E			
MONEY IN THE BANK 2016	Chris Jericho			
NO MERCY 2016	Heath Slater			
CLASH OF CHAMPIONS 2016	Kevin Owens			
SUMMERSLAM 2016	The Miz			

WWE ELITE COLLECTION SERIES 54 (2018)		MIB	LOOSE	VALUE
ELIMINATION CHAMBER 2017	Bray Wyatt			
WRESTLEMANIA 32	Charlotte Flair			
SMACKDOWN – 9/13/2016	Jey Uso			
SMACKDOWN – 9/13/2016	Jimmy Uso			
SMACKDOWN – 1/31/2017	John Cena			
RAW – 12/26/2016	Rich Swann			

WWE ELITE COLLECTION SERIES 55 (2018)		MIB	LOOSE	VALUE
WRESTLEMANIA 33	Big Cass			
WRESTLEMANIA 33	Brock Lesnar			
RAW – 6/27/2016	Enzo Amore			
SMACKDOWN – 12/20/2016	James Ellsworth			
WRESTLEMANIA 33	Neville			
WRESTLEMANIA XIX	The Undertaker			

WWE ELITE COLLECTION SERIES 56 (2018)		MIB	LOOSE	VALUE
SURVIVOR SERIES 2016	AJ Styles			
205 LIVE – 11/29/2016	Gentleman Jack Gallagher			
ROYAL RUMBLE 2017	Karl Anderson			
HELL IN A CELL 2016	Luke Gallows			
FASTLANE 2017	Roman Reigns			
EXTREME RULES 2017	Samoa Joe			

WWE ELITE COLLECTION SERIES 57 (2018)		MIB	LOOSE	VALUE
MONEY IN THE BANK 2017	Baron Corbin			
WRESTLEMANIA 33	Jeff Hardy			
SMACKDOWN – 12/16/1999	Scotty 2 Hotty			
WRESTLEMANIA 33	Seth Rollins			
BACKLASH 2017	Shinsuke Nakamura			
NXT TAKEOVER TORONTO	Tye Dillinger			

WWE ELITE COLLECTION SERIES 58 (2018)		MIB	LOOSE	VALUE
GREAT BALLS OF FIRE 2017	Braun Strowman			
WRESTLEMANIA 33	Cesaro			
EXTREME RULES 2017	Dean Ambrose			
PAYBACK 2017	Matt Hardy			
NXT TAKEOVER TORONTO	Mickie James			
WRESTLEMANIA 33	Sheamus			

WWE ELITE COLLECTION SERIES 59 (2018)		MIB	LOOSE	VALUE
SMACKDOWN – 12/27/2016	Chad Gable			
RAW – 8/15/2016	Finn Bálor			
SMACKDOWN – 12/27/2016	Jason Jordan			
WRESTLEMANIA XIX	Kurt Angle			
WRESLEMANIA 33	The Miz			
BATTLEGROUND 2016	Zack Ryder			

WWE ELITE COLLECTION SERIES 60 (2018)		MIB	LOOSE	VALUE
NXT – 11/17/2016	Elias			
PRIME TIME WRESTLING – 9/8/1986	Giant Machine			
SMACKDOWN – 7/18/2017	John Cena			
SMACKDOWN – 7/4/2017	Kofi Kingston			
WRESTLEMANIA 33	Triple H			
SMACKDOWN – 7/4/2017	Xavier Woods			

WWE ELITE COLLECTION SERIES 61 (2018)		MIB	LOOSE	VALUE
SUMMERSLAM 2017	AJ Styles			
SMACKDOWN – 7/4/2017	BIG E			
SMACKDOWN – 10/10/2017	Fandango			
SMACKDOWN – 8/1/2017	Kevin Owens			
HELL IN A CELL 2017	Shane McMahon			
SMACKDOWN – 10/10/2017	Tyler Breeze			

WWE ELITE COLLECTION SERIES 62 (2018)		MIB	LOOSE	VALUE
NXT TAKEOVER ORLANDO	Akam			
TLC 2017	Braun Strowman			
RAW – 7/14/1997	Dude Love			
NXT TAKEOVER ORLANDO	Rezar			
ROYAL RUMBLE 2018	Roman Reigns			
GREAT AMERICAN BASH 1991	Sting			

WWE ELITE COLLECTION SERIES 63 (2019)		MIB	LOOSE	VALUE
SURVIVOR SERIES 1994	Bob Backlund (Walmart)			
TLC 2017	Dean Ambrose			
SUPERSTARS – 2/7/1986	Dusty Rhodes			
ROYAL RUMBLE 2018	Kane			
SMACKDOWN – 11/14/2017	Sami Zayn			
SMACKDOWN – 8/29/2017	Shelton Benjamin (Standard - Bald)			
WRESTLEMANIA 25	Shelton Benjamin (Chase - Gold Standard)			
NXT TAKEOVER ORLANDO	Shinsuke Nakamura			

WWE ELITE COLLECTION SERIES 64 (2019)		MIB	LOOSE	VALUE
ELIMINATION CHAMBER 2017	Curt Hawkins (Standard - Blue Singlet)			
RAW – 9/25/2017	Curt Hawkins (Chase - Black Singlet)			
HELL IN A CELL 2017	Jey Uso			
HELL IN A CELL 2017	Jimmy Uso			
RAW – 1/22/2018	John Cena			
NXT TAKEOVER CHICAGO	Pete Dunne (Target)			
RAW – 3/13/2017	Samoa Joe			
ROYAL RUMBLE 2018	Seth Rollins			

WWE ELITE COLLECTION SERIES 65 (2019)		MIB	LOOSE	VALUE
CLASH OF CHAMPIONS 2017	Aiden English (Standard – Black Tights)			
SMACKDOWN – 8/22/2017	Aiden English (Chase - Grey on Tights)			
NXT – 4/19/2017	Eric Young			
RAW – 12/11/2017	Nia Jax			
RAW – 11/20/2017	Roman Reigns			
ELIMINATION CHAMBER 2018	Ronda Rousey			
CLASH OF CHAMPIONS 2017	Rusev			
WRESTLEMANIA VI	Sensational Sherri (Walmart)			

WWE ELITE COLLECTION SERIES 66 (2019)		MIB	LOOSE	VALUE
ROYAL RUMBLE 2018	AJ Styles			
NXT – 4/19/2017	Alexander Wolfe (Target)			
SMACKDOWN – 11/21/2017	Harper			
ROYAL RUMBLE 2018	Kevin Owens (Standard - Fight Anyone Shirt)			
WRESTLEMANIA 34	Kevin Owens (Chase - KO-Mania III Shirt)			
SURVIVOR SERIES 2017	Kurt Angle			
NXT – 4/19/2017	Nikki Cross			
SMACKDOWN – 11/21/2017	Rowan			

    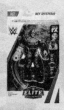  

WWE ELITE COLLECTION SERIES 67 (2019)		MIB	LOOSE	VALUE
WRESTLEMANIA 34	Cedric Alexander			
SMACKDOWN – 7/10/2018	Jeff Hardy (Standard - Blue Camo Sleeves)			
SMACKDOWN – 7/3/2018	Jeff Hardy (Chase - Blue Sleeves)			
SMACKDOWN – 4/3/2018	Randy Orton			
HALLOWEEN HAVOC 1997	Rey Mysterio			
NXT TAKEOVER NEW ORLEANS	Shayna Baszler			
NXT – 5/25/2017	Velveteen Dream			

WWE ELITE COLLECTION SERIES 68 - SUMMERSLAM (2019)		MIB	LOOSE	VALUE
SUMMERSLAM 2018	Braun Strowman			
SUMMERSLAM 2014	Brie Bella			
SUMMERSLAM 2018	Daniel Bryan			
RAW – 6/26/1995	King Mabel (Standard - M On Chest)			
SUMMERSLAM 1995	King Mabel (Chase - Lightning Bolts)			
RAW – 5/10/1999	Pat Patterson (Walmart)			
SUMMERSLAM 2018	Roman Reigns			
SUMMERSLAM 2000	The Undertaker			

WWE ELITE COLLECTION SERIES 69 (2019)		MIB	LOOSE	VALUE
SUPER SHOWDOWN 2019	Ali (Standard - Yellow Tights)			
WRESTLEMANIA 35	Ali (Chase - Red Tights)			
RAW – 4/16/2018	Bobby Lashley			
ROYAL RUMBLE 2018	Liv Morgan (Target)			
SMACKDOWN – 1/22/2019	Rey Mysterio			
NXT TAKEOVER CHICAGO II	Ricochet			
EVOLUTION	Sonya Deville (Target)			
WRESTLEMANIA 34	The Miz			
KING OF THE RING 2000	The Rock (Walmart)			
NXT TAKEOVER CHICAGO II	Tommaso Ciampa			

WWE ELITE COLLECTION SERIES 70 (2019)		MIB	LOOSE	VALUE
SUMMERSLAM 2018	Dolph Ziggler (Standard - Black Tights)			
FASTLANE 2018	Dolph Ziggler (Chase - Pink Tights)			
NAT – 5/9/2018	EC3			
NXT TAKEOVER LONDON	Finn Bálor			
RAW – 5/10/1999	Gerald Brisco (Walmart)			
NXT TAKEOVER BROOKLYN IV	Johnny Gargano			
SUPERSTARS – 9/22/1990	Mr. McMahon			
SUPER SHOWDOWN 2018	Seth Rollins			

WWE ELITE COLLECTION SERIES 71 (2019)		MIB	LOOSE	VALUE
NZT – 6/27/2018	Adam Cole			
SURVIVOR SERIES 1999	Big Show			
HELL IN A CELL 2018	Drew McIntyre			
SMACKDOWN – 7/24/2018	Jeff Hardy			
RAW – 1/7/2019	John Cena			
NXT TAKEOVER PHILADELPHIA	Kassius Ohno (Target)			
EVOLUTION	Nikki Bella (Standard - Bellalution Shirt)			
SMACKDOWN – 3/7/2017	Nikki Bella (Chase - Do More, Fear Less Shirt)			
RAW – 12/11/2017	Paige (Target)			

WWE ELITE COLLECTION SERIES 72 (2020)		MIB	LOOSE	VALUE
WRESTLEMANIA 35	Batista			
SMACKDOWN – 1/1/2019	Becky Lynch			
SURVIVOR SERIES 2018	Buddy Murphy (Standard - Red Gear)			
205 LIVE – 3/27/2018	Buddy Murphy (Chase - Black Gear)			
SURVIVOR SERIES 1987	Gorilla Monsoon (Walmart)			
SMACKDOWN 1000 – 10/16/2018	Rey Mysterio			
NXT TAKEOVER WAR GAMES	Roderick Strong			
NXT – 10/2/2019	Velveteen Dream			

WWE ELITE COLLECTION SERIES 73 (2020)		MIB	LOOSE	VALUE
NXT TAKEOVER WAR GAMES 2018	Aleister Black			
SMACKDOWN – 2/5/2019	Daniel Bryan			
MONEY IN THE BANK 2018	Elias			
RAW – 9/19/2016	Gran Metalik (Standard - Blue Gear)			
205 LIVE – 1/23/2018	Gran Metalik (Chase - Black Gear)			
NXT TAKEOVER BROOKLYN IV	Kairi Sane			
SMACKDOWN – 5/8/2018	Peyton Royce (Target)			
WRESTLEMANIA 34	Triple H			

WWE ELITE COLLECTION SERIES 74 (2020)		MIB	LOOSE	VALUE
ROYAL RUMBLE 2019	AJ Styles			
ROYAL RUMBLE 2019	Andrade			
ROYAL RUMBLE 2019	Finn Bálor			
RAW – 10/29/2003	Goldberg			
SURVIVOR SERIES 1994	Jim "The Anvil" Neidhart (Walmart)			
205 LIVE – 6/5/2018	Lince Dorado (Standard - Black Tights)			
RAW – 1/7/2019	Lince Dorado (Chase - Gold Tights)			
ROYAL RUMBLE 2018	Natalya			

WWE ELITE COLLECTION SERIES 75 (2020)		MIB	LOOSE	VALUE
ELIMINATION CHAMBER 2019	Billie Kay (Target)			
2002	Jeff Hardy			
RAW – 2/4/2019	Kalisto			
SMACKDOWN – 2/19/2019	Mandy Rose			
NXT TAKEOVER BLACKPOOL	Pete Dunne			
ROYAL RUMBLE 2019	Seth Rollins			
SMACKDOWN 5/9/2002	The Hurricane (Standard - Black Boots)			
RAW – 3/10/2003	The Hurricane (Chase - White Boots)			

WWE ELITE COLLECTION SERIES 76 (2020)		MIB	LOOSE	VALUE
WRESTLEMANIA 35	Braun Strowman			
JUDGEMENT DAY 1998	Christian (Standard - White Shirt)			
RAW – 7/26/1999	Christian (Chase - Black Shirt)			
WRESTLEMANIA 35	John Cena			
RAW – 4/29/2019	Lacey Evans			
EXTREME RULES 2019	Otis			
EXTREME RULES 2019	Tucker			

WWE ELITE COLLECTION SERIES 77 - SUMMERSLAM (2020)		MIB	LOOSE	VALUE
SUMMERSLAM 2019	AJ Styles			
WRESTLEMANIA	"Classy" Freddie Blassie (Walmart)			
SUMMERSLAM 1988	Miss Elizabeth			
SUMMERSLAM 1989	"Ravishing" Rick Rude (Standard - Warrior Tights)			
SUPERSTARS – 4/2/1989	"Ravishing" Rick Rude (Chase - IC Title Tights)			
SUMMERSLAM 2018	Ronda Rousey			
SUMMERSLAM 2019	"The Fiend" Bray Wyatt			
SUMMERSLAM 1999	Viscera			

WWE ELITE COLLECTION SERIES 78 (2020)		MIB	LOOSE	VALUE
RAW – 7/29/2019	Drake Maverick			
SMACKDOWN – 10/4/2019	Kofi Kingston			
NXT TAKEOVER XXV	Matt Riddle			
WRESTLEMANIA 33	Naomi (Standard - Black & Green)			
BACKLASH 2017	Naomi (Chase - Pink & Green)			
SUMMERSLAM 2019	Randy Orton			
SMACKDOWN – 1/29/2019	R-Truth			
1987	"Superstar" Billy Graham (Target)			

WWE ELITE COLLECTION SERIES 79 (2020)		MIB	LOOSE	VALUE
SMACKDOWN – 10/11/2019	Big E			
NXT TAKEOVER WAR GAMES '18	Bobby Fish (Standard - Snow Camo)			
WORLDS COLLIDE 2019	Bobby Fish (Chase - Black Trunks)			
MONEY IN THE BANK 2019	Daniel Bryan			
NXT TAKEOVER TORONTO 2019	Io Shirai			
SMACKDOWN – 9/24/2019	Roman Reigns			
EXTREME RULES 2019	The Undertaker (Walmart)			
SMACKDOWN – 10/11/2019	Xavier Woods			

WWE ELITE COLLECTION SERIES 80 (2020)		MIB	LOOSE	VALUE
SMACKDOWN – 10/11/2019	Bayley			
RAW – 5/6/2019	Erik			
RAW – 5/6/2019	Ivar			
SMACKDOWN – 10/4/2019	Kevin Owens			
NXT TAKEOVER WAR GAMES 2018	Kyle O'Reilly (Standard - Snow Camo)			
NXT TAKEOVER TORONTO 2019	Kyle O'Reilly (Chase - Black Trunks)			
RAW – 8/12/2019	Ricochet			
1983	Rocky Johnson (Target)			

WWE ELITE COLLECTION SERIES 81 (2021)		MIB	LOOSE	VALUE
RAW – 7/1/2019	Angelo Dawkins			
NXT TAKEOVER PHOENIX	Bianca Belair			
RAW – 10/11/1999	Mae Young (Walmart)			
RAW – 7/1/2019	Montez Ford			
SURVIVOR SERIES 2019	Shinsuke Nakamura (Standard - Blue Suit)			
SMACKDOWN – 11/22/2019	Shinsuke Nakamura (Chase - Black Suit)			
SLAMBOREE 1993	"Stunning" Steve Austin			
SMACKDOWN – 10/4/2019	The Rock			

WWE ELITE COLLECTION SERIES 82 (2021)		MIB	LOOSE	VALUE
HELL IN A CELL 2019	Alexa Bliss			
SURVIVOR SERIES 1987	Davey Boy Smith (Target)			
NXT WORLDS COLLIDE 2020	Finn Bálor			
SUMMERSLAM 1993	Jerry "The King" Lawler			
ROYAL RUMBLE 2020	John Morrison			
NXT – 1/22/2020	Keith Lee (Standard - Black Gear)			
NXT – 1/8/2020	Keith Lee (Chase - White Gear)			
WRESTLEMANIA 36	Rob Gronkowski			

WWE ELITE COLLECTION SERIES 83 (2021)		MIB	LOOSE	VALUE
WRESTLEMANIA 36	Drew McIntyre			
SNME – 11/13/1990	Dusty Rhodes			
WRESTLEMANIA 36	Edge (Standard - Grey Tights)			
RAW – 1/27/2020	Edge (Chase - Black Tights)			
ROYAL RUMBLE 2020	King Corbin			
WCCW – 5/11/1985	Michael P.S. Hayes (Walmart)			
RAW – 8/26/2019	Sasha Banks			

WWE ELITE COLLECTION SERIES 84 (2021)		MIB	LOOSE	VALUE
205 LIVE – 10/24/2019	Angel Garza			
SMACKDOWN – 3/5/2019	Jeff Hardy (Standard - Blue Face Paint)			
ROYAL RUMBLE 2019	Jeff Hardy (Chase - Red Face Paint)			
RAW – 4/27/2020	Murphy			
NXT – 1/8/2020	Rhea Ripley			
CLASH 2019/SUMMERSLAM 2020	Roman Reigns			
SMACKDOWN – 1/3/2020	Sheamus			
RAW – 11/4/2019	Zelina Vega (Target)			

WWE ELITE COLLECTION SERIES 85 (2021)		MIB	LOOSE	VALUE
WRESTLEMANIA 36	Aleister Black (Standard - All Black Gear)			
WRESTLEMANIA 35	Aleister Black (Chase - White On Knee Pad)			
WRESTLEMANIA 36	Becky Lynch			
RAW – 6/10/2019	Bray Wyatt			
SUMMERSLAM 1995	Kama (Walmart)			
NXT – 5/6/2020	Karrion Kross			
ROYAL RUMBLE 2020	Liv Morgan			
WRESTLEMANIA 36	The Undertaker			

WWE ELITE COLLECTION SERIES 86 - SUMMERSLAM (2021)		MIB	LOOSE	VALUE
SUMMERSLAM 2018	Carmella			
SUMMERSLAM 1991	Colonel Mustafa (Target)			
SUMMERSLAM 2020	Seth Rollins			
SS 1991/CLASH XII	Sid Justice			
SUMMERSLAM 2020	"The Fiend" Bray Wyatt			
SUMMERSLAM 2018	The Miz			
SUMMERSLAM 1998	Triple H (Standard - Purple Tights)			
RAW – 1/11/1999	Triple H (Chase - Red Tights)			

WWE ELITE COLLECTION SERIES 87 (2021)		MIB	LOOSE	VALUE
PAYBACK 2020	Apollo Crews (Standard - Blue)			
SUMMERSLAM 2020	Apollo Crews (Chase - White Trunks)			
WRESTLEMANIA 36	Asuka			
SUMMERSLAM 2020	Braun Strowman			
NXT TAKEOVER: IN YOUR HOUSE 2020	Candice Lerae			
SMACKDOWN – 8/28/2020	Otis			
NXT – 6/24/2020	Santos Escobar			
WRESTLEMANIA V	Warlord (Walmart)			

WWE ELITE COLLECTION SERIES 88 (2021)		MIB	LOOSE	VALUE
NXT – 5/1/2019	Kushida			
EXTREME RULES 2020	MVP			
PAYBACK 2020	Rey Mysterio			
NXT TAKEOVER PORTLAND	Riddle			
HELL IN A CELL 2020	Roman Reigns			
SURVIVOR SERIES 2001	Trish Stratus (Standard - Pink Hat)			
WRESTLEMANIA X8	Trish Stratus (Chase - White Hat)			
WCW SATURDAY NIGHT – 9/9/1995	Zodiac (Target)			

WWE ELITE COLLECTION SERIES 89 (2022)		MIB	LOOSE	VALUE
SURVIVOR SERIES 2020	Bobby Lashley			
NXT TAKEOVER 31	Damian Priest			
RAW – 9/7/2020	Dominik Mysterio			
SURVIVOR SERIES 2020	Drew McIntyre			
MONEY IN THE BANK 2020	Nia Jax (Standard - Red Suit)			
BACKLASH 2020	Nia Jax (Chase - Purple Suit)			
SUMMERSLAM 1991	Sgt. Slaughter			
SUPERSTARS – 7/20/1995	The Goon (Walmart)			

WWE ELITE COLLECTION SERIES 90 (2022)		MIB	LOOSE	VALUE
SUPERSTARS – 7/18/1992	Big Boss Man (Standard - Blue Shirt)			
WCW STARRCADE 1992	Big Boss Man (Chase - The Boss)			
NXT TAKEOVER XXX	Bronson Reed			
	Chief Jay Strongbow (Target - **CANCELED**)			
HELL IN A CELL 2020	Jey Uso			
RAW – 10/19/2020	Mustafa Ali			
WRESTLEMANIA 37	Randy Orton			
RAW – 11/30/2020	Reckoning			

WWE ELITE COLLECTION SERIES 91 (2022)		MIB	LOOSE	VALUE
NXT – 3/17/2021	Austin Theory			
ROYAL RUMBLE 2021	Bianca Bel Air			
SUMMERSLAM 2005	Hulk Hogan			
ROYAL RUMBLE 2021	Kevin Owens			
ECW GUILTY AS CHARGEd '01	Rob Van Dam (Standard - Tiger Stripes)			
	Rob Van Dam (Chase - Rising Sun - **CANCELED**)			
SMACKDOWN – 12/25/2020	Sami Zayn			

WWE ELITE COLLECTION SERIES 92 (2022)		MIB	LOOSE	VALUE
NXT STAND & DELIVER 2021	Adam Cole (Standard - Green Trunks)			
NXT TAKEOVER WAR GAMES '18	Adam Cole (Chase - Snow Camo Trunks)			
ROYAL RUMBLE 2021	Charlotte Flair			
FASTLANE 2021	"The Fiend" Bray Wyatt			
SMACKDOWN – 2/12/2021	Rey Mysterio			
CLASH OF CHAMPIONS XXXII	Ric Flair			
NXT - 12/9/2020	Scarlett			

WWE ELITE COLLECTION SERIES 93 (2022)		MIB	LOOSE	VALUE
WRESTLEMANIA 37	Cesaro			
TAKEOVER: STAND & DELIVER '21	Karrion Kross			
TAKEOVER: STAND & DELIVER '21	Raquel Gonzalez			
WCW FALL BRAWL 1993	Ricky Steamboat (Standard - White Tights)			
WCW SPRING STAMPEDE 1994	Ricky Steamboat (Chase - Yellow Tights)			
WRESTLEMANIA 37	Seth Rollins			
RAW – 10/19/2020	T-Barr			

WWE ELITE COLLECTION SERIES 94 (2022)		MIB	LOOSE	VALUE
SUMMERSLAM 1992	Bret "Hitman" Hart (Standard - Pink Tights)			
SUMMERSLAM 1991	Bret "Hitman" Hart (Chase - Black Tights)			
SUMMERSLAM 1992	British Bulldog (Walmart)			
WRESTLEMANIA 37	Edge			
RAW – 10/19/2020	Mace			
TAKEOVER: STAND & DELIVER	Nash Carter			
RAW – 8/21/2000	Stephanie McMahon-Helmsley			
TAKEOVER- STAND & DELIVER	Wes Lee			

WWE ELITE COLLECTION SERIES 95 (2022)		MIB	LOOSE	VALUE
RAW – 9/12/2021	Big E			
SUMMERSLAM 2021	Bobby Lashley			
SMACKDOWN – 1/30/2003	Eddie Guerrero (Standard - Green Tights)			
SMACKDOWN – 1/2/2003	Eddie Guerrero (Chase - Black Tights)			
MONEY IN THE BANK 2021	Jimmy Uso			
MONEY IN THE BANK 2021	John Cena			
TAKEOVER: VENGEANCE DAY	Shotzi Blackheart			

WWE ELITE COLLECTION SERIES 96 (2022)		MIB	LOOSE	VALUE
CROWN JEWEL 2021	Brock Lesnar			
RAW – 6/14/2021	Doudrop (Standard - Blue Gear)			
SUMMERSLAM 2021	Doudrop (Chase - Green Gear)			
WRESTLING CHALLENGE – 9/4/1988	Hulk Hogan			
NXT – 8/10/2021	Ilja Dragunov			
MONEY IN THE BANK 2021	Kofi Kingston			
MONEY IN THE BANK 2021	Shinsuke Nakamura			

WWE ELITE COLLECTION SERIES 97 (2023)		MIB	LOOSE	VALUE
SUMMERSLAM 2021	Alexa Bliss			
RAW – 12/29/1997	Chainsaw Charlie			
MONEY IN THE BANK 2021	Omos			
ROYAL RUMBLE 2022	Ronda Rousey			
RAW – 7/21/2021	Sheamus			
SMACKDOWN – 10/29/2021	Xavier Woods (Standard - White Tights)			
RAW – 10/20/2021	Xavier Woods (Chase – He-Man Tights)			

WWE ELITE COLLECTION SERIES 98 (2023)		MIB	LOOSE	VALUE
DAY 1 – 1/1/2022	Big E			
RAW – 8/5/1996 & 9/16/1996	Faarooq Asaad			
EXTREME RULES 2021	Finn Bálor			
NXT HALLOWEEN HAVOC 2021	Mandy Rose			
SUMMERSLAM 2021	Randy Orton			
SMACKDOWN – 8/27/2021	Rick Boogs (Standard - Overalls Singlet)			
ROYAL RUMBLE 2022	Rick Boogs (Chase - Red Singlet)			

WWE ELITE COLLECTION SERIES 99 (2023)		MIB	LOOSE	VALUE
ECW – 12/30/2008	Boogeyman (Standard – Red & Yellow Paint)			
ECW – 8/7/2007	Boogeyman (Chase – All Red Paint)			
SMACKDOWN – 12/10/2021	Brock Lesnar (Standard – Brown Overalls)			
SMACKDOWN – 12/17/2021	Brock Lesnar (Chase – Blue Overalls)			
SMACKDOWN 11/26/2021	Happy Corbin			
RAW – 12/6/2021	Queen Zelina			
CROWN JEWEL 2021	Matt Riddle			
RAW – 10/25/2021	Seth Rollins			

WWE ELITE COLLECTION SERIES 100 (2023)		MIB	LOOSE	VALUE
SUPERSTARS – 2/7/1987	Andre The Giant (Standard – Checkered Jacket)			
SUPERSTARS – 3/21/1987	Andre The Giant (Chase – Blue Jacket)			
EXTREME RULES 2021	Becky Lynch			
SMACKDOWN – 4/15/2005	John Cena			
BASH AT THE BEACH 1998	Rey Mysterio			
ROYAL RUMBLE 2001	The Rock			
HALLOWEEN HAVOC 1991	"Stunning" Steve Austin			

WWE ELITE COLLECTION SERIES 101 (2023)		MIB	LOOSE	VALUE
RAW – 4/18/2022	Cody Rhodes			
WRESTLEMANIA 38	Johnny Knoxville			
RAW 3/21/2022 & WM 38	Kevin Owens			
SMACKDOWN – 5/1/2003	Mr. America (Standard – Star Mask)			
SMACKDOWN – 6/26/2003	Mr. America (Chase – Stars & Stripes Mask)			
SMACKDOWN – 3/3/2022	Ricochet			
SMACKDOWN – 12/10/2021	Sonya Deville			

WWE ELITE COLLECTION SERIES 102 (2023)		MIB	LOOSE	VALUE
HELL IN A CELL 2022	Austin Theory (Standard - America Gear)			
WRESTLEMANIA 38	Austin Theory (Chase - Black Gear)			
RAW – 6/26/2000	Commissioner Foley			
HELL IN A CELL 2022	Edge			
SMACKDOWN – 4/8/2022	Gunther			
HELL IN A CELL 2022	Rhea Ripley			
WRESTLEMANIA 38	Sami Zayn			

WWE ELITE COLLECTION SERIES 103 (2023)		MIB	LOOSE	VALUE
RAW – 7/4/2022	Angelo Dawkins			
SUMMERSLAM 2022	Bobby Lashley			
MONEY IN THE BANK 2022	Liv Morgan			
SMACKDOWN – 7/1/2022	Montez Ford			
WRESTLEMANIA 38	Roman Reigns			
WRESTLEMANIA 32	Stardust (Standard - Polka Dots)			
RAW – 7/13/2015	Stardust (Chase - Blue Star Suit)			

WWE ELITE COLLECTION SERIES 104 (2023)		MIB	LOOSE	VALUE
RAW – 8/22/2022	AJ Styles			
NXT SPRING BREAKIN' 2022	Bron Breakker (Standard - Pink Singlet)			
NXT HALLOWEEN HAVOC 2022	Bron Breakker (Chase - Yellow Singlet)			
RAW – 9/12/2022	Dakota Kai			
CLASH AT THE CASTLE	Drew McIntyre			
NITRO – 7/5/1999	Rick Steiner			
SMACKDOWN – 9/9/2022	Solo Sikoa			

WWE ELITE COLLECTION SERIES 105 (2024)		MIB	LOOSE	VALUE
SMACKDOWN – 10/14/2022	Braun Strowman			
NXT 2.0 – 3/1/2022	Carmelo Hayes (Standard – Purple Shorts)			
NXT 2.0: VENGEANCE DAY 2022	Carmelo Hayes (Chase – Pink Shorts)			
RAW – 9/12/2022	Dominik Mysterio			
SMACKDWON – 10/14/2022	Iyo Sky			
RAW – 9/12/2022	Johnny Gargano			
BAD BLOOD 2003	Scott Steiner			

WWE ELITE COLLECTION SERIES 106 (2024)		MIB	LOOSE	VALUE
RAW – 3/27/2023	Chad Gable			
SURVIVOR SERIES 2022	Jey Uso			
SURVIVOR SERIES 2022	Jimmy Uso			
SUMMERSLAM 1994	Paul Bearer (Standard - Black Suit)			
RAW – 6/26/1998	Paul Bearer (Chase - Blue Suit)			
NXT – 12/13/2022	Roxanne Perez			
RAW – 3/6/2023	Sami Zayn			

WWE ELITE COLLECTION SERIES 107 (2024)		MIB	LOOSE	VALUE
NXT – 5/16/2023	Cora Jade			
SURVIVOR SERIES 2022	Finn Bálor			
NXT DEADLINE 2022	Grayson Waller (Standard - White Gear)			
NXT STAND & DELIVER 2023	Grayson Waller (Chase - Black Gear)			
RAW – 4/10/2023	Otis			
SURVIVOR SERIES 2022	Solo Sikoa			
RAW XXX	The Undertaker			

WWE ELITE COLLECTION SERIES 108 (2024)		MIB	LOOSE	VALUE
SUMMERSLAM 2022	Brock Lesnar			
BACKLASH 2023	Bronson Reed			
RAW – 3/27/2023	Chelsea Green (Standard - Blue Gear)			
ROYAL RUMBLE 2023	Chelsea Green (Chase - Orange Gear)			
TRIBUTE TO THE TROOPS 2022	LA Knight			
WRESTLEMANIA 39	Omos			
IWA 1995 & BURIED ALIVE 1996	Terry "Bam Bam" Gordy/The Executioner			

WWE ELITE COLLECTION SERIES 109 (2024)		MIB	LOOSE	VALUE
SMACKDOWN – 6/9/2023	Bayley			
RAW – 7/24/2023	Cody Rhodes			
ELIMINATION CHAMBER 2023	Damien Priest			
RAW – 1/9/2023	Dominik Mysterio			
MONEY IN THE BANK 2023	Seth Freakin' Rollins			
RAW – 8/7/2023	Shinsuke Nakamura (Standard – Black/White)			
PRO WRESTLING NOAH 1/1/24	Shinsuke Nakamura (Chase – Black/Red)			

WWE ELITE COLLECTION SERIES 110 (2024)		MIB	LOOSE	VALUE
	Austin Theory			
	Bruno Sammartino			
	Butch (Standard – White Singlet)			
	Butch (Chase – Green Singlet)			
	Elton Prince			
	Kit Wilson			
	Rhea Ripley			
	Roman Reigns			

WWE ELITE COLLECTION SERIES 111 (2024)	MIB	LOOSE	VALUE
Cody Rhodes			
Finn Bálor			
Ricochet			
Sandman (Standard – Black & White)			
Sandman (Chase – Red, White & Blue)			
Tony D'Angelo			
Trish Stratus			

WWE ELITE COLLECTION SERIES 112 (2024)	MIB	LOOSE	VALUE
Becky Lynch (Standard – Green & Yellow)			
Becky Lynch (Chase – Black & White)			
Bray Wyatt			
Channing "Stacks" Lorenzo			
JD McDonough			
Seth Freakin' Rollins			
Xavier Woods			

WWE ELITE COLLECTION SERIES 113 (2024)	MIB	LOOSE	VALUE
Carlito (Standard – White Gear)			
Carlito (Chase – Purple Gear)			
CM Punk			
Dragon Lee			
Kofi Kingston			
Tiffany Stratton			
Trick Williams			

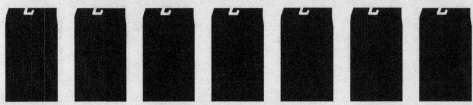

WWE ELITE COLLECTION SERIES 114 (2024)	MIB	LOOSE	VALUE
Bron Breakker			
Ilja Dragunov			
Jey Uso			
Jimmy Uso			
Tommaso Ciampa			
Zoey Stark			

WWE ELITE COLLECTION SERIES 115 (2025)	MIB	LOOSE	VALUE
Kairi Sane			
R-Truth			
The Rock			

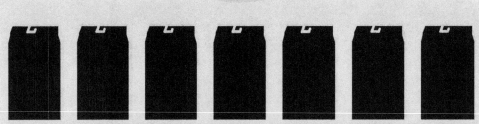

WWE ELITE COLLECTION SERIES 116 (2025)	MIB	LOOSE	VALUE

WWE ELITE COLLECTION SERIES 117 (2025)		MIB	LOOSE	VALUE

WWE ELITE COLLECTION SERIES 118 (2025)		MIB	LOOSE	VALUE

WWE ELITE COLLECTION SERIES 119 (2025)		MIB	LOOSE	VALUE

2010 WRESTLEMANIA 26 (TOYS 'R' US)	MIB	LOOSE	VALUE
Jack Swagger			
Rey Mysterio			
Triple H			
The Undertaker			

2011 WRESTLEMANIA 27 (TOYS 'R' US)	MIB	LOOSE	VALUE
Kofi Kingston			
Stone Cold Steve Austin			
The Miz			
The Rock			
The Undertaker			

2012 BEST OF PAY-PER-VIEW (TOYS 'R' US)		MIB	LOOSE	VALUE
SUMMERSLAM 2010	Bret "Hit Man" Hart			
SUMMERSLAM 2010	Daniel Bryan			
WRESTLEMANIA 27	John Cena			
WRESTLEMANIA 27	Triple H			
BUILD-A-FIGURE	Michael Cole			

2012 WRESTLEMANIA 28 (TOYS 'R' US)		MIB	LOOSE	VALUE
WRESTLEMANIA 28	Big Show			
WRESTLEMANIA 28	CM Punk			
WRESTLEMANIA 28	Shawn Michaels			
WRESTLEMANIA 28	The Miz			
BUILD-A-FIGURE	Ricardo Rodriguez			

2013 BEST OF PAY-PER-VIEW (TOYS 'R' US)		MIB	LOOSE	VALUE
NO WAY OUT	Christian			
EXTREME RULES	John Cena			
MONEY IN THE BANK	Sheamus			
NO WAY OUT	Sin Cara			
BUILD-A-FIGURE	John Laurinaitis			

2013 WRESTLEMANIA 29 (TOYS 'R' US)		MIB	LOOSE	VALUE
WRESTLEMANIA 29	Brock Lesnar			
WRESTLEMANIA 29	CM Punk			
WRESTLEMANIA 29	Daniel Bryan			
WRESTLEMANIA 29	John Cena			
BUILD-A-FIGURE	Paul Heyman			

2014 WRESTLEMANIA 30		MIB	LOOSE	VALUE
WRESTLEMANIA 10	Bret "Hit Man" Hart			
WRESTLEMANIA 14	Shawn Michaels			

2014 BEST OF PAY-PER-VIEW (TOYS 'R' US)		MIB	LOOSE	VALUE
PAYBACK	Alberto Del Rio			
MONEY IN THE BANK	CM Punk			
PAYBACK	Curtis Axel			
MONEY IN THE BANK	Randy Orton			
BUILD-A-FIGURE	Jim Ross			

2014 WRESTLEMANIA XXX (TOYS 'R' US)		MIB	LOOSE	VALUE
WRESTLEMANIA 30	Bray Wyatt			
WRESTLEMANIA 30	Daniel Bryan			
WRESTLEMANIA 30	John Cena			
WRESTLEMANIA 30	The Undertaker			
BUILD-A-FIGURE	Corporate Kane			

2015 WRESTLEMANIA 31		MIB	LOOSE	VALUE
WRESTLEMANIA 16	Kane			
WRESTLEMANIA 7	The Undertaker			

2016 WRESTLEMANIA 32		MIB	LOOSE	VALUE
WRESTLEMANIA 20	Brock Lesnar			
WRESTLEMANIA 31	The Undertaker			

2017 WRESTLEMANIA 33		MIB	LOOSE	VALUE
WRESTLEMANIA 12	Shawn Michaels			
WRESTLEMANIA 32	Triple H			

2017 SUMMERSLAM		MIB	LOOSE	VALUE
SUMMERSLAM 2016	Finn Balor			
SUMMERSLAM 1999	Mankind			

2018 WRESTLEMANIA 34		MIB	LOOSE	VALUE
WRESTLEMANIA 9	Brutus "The Barber" Beefcake			
WRESTLEMANIA 23	John Cena			
WRESTLEMANIA 33	Kevin Owens			
WRESTLEMANIA 33	Randy Orton			

2018 SUMMERSLAM (WALMART)		MIB	LOOSE	VALUE
SUMMERSLAM 2017	Dean Ambrose			
SUMMERSLAM 1998	Edge			
SUMMERSLAM 2004	Matt Hardy			
SUMMERSLAM 2017	Seth Rollins			

2018 SURVIVOR SERIES (WALMART)		MIB	LOOSE	VALUE
SUMMERSLAM 2018	AJ Styles			
SUMMERSLAM 2018	Alexa Bliss			
SUMMERSLAM 2018	Bobby Roode			

2019 WRESTLEMANIA 35		MIB	LOOSE	VALUE
WRESTLEMANIA 32	Sasha Banks			
WRESTLEMANIA 18	Scott Hall			
WRESTLEMANIA 19	Triple H			
WRESTLEMANIA 33	The Undertaker			

2019 SURVIVOR SERIES (WALMART)		MIB	LOOSE	VALUE
SURVIVOR SERIES 2017	Alicia Fox			
SURVIVOR SERIES 1987	Don Muraco			
SURVIVOR SERIES 2006	Jeff Hardy			
SURVIVOR SERIES 2017	Shinsuke Nakamura			

2020 ROYAL RUMBLE (TARGET)		MIB	LOOSE	VALUE
ROYAL RUMBLE 2007	Bobby Lashley			
ROYAL RUMBLE 2006	Lita			
ROYAL RUMBLE 1991	"Macho King" Randy Savage			
ROYAL RUMBLE 2013	The Rock			

2020 WRESTLEMANIA 36		MIB	LOOSE	VALUE
WRESTLEMANIA 19	Booker T			
WRESTLEMANIA 35	Kofi Kingston			
WRESTLEMANIA 22	Mick Foley			
WRESTLEMANIA 34	"Woken" Matt Hardy			
BUILD-A-FIGURE	"Dangerous" Danny Davis			

2020 SURVIVOR SERIES		MIB	LOOSE	VALUE
SURVIVOR SERIES 2018	Drew McIntyre			
SURVIVOR SERIES 2007	John Morrison			
SURVIVOR SERIES 2001	Kane			
SURVIVOR SERIES 2018	Samoa Joe			

2021 ROYAL RUMBLE (TARGET)		MIB	LOOSE	VALUE
ROYAL RUMBLE 2002	Stone Cold Steve Austin			
GREATEST RUMBLE	Titus O'Neil			
ROYAL RUMBLE 1990	Ultimate Warrior			
ROYAL RUMBLE 2008	Umaga			

2021 WRESTLEMANIA 37		MIB	LOOSE	VALUE
WRESTLEMANIA 17	Chyna			
WRESTLEMANIA 22	Edge			
WRESTLEMANIA 36	Goldberg			
WRESTLEMANIA 9	Shawn Michaels			
BUILD-A-FIGURE	Paul Ellering			

2021 SURVIVOR SERIES		MIB	LOOSE	VALUE
SURVIVOR SERIES 2019	Bayley			
SURVIVOR SERIES 1996	Bret "Hit Man" Hart			
SURVIVOR SERIES 1989	Hulk Hogan			
SURVIVOR SERIES 2019	Keith Lee			

2022 ROYAL RUMBLE (TARGET)		MIB	LOOSE	VALUE
ROYAL RUMBLE 2020	Big E			
ROYAL RUMBLE 2020	Dakota Kai			
ROYAL RUMBLE 1990	Earthquake			
ROYAL RUMBLE 1993	Yokozuna			
BUILD-A-FIGURE	Jimmy Hart			

2022 WRESTLEMANIA 38		MIB	LOOSE	VALUE
WRESTLEMANIA 36	AJ Styles			
WRESTLEMANIA 26	Bret "Hit Man" Hart			
WRESTLEMANIA 26	Shawn Michaels			
WRESTLEMANIA 19	Stone Cold Steve Austin			
BUILD-A-FIGURE	Vince McMahon			

2022 SUMMERSLAM		MIB	LOOSE	VALUE
SUMMERSLAM 2005	Randy Orton			
SUMMERSLAM 2005	Rey Mysterio			
SUMMERSLAM 1992	Sensational Sherri			
SUMMERSLAM 2005	Shawn Michaels			
BUILD-A-FIGURE	Dominik Mysterio			

    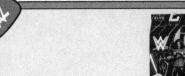

2022 SURVIVOR SERIES		MIB	LOOSE	VALUE
SURVIVOR SERIES 2020	AJ Styles			
SURVIVOR SERIES 2021	Becky Lynch			
SURVIVOR SERIES 2009	Drew McIntyre			
SURVIVOR SERIES 1990	Ultimate Warrior			
BUILD-A-FIGURE	Rick Rude			

2023 ROYAL RUMBLE (TARGET)		MIB	LOOSE	VALUE
ROYAL RUMBLE 2018	Brie Bella			
ROYAL RUMBLE 2021	Damian Priest			
ROYAL RUMBLE 2006	Rey Mysterio			
ROYAL RUMBLE 1996	Vader			
BUILD-A-FIGURE	Dok Hendrix			

2023 WRESTLEMANIA 39		MIB	LOOSE	VALUE
WRESTLEMANIA 6	Dusty Rhodes			
WRESTLEMANIA 18	"Hollywood" Hulk Hogan			
WRESTLEMANIA 6	"Macho King" Randy Savage			
WRESTLEMANIA 18	The Rock			
BUILD-A-FIGURE	"Mean" Gene Okerlund			

2023 SUMMERSLAM		MIB	LOOSE	VALUE
SUMMERSLAM 2019	Dolph Ziggler			
SUMMERSLAM 1991	Hulk Hogan			
SUMMERSLAM 2021	Jey Uso			
SUMMERSLAM 1989	Zeus			
BUILD-A-FIGURE	Mr. Perfect			

2023 SURVIVOR SERIES		MIB	LOOSE	VALUE
SURVIVOR SERIES 2021	Charlotte Flair			
SURVIVOR SERIES 1996	Jerry "The King" Lawler			
SURVIVOR SERIES 2021	Kevin Owens			
SURVIVOR SERIES 2002	Shawn Michaels			
BUILD-A-FIGURE	British Bulldog			

2024 ROYAL RUMBLE		MIB	LOOSE	VALUE
ROYAL RUMBLE 2005	Batista			
ROYAL RUMBLE 2022	Beth Phoenix			
ROYAL RUMBLE 2022	Brock Lesnar			
ROYAL RUMBLE 2022	Ridge Holland			
BUILD-A-FIGURE	Virgil			

2024 WRESTLEMANIA XL		MIB	LOOSE	VALUE
WRESTLEMANIA XXVII	John Cena			
WRESTLEMANIA 38	Pat McAfee			
SURVIVOR SERIES 2011	The Rock			
WRESTLEMANIA XXVII	Trish Stratus			
BUILD-A-FIGURE	Nicholas			

2024 SUMMERSLAM		MIB	LOOSE	VALUE
SUMMERSLAM 2004	Kane			
SUMMERSLAM 1993	Lex Luger			
SUMMERSLAM 2015	The Undertaker			
SUMMERSLAM 1998	X-Pac			
BUILD-A-FIGURE	John Cone			

2024 SURVIVOR SERIES		MIB	LOOSE	VALUE
SURVIVOR SERIES 1993	Bushwhacker Butch			
SURVIVOR SERIES 1993	Bushwhacker Luke			
SURVIVOR SERIES 2022	Kevin Owens			
SURVIVOR SERIES 2022	Sami Zayn			
BUILD-A-FIGURE	Adam Pearce			

2025 ROYAL RUMBLE		MIB	LOOSE	VALUE
ROYAL RUMBLE				
ROYAL RUMBLE				
ROYAL RUMBLE				
ROYAL RUMBLE				
BUILD-A-FIGURE				

2025 WRESTLEMANIA 41		MIB	LOOSE	VALUE
WRESTLEMANIA				
WRESTLEMANIA				
WRESTLEMANIA				
WRESTLEMANIA				
BUILD-A-FIGURE				

2025 SUMMERSLAM		MIB	LOOSE	VALUE
SUMMERSLAM				
SUMMERSLAM				
SUMMERSLAM				
SUMMERSLAM				
BUILD-A-FIGURE				

BEST OF 2010		MIB	LOOSE	VALUE
ELITE SERIES 3	John Cena			
ELITE SERIES 4	Kane			
ELITE SERIES 2	Randy Orton			
ELITE SERIES 1	Rey Mysterio			
ELITE SERIES 2	Triple H			
ELITE SERIES 1	The Undertaker			

BEST OF 2011		MIB	LOOSE	VALUE
ELITE SERIES 11	John Cena			
ELITE SERIES 10	John Morrison			
ELITE SERIES 9	Randy Orton			
ELITE SERIES 11	Rey Mysterio			
ELITE SERIES 8	Sheamus			

TOP PICKS 2018	MIB	LOOSE	VALUE
AJ Styles			
Braun Strowman			
Finn Balor			
Seth Rollins			

TOP PICKS 2019	MIB	LOOSE	VALUE
AJ Styles			
Braun Strowman			
Finn Balor			
Seth Rollins			

TOP PICKS 2020	MIB	LOOSE	VALUE
Braun Strowman			
Ricochet			
Roman Reigns			
Seth Rollins			

	TOP PICKS 2021	MIB	LOOSE	VALUE
WAVE 1	Drew McIntyre			
	Kofi Kingston			
	Roman Reigns			
	"The Fiend" Bray Wyatt			
WAVE 2	Drew McIntyre			
	John Cena			
	Rey Mysterio			
	Roman Reigns			

	TOP PICKS 2022	MIB	LOOSE	VALUE
WAVE 1	Goldberg			
	Jeff Hardy			
	Roman Reigns			
WAVE 2	Rey Mysterio			
	The Rock			
	The Undertaker			
WAVE 3	Drew McIntyre			
	John Cena			
	Randy Orton			
	Rey Mysterio			

	TOP PICKS 2023	MIB	LOOSE	VALUE
WAVE 1	Rey Mysterio			
	Roman Reigns			
	Seth Rollins			
WAVE 2	Bobby Lashley			
	John Cena			
	Ronda Rousey			
WAVE 3	Jimmy Uso			
	Roman Reigns			
	The Rock			
WAVE 4	Cody Rhodes			
	Rey Mysterio			
	Riddle			

	TOP PICKS 2024	MIB	LOOSE	VALUE
WAVE 1	John Cena			
	Roman Reigns			
	Seth Rollins			
WAVE 2	Cody Rhodes			
	Logan Paul			
	Sheamus			
WAVE 3	Gunther			
	Rey Mysterio			
	Roman Reigns			
WAVE 4	Cody Rhodes			
	The Rock			
	Solo Sikoa			

	TOP PICKS 2025	MIB	LOOSE	VALUE
WAVE 1	John Cena			
	Roman Reigns			
	Seth Rollins			
WAVE 2	Cody Rhodes			
	Logan Paul			
	Sheamus			
WAVE 3	Gunther			
	Rey Mysterio			
	Roman Reigns			
WAVE 4	Cody Rhodes			
	The Rock			
	Solo Sikoa			

	LOST LEGENDS	MIB	LOOSE	VALUE
ELITE SERIES 20	Chris Jericho			
LEGENDS 2	Kamala			
	Magnum T.A.			
ELITE SERIES 19	Shawn Michaels			
LEGENDS 6	Ultimate Warrior			
ELITE SERIES 23	The Undertaker			

	GREATEST HITS SERIES 1	MIB	LOOSE	VALUE
LEGENDS 5	Bam Bam Bigelow			
FLASHBACK 3	Jake "The Snake" Roberts			
ELITE 24	Rey Mysterio			
HALL OF CHAMPIONS 1	Rikishi			
BEST OF ATTITUDE ERA	The Rock			
ELITE 8	The Undertaker			

GREATEST HITS SERIES 2		MIB	LOOSE	VALUE
ELITE 33	Batista			
LEGENDS 10	Diamond Dallas Page			
FLASHBACK 3	King Harley Race			
ELITE WM 31	Seth Rollins			
ELITE WM XXX	Shawn Michaels			
HALL OF CHAMPIONS 1	The Undertaker			

GREATEST HITS SERIES 3		MIB	LOOSE	VALUE
LEGENDS 19	Brutus "The Barber" Beefcake			
THEN, NOW, FOREVER 2	Earthquake			
ELITE 10	R-Truth			
HOLLYWOOD SERIES 1	"Rowdy" Roddy Piper as John Nada			
ELITE 33	Seth Rollins			
HOLLYWOOD SERIES 2	The Rock as The Scorpion King			
THEN, NOW, FOREVER 2	Typhoon			

GREATEST HITS SERIES 4		MIB	LOOSE	VALUE
	AJ Styles			
	Hulk Hogan			
	Rey Mysterio			
	Randy Orton			

GREATEST HITS SERIES 5		MIB	LOOSE	VALUE

FROM THE VAULT SERIES 1 (RINGSIDE COLLECTIBLES)		MIB	LOOSE	VALUE
ELITE 45	Bubba Ray Dudley			
ELITE 45	D-Von Dudley			
DEFINING MOMENTS	John Cena			
RINGSIDE EXCLUSIVE	Kane			
ELITE 7	Shawn Michaels			
ELITE 7	Triple H			
HALL OF CHAMPIONS 3	Ultimate Warrior			
DEFINING MOMENTS	The Undertaker			

FROM THE VAULT SERIES 2 (RINGSIDE COLLECTIBLES)		MIB	LOOSE	VALUE
HALL OF CHAMPIONS 3	Billy Gunn			
ELITE 16	Diesel			
LEGENDS 6	Eddie Guerrero			
TRIBAL CHIEF VS. BEAST	Paul Heyman			
ELITE 27	Rikishi			
HALL OF CHAMPIONS 3	Road Dogg			
RINGSIDE EXCLUSIVE	Shawn Michaels			
RINGSIDE EXCLUSIVE	The Undertaker (as Kane)			

DEFINING MOMENTS (ORIGINAL)		MIB	LOOSE	VALUE
WAVE 1	"Macho Man" Randy Savage			
	Shawn Michaels			
WAVE 2	The Rock			
	Ultimate Warrior			
WAVE 3	Ricky "The Dragon" Steamboat			
	Triple H			
WAVE 4	Stone Cold Steve Austin			
	The Undertaker			
WAVE 5	Bret "Hit Man" Hart			
	John Cena			

	DEFINING MOMENTS (REVIVAL)	MIB	LOOSE	VALUE
2014	Ric Flair			
2015	Hulk Hogan			
	Razor Ramon			
	Sting			
	The Undertaker			
2016	Stone Cold Steve Austin			
	Sting			
	Ultimate Warrior			
	John Cena			
2017	Ric Flair (Closed Robe)			
	Ric Flair (Open Robe)			
	Shinsuke Nakamura			
	"Macho Man" Randy Savage			
	Chris Jericho			

DEFINING MOMENTS ULTIMATE WARRIOR EXCLUSIVES			MIB	LOOSE	VALUE
ULTIMATE WARRIOR.COM	1 OF 15	Ultimate Warrior (One Warrior Nation)			
	1 OF 15	Ultimate Warrior (Granite)			
	1 OF 15	Ultimate Warrior (2K14 Commercia)			

DEFINING MOMENTS RINGSIDE EXCLUSIVE 4-PACK SERIES 1		MIB	LOOSE	VALUE
	Bret "Hit Man" Hart			
	Cody Rhodes			
	Mankind			
	Shawn Michaels			

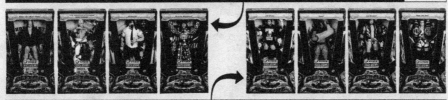

DEFINING MOMENTS RINGSIDE EXCLUSIVE 4-PACK SERIES 2		MIB	LOOSE	VALUE
	CM Punk			
	Kane			
	LA Knight			
	Rob Van Dam			

HALL OF FAME SERIES 1 (TARGET)		MIB	LOOSE	VALUE
CLASS OF 2004	Sgt. Slaughter			
CLASS OF 2009	Stone Cold Steve Austin			
CLASS OF 2013	Trish Stratus			
CLASS OF 2014	Ultimate Warrior			

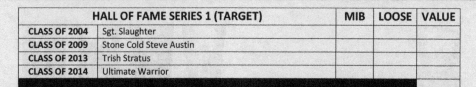

HALL OF FAME SERIES 2 (TARGET)		MIB	LOOSE	VALUE
CLASS OF 2006	Eddie Guerrero			
CLASS OF 2005	Hulk Hogan			
CLASS OF 2004	Tito Santana			
CLASS OF 2012	Yokozuna			

HALL OF FAME SERIES 3 (TARGET)		MIB	LOOSE	VALUE
CLASS OF 2013	Cactus Jack (Stop Release)			
CLASS OF 2015	"Macho King" Randy Savage			
CLASS OF 2010	"Million Dollar Man" Ted Dibiase			
CLASS OF 2005	"The Mouth Of The South" Jimmy Hart			

HALL OF FAME SERIES 4 (TARGET)		MIB	LOOSE	VALUE
CLASS OF 2012	Edge			
CLASS OF 2007	Jerry "The King" Lawler			
CLASS OF 2013	King Booker			
CLASS OF 2016	Sting			

HALL OF FAME SERIES 5 (TARGET)		MIB	LOOSE	VALUE
CLASS OF 2015	Diesel			
CLASS OF 1995	George "The Animal" Steele			
CLASS OF 2014	Jake "The Snake" Roberts			
CLASS OF 2005	"Rowdy" Roddy Piper			

HALL OF FAME 2-PACKS (TARGET)		MIB	LOOSE	VALUE
CLASS OF 2016	Papa Shango			
CLASS OF 2014	Ultimate Warrior			
CLASS OF 2007	Afa			
CLASS OF 2007	Sika			

HALL OF FAME - FOUR HORSEMEN (TARGET)		MIB	LOOSE	VALUE
CLASS OF 2012	Ric Flair			
CLASS OF 2012	Arn Anderson			
CLASS OF 2012	Barry Windham			
CLASS OF 2012	Tully Blanchard			

HALL OF FAME - HEENAN FAMILY (TARGET)		MIB	LOOSE	VALUE
CLASS OF 1993	Andre The Giant			
CLASS OF 2004	Bobby Heenan			
CLASS OF 2007	Mr. Perfect			
CLASS OF 2004	Big John Studd			

HALL OF FAME – NITRO NOTABLES (TARGET)		MIB	LOOSE	VALUE
CLASS OF 2006	Eddie Guerrero			
CLASS OF 2015	Kevin Nash			
CLASS OF 2014	Scott Hall			
CLASS OF 2015	Larry Zybysko			

NXT TAKEOVER SERIES 1 (TARGET)	MIB	LOOSE	VALUE
Austin Aries			
Bayley			
No Way Jose			
Seth Rollins			

NXT TAKEOVER SERIES 2 (TARGET)	MIB	LOOSE	VALUE
Asuka			
Dash Wilder			
Scott Dawson			
Shinsuke Nakamura			

NXT TAKEOVER SERIES 3 (TARGET)	MIB	LOOSE	VALUE
Alexander Rusev			
Bobby Roode			
Ember Moon			
Roman Reigns			

NXT TAKEOVER SERIES 4 (TARGET)	MIB	LOOSE	VALUE
Aleister Black			
Drew McIntyre			
Killian Dain			
Ruby Riott			

NXT TAKEOVER SERIES 5	MIB	LOOSE	VALUE
Andrade "Cien" Almas (Ringside Collectibles)			
Hideo Itami		CANCELLED	
Roderick Strong		CANCELLED	
Titus O'Neil		CANCELLED	

THEN, NOW, FOREVER SERIES 1 (WALMART)	MIB	LOOSE	VALUE
Bam Bam Bigelow			
Rusev			
The Rock			
Tyler Breeze			

THEN, NOW, FOREVER SERIES 2 (WALMART)	MIB	LOOSE	VALUE
Earthquake			
"Macho Man" Randy Savage			
Sami Zayn			
Typhoon			

THEN, NOW, FOREVER SERIES 3 (WALMART)	MIB	LOOSE	VALUE
Chad Gable			
Jason Jordan			
Miss Elizabeth			
Seth Rollins			

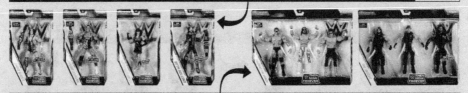

THEN, NOW, FOREVER 3-PACKS (WALMART)		MIB	LOOSE	VALUE
BASH AT THE BEACH	Lex Luger			
	"Macho Man" Randy Savage			
	Sting			
THE SHIELD	Seth Rollins			
	Dean Ambrose			
	Roman Reigns			

NETWORK SPOTLIGHT SERIES 1 (TOYS 'R' US)	MIB	LOOSE	VALUE
AJ Styles			
Bayley			
Big Boss Man			
Dean Ambrose			
Finn Balor			
Hunter Hearst Helmsley			
Mr. McMahon			
Roman Reigns			
Shawn Michaels			
The Ringmaster			
The Undertaker			
TJ Perkins			

NETWORK SPOTLIGHT SERIES 2 (TARGET)	MIB	LOOSE	VALUE
Asuka			
Diesel			
Jinder Mahal			
Rey Mysterio			

NETWORK SPOTLIGHT SERIES 3 (TARGET)	MIB	LOOSE	VALUE
Kurt Angle			
Ricochet			
Wendi Richter			
"Woken" Matt Hardy			

WOMEN'S DIVISION (WALGREENS)	MIB	LOOSE	VALUE
Sasha Banks			
Becky Lynch			
Maryse			
Alexa Bliss			
Paige		CANCELLED	

FLASHBACK SERIES 1 (WALMART)	MIB	LOOSE	VALUE
Mean Gene Okerlund			
Syxx			
Ultimate Warrior			
Yokozuna			

FLASHBACK SERIES 2 (WALMART)	MIB	LOOSE	VALUE
Alundra Blayze			
Doink The Clown			
Razor Ramon			
Shawn Michaels			

	FLASHBACK SERIES 3 (WALMART)	MIB	LOOSE	VALUE
	Jake "The Snake" Roberts			
	King Harley Race			
	Ricky "The Dragon" Steamboat			
	Stone Cold Steve Austin			
BUILD-A-FIGURE	Commissioner Shawn Michaels			

	HALL OF CHAMPIONS SERIES 1 (TARGET)	MIB	LOOSE	VALUE
2005	Batista			
1997	Eddie Guerrero			
2000	Rikishi			
1999	The Undertaker			

	HALL OF CHAMPIONS SERIES 2 (TARGET)	MIB	LOOSE	VALUE
2016	Johnny Gargano			
1998	Kane			
1992	Ron Simmons			
2016	Tommaso Ciampa			

HALL OF CHAMPIONS SERIES 3 (TARGET)		MIB	LOOSE	VALUE
1998	Billy Gunn			
1991	Paul Bearer			
1998	Road Dogg			
1990	Ultimate Warrior			

BEST OF ATTITUDE ERA (AMAZON)	MIB	LOOSE	VALUE
Chris Jericho			
Stone Cold Steve Austin			
The Rock			
Triple H			

RETROFEST (GAMESTOP)		MIB	LOOSE	VALUE
SERIES 1	"Macho Man" Randy Savage			
	Shawn Michaels			
SERIES 2	"Hacksaw" Jim Duggan			
	Honky Tonk Man			
	Ric Flair			

RETROFEST SERIES 3 (TARGET.COM)	MIB	LOOSE	VALUE
Iron Sheik			
Mr. Perfect			

FAN CENTRAL SERIES 1 (TOYS 'R' US)	MIB	LOOSE	VALUE
Big Show			
Bobby "The Brain" Heenan			
Mark Henry			
Triple H			

FAN CENTRAL SERIES 2 (WALMART)	MIB	LOOSE	VALUE
Akira Tozawa			
Carmella			
Daniel Bryan			
Mojo Rawley			

ENTRANCE GREATS		MIB	LOOSE	VALUE
SERIES 1	Jeff Hardy			
	Kurt Angle			
SERIES 2	Bobby Roode			
	Finn Balor			
SERIES 3	Elias			
	Goldberg			

GHOSTBUSTERS (WALMART)	MIB	LOOSE	VALUE
John Cena			
Shawn Michaels			
Stone Cold Steve Austin			
The Rock			
The Undertaker			

DECADE OF DOMINATION SERIES 1 (WALMART)	MIB	LOOSE	VALUE
John Cena			
Mark Henry			
Natalya			
Randy Orton			
The Undertaker			

DECADE OF DOMINATION SERIES 2 (WALMART)	MIB	LOOSE	VALUE
Beth Phoenix			
Big Show			
Kane (w/ Clean Shaven Alternate Head)			
Kane (w/ Goatee on Alternate Head)			
Kofi Kingston			
Triple H			

FAN TAKEOVER SERIES 1 (AMAZON)	MIB	LOOSE	VALUE
Adam Cole			
Ricky "The Dragon" Steamboat			
Seth Rollins			
Shayna Baszler			

FAN TAKEOVER SERIES 2 (AMAZON)	MIB	LOOSE	VALUE
Christian			
Johnny Gargano			
Randy Orton			
X-Pac			

HOLLYWOOD SERIES 1 (WALMART)	MIB	LOOSE	VALUE
John Cena as Jakob Toretto			
"Rowdy" Roddy Piper as John Nada			
The Rock as Luke Hobbs			

HOLLYWOOD SERIES 2 (WALMART)	MIB	LOOSE	VALUE
Andre The Giant as Bigfoot			
Roman Reigns as Matteo Hobbs			
The Rock as The Scorpion King			

RUTHLESS AGGRESSION SERIES 1 (WALMART)		MIB	LOOSE	VALUE
RA 2	Batista			
RA 1	Brock Lesnar			
RA 29	Shawn Michaels			

RUTHLESS AGGRESSION SERIES 2 (WALMART)		MIB	LOOSE	VALUE
RA 9	Booker T			
RA 1	Rey Mysterio			
RA 21	Rob Van Dam			

RUTHLESS AGGRESSION SERIES 3 (WALMART)		MIB	LOOSE	VALUE
RA 38	John Cena			
RA 5	Kevin Nash			
RA 13	Shelton Benjamin			

RUTHLESS AGGRESSION SERIES 4 (WALMART)		MIB	LOOSE	VALUE
RA 1/PPV 12	Eric Bischoff			
RA 9	Stone Cold Steve Austin			
RA 4	The Undertaker			

RUTHLESS AGGRESSION SERIES 5 (WALMART)		MIB	LOOSE	VALUE
RA 35.5	Edge			
PPV 10	JBL			
RA 4	Torrie Wilson			

RUTHLESS AGGRESSION SERIES 6 (WALMART)		MIB	LOOSE	VALUE
RA 28	The Miz			
DA 14	MVP			
RA 4	The Rock			

MONDAY NIGHT WAR SERIES 1 (WALMART)		MIB	LOOSE	VALUE
NITRO	Hulk Hogan			
NITRO	Scott Hall			
RAW	Stone Cold Steve Austin			
RAW	The Undertaker			
BUILD-A-FIGURE	Lex Luger			

MONDAY NIGHT WAR SERIES 2 (WALMART)		MIB	LOOSE	VALUE
RAW	"Diesel"			
NITRO	Kevin Nash			
NITRO	Rey Mysterio Jr.			
RAW	Triple H			
BUILD-A-FIGURE	Teddy Long			

MONDAY NIGHT WAR SERIES 3 (WALMART)		MIB	LOOSE	VALUE
NITRO	Booker T (Standard – Black Gear)			
NITRO	Booker T (Chase – Blue Gear)			
RAW	Rob Van Dam			
NITRO	Stevie Ray (Standard – Black Gear)			
NITRO	Stevie Ray (Chase – Blue Gear)			
RAW	The Rock			
BUILD-A-FIGURE	The Disciple			

MONDAY NIGHT WAR SERIES 4 (WALMART)		MIB	LOOSE	VALUE
RAW	Big Boss Man			
NITRO	Curt Hennig			
NITRO	Diamond Dallas Page (Standard -)			
NITRO	Diamond Dallas Page (Chase -)			
RAW	Stone Cold Steve Austin			
BUILD-A-FIGURE	Commissioner Michaels			

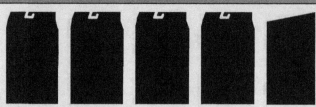

MONDAY NIGHT WAR SERIES 5 (WALMART)		MIB	LOOSE	VALUE
RAW				
NITRO				
NITRO				
RAW				
BUILD-A-FIGURE				

MONDAY NIGHT WAR SERIES 6 (WALMART)		MIB	LOOSE	VALUE
RAW				
NITRO				
NITRO				
RAW				
BUILD-A-FIGURE				

BEST OF MONDAY NIGHT WAR SERIES 1 (WALMART)		MIB	LOOSE	VALUE
RAW				
NITRO				
NITRO				
RAW	Triple H			
BUILD-A-FIGURE	Vincent			

TEENAGE MUTANT NINJA TURTLES X WWE (TARGET)			MIB	LOOSE	VALUE
SERIES 1	MICHELANGELO	Kofi Kingston			
	SHREDDER	Roman Reigns			
	DONATELLO	Xavier Woods			
SERIES 2	CASEY JONES	Cody Rhodes			
	RAPHAEL	Rey Mysterio			
	LEONARDO	Seth Rollins			

2010-2012 RINGSIDE COLLECTIBLES EXCLUSIVES		MIB	LOOSE	VALUE
2010	Rey Mysterio			
2011	CM Punk			
	Kane			
2012	Bret "Hit Man" Hart			
	"Macho Man" Randy Savage			
	Stone Cold Steve Austin			

2013-2014 RINGSIDE COLLECTIBLES EXCLUSIVES		MIB	LOOSE	VALUE
2013	Brock Lesnar			
	Cactus Jack			
	Kane			
2014	CM Punk			
	Edge			
	The Rock			

2015-2016 RINGSIDE COLLECTIBLES EXCLUSIVES		MIB	LOOSE	VALUE
2015	Hulk Hogan			
	Scott Hall			
	Shawn Michaels			
2016	Kevin Nash			
	"Macho Man" Randy Savage			
	Sting			

2017-2018 RINGSIDE COLLECTIBLES EXCLUSIVES		MIB	LOOSE	VALUE
2017	Chris Jericho			
	Finn Balor			
	Shane McMahon			
2018	Shawn Michaels			
	Bret Hart			
	Kurt Angle			
	Matt Hardy			
	The Brian Kendrick			
	Tyler Bate			

	2019-2020 RINGSIDE COLLECTIBLES EXCLUSIVES	MIB	LOOSE	VALUE
2019	Jeff Hardy			
	Matt Hardy			
	The Undertaker (As Kane)			
2020	Bray Wyatt			
	Edgeheads (Edge, Zack Ryder & Curt Hawkins)			
	Walter			

	2021-2022 RINGSIDE COLLECTIBLES EXCLUSIVES	MIB	LOOSE	VALUE
2021	Ultimate Warrior			
	John Cena			
	Cactus Jack			
	Tomasso Ciampa			
2022	The Undertaker			
	"Hollywood" Hulk Hogan			
	Cameron Grimes			
	"Macho Man" Randy Savage			
	Hulk Hogan			

	2023-2024 RINGSIDE COLLECTIBLES EXCLUSIVES	MIB	LOOSE	VALUE
2024	Cactus Jack			
	Dude Love			
	Mankind			

2024 ELITE MATTEL CREATIONS EXCLUSIVES		MIB	LOOSE	VALUE
MADE-TO-ORDER	CM Punk			
DUDLEY BOYZ	Bubba Ray Dudley			
	D-Von Dudley			
HEADBANGERS	Mosh			
	Thrasher			
IMPERIUM	Giovanni Vinci			
	Ludwig Kaiser			
LEGENDS OF THE TERRITORY ERA	Muhammad Ali			
	Gorilla Monsoon			
	Harley Race			
	"Superstar" Billy Graham			

AMAZON EXCLUSIVES		MIB	LOOSE	VALUE
2014	Mankind			
2017	Andre The Giant			
2024	Shawn Michaels			
	Razor Ramon			

GAMESTOP EXCLUSIVES		MIB	LOOSE	VALUE
2016	Brock Lesnar			
	Samoa Joe			
2017	Chris Jericho			

K-MART EXCLUSIVES		MIB	LOOSE	VALUE
2012	John Cena			

SAN DIEGO COMIC CON EXCLUSIVES		MIB	LOOSE	VALUE
2010	The Undertaker			
2016	The Shockmaster			
2017	Isaac Yankem			
2019	"Macho Man" Randy Savage			
2020	Mr. T			

	TARGET EXCLUSIVES	MIB	LOOSE	VALUE
2014	Rocky Maivia			
2018	The Shark			
2019	Red Rooster			

	WALGREENS EXCLUSIVES	MIB	LOOSE	VALUE
2015	Shawn Michaels			
	Triple H			

	TOYS 'R' US EXCLUSIVES	MIB	LOOSE	VALUE
2011	Mr. McMahon			
2012	The Undertaker			
	Triple H			
2013	Triple H			
2014	Brock Lesnar			
2015	Seth Rollins			
	John Cena			
2017	Virgil			

ALL-STARS 2-PACKS	MOC	LOOSE	VALUE
Jake "The Snake" Roberts			
Randy Orton			
"Macho Man" Randy Savage			
John Morrison			
Stone Cold Steve Austin			
CM Punk			

ELITE COLLECTION 2-PACKS 2015-2019		MIB	LOOSE	VALUE
2015 (K-MART)	Faarooq			
	The Rock			
2017 (TOYS 'R' US)	Chris Jericho			
	Kevin Owens			
2018 (WWESHOP)	Matt Hardy			
	Jeff Hardy			
2019	Jeff Hardy			
	Matt Hardy			
	AJ Styles			
	Finn Bálor			

ELITE COLLECTION 2-PACKS 2020		MIB	LOOSE	VALUE
WRESTLEMANIA MOMENT!	Rey Mysterio			
	Samoa Joe			
DX	Chyna			
	Triple H			
MONDAY NITRO	Bret "Hit Man" Hart			
	Goldberg			
WRESTLEMANIA 2	Mr. T			
	"Rowdy" Roddy Piper			

ELITE COLLECTION 2-PACKS 2021		MIB	LOOSE	VALUE
SMACKDOWN!	Triple H			
	Jeff Hardy			
ROCK 'N' SOCK	The Rock			
	Mankind			

ELITE COLLECTION 3-PACKS 2017-2019		MIB	LOOSE	VALUE
BOOTY-O'S (2017)	Big E			
	Kofi Kingston			
	Xavier Woods			
THE SHIELD (2018)	Dean Ambrose			
	Roman Reigns			
	Seth Rollins			
MILK-O-MANIA (2018)	Stephanie McMahon			
	Kurt Angle			
	Stone Cold Steve Austin			
UNDISPUTED ERA (2019)	Kyle O'Reilly			
	Adam Cole			
	Bobby Fish			

ELITE COLLECTION 3-PACKS 2022-2024		MIB	LOOSE	VALUE
HEAD OF THE TABLE VS. BEAST (AMAZON)	Brock Lesnar			
	Roman Reigns			
	Paul Heyman			
RAW 30TH (TARGET)	The Undertaker			
	Razor Ramon			
	1-2-3 Kid			
40th ANNIVERSARY OF HULKAMANIA (TARGET)	Hulk Hogan (Hulkamania)			
	"Hollywood" Hulk Hogan (nWo)			
	Hulk Hogan (Hulk Still Rules)			
MAIVIA LEGACY (WALMART)	Peter Maivia			
	The Rock			
	Rocky Johnson			

ELITE COLLECTION BOXED SETS 2023-2024		MIB	LOOSE	VALUE
WWE 60TH ANNIVERSARY (TARGET)	Becky Lynch			
	Hulk Hogan			
	The Rock			
	Stone Cold Steve Austin			
THEN, NOW, FOREVER, TOGETHER (TARGET)	Becky Lynch			
	Hulk Hogan			
	The Rock			
	Stone Cold Steve Austin			
SMACKDOWN 25th ANNIVERSARY (TARGET)	Booker T			
	Stone Cold Steve Austin			
	John Cena			
	Eddie Guerrero			
LATINO WORLD ORDER (MATTEL CREATIONS)	Cruz Del Toro			
	Rey Mysterio			
	Zelina Vega			
	Santos Escobar			
	Joaquin Wilde			

WWE LEGENDS SERIES 1	MOC	LOOSE	VALUE
Dusty Rhodes			
Ricky "The Dragon" Steamboat			
Road Warrior Animal			
Road Warrior Hawk			
Sgt. Slaughter			
Stone Cold Ateve Austin			

WWE LEGENDS SERIES 1 TAG TEAMS (TOYS 'R' US)	MOC	LOOSE	VALUE
Bushwhacker Luke			
Bushwhacker Butch			
Iron Sheik			
Nikolai Volkoff			
"Rowdy" Roddy Piper			
"Cowboy" Bob Orton			

WWE LEGENDS SERIES 2	MOC	LOOSE	VALUE
Iron Sheik			
Jake "The Snake" Roberts			
Jimmy "Superfly" Snuka			
Kamala			
"Ravishing" Rick Rude			
Terry Funk			

WWE LEGENDS HALL OF FAME (K-MART)		MOC	LOOSE	VALUE
CLASS OF 2007	"The American Dream" Dusty Rhodes			
CLASS OF 1996	Jimmy "Superfly" Snuka			
CLASS OF 2009	Ricky "The Dragon" Steamboat			
CLASS OF 2004	Sgt. Slaughter			
CLASS OF 2009	Stone Cold Steve Austin			
CLASS OF 2009	Terry Funk			

WWE LEGENDS SERIES 3	MOC	LOOSE	VALUE
Brian Pillman			
"British Bulldog" Davey Boy Smith			
"Hacksaw" Jim Duggan			
Mr. Perfect			
The Rock			
Vader			

WWE LEGENDS SERIES 4	MOC	LOOSE	VALUE
Demolition Ax			
Demolition Smash			
George "The Animal" Steele			
Hillbilly Jim			
"Mr. Wonderful" Paul Orndorff			
Ultimate Warrior			

WWE LEGENDS SERIES 5	MOC	LOOSE	VALUE
Akeem			
Bam Bam Bigelow			
"Macho Man" Randy Savage			
Rick Martel			

WWE LEGENDS SERIES 6	MOC	LOOSE	VALUE
Eddie Guerrero			
Kerry Von Erich			
Kevin Von Erich			
Texas Tornado			
Ultimate Warrior			

	WWE LEGENDS SERIES 7 (TARGET)	MIB	LOOSE	VALUE
	Bobby "The Brain" Heenan			
	Greg "The Hammer" Valentine (Black Trunks)			
CHASE	Greg "The Hammer" Valentine (Yellow Trunks)			
	Razor Ramon			

	WWE LEGENDS SERIES 8 (TARGET)	MIB	LOOSE	VALUE
	Eddie Guerrero			
	Jake "The Snake" Roberts (Maroon Tights)			
CHASE	Jake "The Snake" Roberts (Green Tights)			
	"Mr. Wonderful" Paul Orndorff			
	Ultimate Warrior			

	WWE LEGENDS SERIES 9 (TARGET)	MIB	LOOSE	VALUE
	"Million Dollar Man" Ted Dibiase (Black Suit)			
CHASE	"Million Dollar Man" Ted Dibiase (Silver Suit)			
	Nikolai Volkoff			
	Tatanka			
	The Undertaker			

	WWE LEGENDS SERIES 10 (TARGET)	MIB	LOOSE	VALUE
	Big Van Vader			
	Brutus "The Barber" Beefcake (Yellow Tights)			
CHASE	Brutus "The Barber" Beefcake (Blue Tights)			
	Diamond Dallas Page			
	John Cena			

	WWE LEGENDS SERIES 11 (TARGET)	MIB	LOOSE	VALUE
	Bam Bam Bigelow			
	Big John Studd			
	"Macho Man" Randy Savage (Pink Trunks)			
CHASE	"Macho Man" Randy Savage (Yellow Trunks)			
	Scott Hall			

	WWE LEGENDS SERIES 12 (TARGET)	MIB	LOOSE	VALUE
	Billy Gunn			
	Junkyard Dog (Red Tights)			
CHASE	Junkyard Dog (Blue Tights)			
	Kevin Nash			
	"Rowdy" Roddy Piper			

	WWE LEGENDS SERIES 13 (TARGET)	MIB	LOOSE	VALUE
	"Cowboy" Bob Orton			
	Jake "The Snake" Roberts (Blue Tights)			
CHASE	Jake "The Snake" Roberts (Grey Tights)			
	The Hurricane			
	Triple H			

	WWE LEGENDS SERIES 14 (TARGET)	MIB	LOOSE	VALUE
	Chyna			
	Edge (White Tights)			
CHASE	Edge (Red Tights)			
	"Mean" Mark Callous			
	Road Dogg			

	WWE LEGENDS SERIES 15 (TARGET)	MIB	LOOSE	VALUE
	Kane			
	Lex Luger (Black Trunks)			
CHASE	Lex Luger (Orange Trunks)			
	Stacy Kiebler			
	X-Pac			

	WWE LEGENDS SERIES 16 (TARGET)	MIB	LOOSE	VALUE
	Bradshaw			
	Faarooq			
	Molly Holly (Pink Gear)			
CHASE	Molly Holly (Blue Gear)			
	Rey Mysterio			

	WWE LEGENDS SERIES 17 (TARGET)	MIB	LOOSE	VALUE
	AJ Styles			
	Dingo Warrior			
	Ken Shamrock (Green Trunks)			
CHASE	Ken Shamrock (Blue Trunks)			
	Shawn Michaels			

	WWE LEGENDS SERIES 18 (TARGET)	MIB	LOOSE	VALUE
	Fatu (Black Tights)			
CHASE	Fatu (Floral Tights)			
	Hulk Hogan			
	Paul E. Dangerously			
	Samu (Black Tights)			
CHASE	Samu (Floral Tights)			

	WWE LEGENDS SERIES 19 (TARGET)	MIB	LOOSE	VALUE
	Brother Love			
	D'Lo Brown (Nation of Domination)			
CHASE	D'Lo Brown (Black & Blue Gear)			
	Kama Mustafa			
	The Undertaker			

	WWE LEGENDS SERIES 20 (TARGET)	MIB	LOOSE	VALUE
	Greg "The Hammer" Valentine			
	"Million Dollar Man" Ted Dibiase (Green Suit)			
CHASE	"Million Dollar Man" Ted Dibiase (White Suit)			
	Mr. Perfect			
	Triple H			

	WWE LEGENDS SERIES 21 (TARGET)	MIB	LOOSE	VALUE
	Andre The Giant (Yellow Trunks)			
CHASE	Andre The Giant (Red Trunks)			
	Hulk Hogan			
	Iron Sheik			
	"The Mouth of The South" Jimmy Hart			

	WWE LEGENDS SERIES 22 (TARGET)	MIB	LOOSE	VALUE
	Captain Lou Albano			
	Hulk Hogan (Black Knee Pads)			
CHASE	Hulk Hogan (Red Knee Pads)			
	Muhammad Ali			
	The Sultan			

	WWE LEGENDS SERIES 23 (TARGET)	MIB	LOOSE	VALUE
	Big Bubba Rogers (White Shirt)			
CHASE	Big Bubba Rogers (Light Blue Shirt)			
	Hulk Hogan			
	Jamal			
	Rosey			

	WWE LEGENDS SERIES 24 (TARGET)	MIB	LOOSE	VALUE
	Faarooq (Red, Yellow, Green Singlet Design)			
CHASE	Faarooq (Purple, Yellow, White Singlet Design)			
	Hulk Hogan			
	Jim "The Anvil" Neidhart			
	Kurt Angle			

	WWE LEGENDS GREATEST HITS SERIES 1	MIB	LOOSE	VALUE
LEGENDS 3	British Bulldog			
ELITE 25	Bruno Sammartino			
RETROFEST	Honky Tonk Man			
ELITE 41	Terry Funk			
FLASHBACK 1	Ultimate Warrior			

	WWE LEGENDS GREATEST HITS SERIES 2	MIB	LOOSE	VALUE
ELITE 40	Irwin R. Schyster			
HALL OF FAME 4	King Booker			
ELITE 44	Tugboat			
LEGENDS 4	Ultimate Warrior			
ELITE 50	Warlord			

	WWE LEGENDS EXCLUSIVES	MOC	LOOSE	VALUE
MATTY COLLECTOR	Shawn Michaels (The Rockers)			
	Marty Jannetty (The Rockers)			
	Andre The Giant			
	Diamond Dallas Page			
	Bundy			
	Arn Anderson			
	Tully Blanchard			
RINGSIDE COLLECTIBLES	"Macho King" Randy Savage			
ULTIMATEWARRIOR.COM	Ultimate Warrior (1 of 5)			

LEGENDS INTERCONTINENTAL TITLE COMBO PACK (BASIC)	MIB	LOOSE	VALUE
The Rock			
Stone Cold Steve Austin			

ULTIMATE EDITION SERIES 1		MIB	LOOSE	VALUE
WRESTLEMANIA 34	Ronda Rousey			
WCW HALLOWEEN HAVOC 1998	Ultimate Warrior			

ULTIMATE EDITION SERIES 2		MIB	LOOSE	VALUE
WRESTLEMANIA 34	Shinsuke Nakamura			
KING OF THE RING 1994	Bret "Hit Man" Hart			

ULTIMATE EDITION SERIES 3		MIB	LOOSE	VALUE
SUMMERSLAM 2018	Finn Bálor			
SUMMERSLAM 1999	Triple H			

ULTIMATE EDITION SERIES 4		MIB	LOOSE	VALUE
SUMMERSLAM 2019	Brock Lesnar			
SURVIVOR SERIES 1997	Shawn Michaels			

ULTIMATE EDITION SERIES 5		MIB	LOOSE	VALUE
WRESTLEMANIA 35	Becky Lynch			
ROYAL RUMBLE 2008	John Cena			

ULTIMATE EDITION SERIES 6		MIB	LOOSE	VALUE
SUMMERSLAM 2018	Charlotte Flair (Ringside Collectibles)			
SURVIVOR SERIES 1998	The Rock (Amazon)			

ULTIMATE EDITION SERIES 7		MIB	LOOSE	VALUE
ROYAL RUMBLE 2020	"The Fiend" Bray Wyatt			
WCW HOG WILD 1996	"Hollywood" Hulk Hogan			

ULTIMATE EDITION SERIES 8		MIB	LOOSE	VALUE
ROYAL RUMBLE 2020	Edge			
SNME – 2/8/1992	"Macho Man" Randy Savage			

ULTIMATE EDITION SERIES 9		MIB	LOOSE	VALUE
WCW – 3/11/1989	Ric Flair			
WRESTLEMANIA 13	Stone Cold Steve Austin			

ULTIMATE EDITION SERIES 10		MIB	LOOSE	VALUE
WRESTLEMANIA 29	The Rock			
WRESTLEMANIA 22	John Cena			

ULTIMATE EDITION SERIES 11		MIB	LOOSE	VALUE
IN YOUR HOUSE: BADD BLOOD 1997	Kane			
WRESTLEMANIA XIV	The Undertaker			

ULTIMATE EDITION SERIES 12		MIB	LOOSE	VALUE
RAW – 1/18/2021	Alexa Bliss			
WRESTLEMANIA 37	"The Fiend" Bray Wyatt			

ULTIMATE EDITION SERIES 13		MIB	LOOSE	VALUE
WRESTLEMANIA	Hulk Hogan			
WRESTLEMANIA	Mr. T			

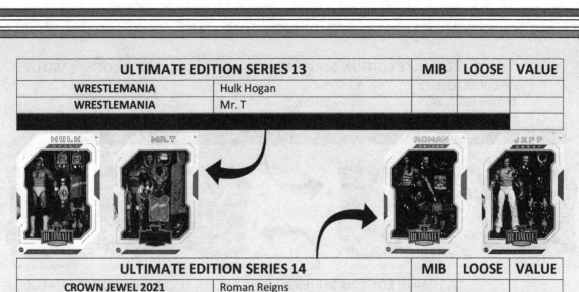

ULTIMATE EDITION SERIES 14		MIB	LOOSE	VALUE
CROWN JEWEL 2021	Roman Reigns			
RAW – 11/11/2002	Jeff Hardy			

ULTIMATE EDITION SERIES 15		MIB	LOOSE	VALUE
DAY 1	Brock Lesnar			
WRESTLEMANIA VII	Ultimate Warrior			

ULTIMATE EDITION SERIES 16		MIB	LOOSE	VALUE
WRESTLEMANIA 38	AJ Styles			
SUPERSTARS – 8/15/1992	Razor Ramon (Standard - Yellow Vest)			
SUPERSTARS – 1/8/1994	Razor Ramon (Chase - Purple Vest)			

ULTIMATE EDITION SERIES 17		MIB	LOOSE	VALUE
MONEY IN THE BANK 2022	Seth Rollins			
WRESTLEMANIA III	Andre The Giant			

ULTIMATE EDITION SERIES 18		MIB	LOOSE	VALUE
WRESTLEMANIA 38	Randy Orton			
WRESTLEMANIA VII	"Macho Man" Randy Savage		CANCELED	

ULTIMATE EDITION SERIES 19		MIB	LOOSE	VALUE
HELL IN A CELL 2022	Bianca Belair			
CROWN JEWEL 2023	Bobby Lashley			
ROYAL RUMBLE 2001	Kurt Angle			

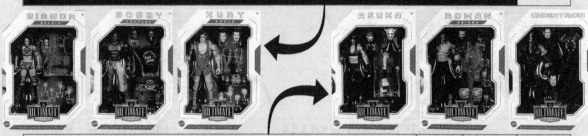

ULTIMATE EDITION SERIES 20		MIB	LOOSE	VALUE
ROYAL RUMBLE 2023	Asuka			
WRESTLEMANIA 39	Roman Reigns			
WRESTLEMANIA XIV	The Undertaker (Greatest Hits)			

ULTIMATE EDITION SERIES 21		MIB	LOOSE	VALUE
WRESTLEMANIA 39	Cody Rhodes			
WRESTLEMANIA 39	Kevin Owens			
WRESTLEMANIA 39	Sami Zayn			

ULTIMATE EDITION SERIES 22		MIB	LOOSE	VALUE
	Gunther			
SUMMERSLAM 2023	Jey Uso			
CROWN JEWEL 2023	John Cena			

ULTIMATE EDITION SERIES 23		MIB	LOOSE	VALUE
WRESTLEMANIA 39	Dominik Mysterio			
	LA Knight			
WRESTLEMANIA 39	Rey Mysterio			

ULTIMATE EDITION SERIES 24		MIB	LOOSE	VALUE
ROYAL RUMBLE 2023	Bray Wyatt			

ULTIMATE EDITION SERIES 25		MIB	LOOSE	VALUE
	Damien Priest			
	The Great Muta			

ULTIMATE EDITION GREATEST HITS SERIES 1		MIB	LOOSE	VALUE
KING OF THE RING 1994	Bret "Hit Man" Hart			
SUMMERSLAM 1999	Triple H			

ULTIMATE EDITION GREATEST HITS SERIES 2		MIB	LOOSE	VALUE
WRESTLEMANIA 13	Stone Cold Steve Austin			
WCW HALLOWEEN HAVOC 1998	Ultimate Warrior			

ULTIMATE EDITION GREATEST HITS SERIES 3		MIB	LOOSE	VALUE
WCW HOG WILD 1996	"Hollywood" Hulk Hogan			
SUMMERSLAM 2018	Charlotte Flair			

ULTIMATE EDITION GREATEST HITS SERIES 4		MIB	LOOSE	VALUE
BACKLASH 2005	Batista (White Box)			
BACKLASH 2005	Batista (Red Box)			
SURVIVOR SERIES 1998	The Rock (White Box)			
SURVIVOR SERIES 1998	The Rock (Red Box)			

2022 ULTIMATE EDITION FAN TAKEOVER (AMAZON)		MIB	LOOSE	VALUE
WRESTLEMANIA 9	Hulk Hogan			
SMACKDOWN 12/19/08	Jeff Hardy			
WRESTLEMANIA 6	Ultimate Warrior			
SURVIVOR SERIES 2006	Triple H			
SURVIVOR SERIES 1995	Shawn Michaels			
WCW AUGUST 1998	Goldberg			

2024 ULTIMATE EDITION FAN TAKEOVER (AMAZON)	MIB	LOOSE	VALUE
Rey Mysterio			
Seth Rollins			

2025 ULTIMATE EDITION FAN TAKEOVER (AMAZON)	MIB	LOOSE	VALUE
John Cena			
Randy Orton			

	ULTIMATE EDITION LEGENDS (TARGET)	MIB	LOOSE	VALUE
	Batista			
	"Macho Man" Randy Savage			
	Bret "Hit Man" Hart			
	The Rock			
	Ultimate Warrior			
	Yokozuna (Black Sarong)			
CHASE	Yokozuna (White Sarong)			
	The Undertaker			
	Dusty Rhodes			
	Vader (Black Mask)			
CHASE	Vader (Red Mask)			

ULTIMATE RUTHLESS AGGRESSION 1 (WALMART)		MIB	LOOSE	VALUE
Eddie Guerrero				
Rey Mysterio				

ULTIMATE RUTHLESS AGGRESSION 2 (WALMART)		MIB	LOOSE	VALUE
Brock Lesnar				
Rob Van Dam				

ULTIMATE MONDAY NIGHT WARS 1 (WALMART)		MIB	LOOSE	VALUE
RAW	Bret "Hit Man" Hart			
NITRO	"Rowdy" Roddy Piper			

ULTIMATE MONDAY NIGHT WARS 2 (WALMART)		MIB	LOOSE	VALUE
NITRO	Eddie Guerrero			
RAW	Mankind			

ULTIMATE AMAZON EXCLUSIVES		MIB	LOOSE	VALUE
2023	Gobbledy Gooker			
	The Undertaker			

ULTIMATE EDITION RINGSIDE COLLECTIBLES EXCLUSIVES		MIB	LOOSE	VALUE
2022	Raw Ring w/ Kane			
2023	Jey Uso			
	Jimmy Uso			
2024	Nitro Ring w/ Eric Bischoff			
	Kevin Nash			
	Scott Hall			
	Rick Steiner			
	Scott Steiner			

ULTIMATE SAN DIEGO COMIC CON EXCLUSIVES		MIB	LOOSE	VALUE
2021	Sgt. Slaughter (Standard Edition – Blue Card)			
	Sgt. Slaughter (Chase Edition – Black Card)			
2022	Rip			
	Zeus			
2023	Muhammad Ali (Ring Gear)			
	Muhammad Ali (Referee)			
2024	Shawn Michaels			

ULTIMATE EDITION MATTEL CREATIONS EXCLUSIVES		MIB	LOOSE	VALUE
	Cody Rhodes			
	Logan Paul			
NEW GENERATION ARENA	Diesel			
	"Macho Man" Randy Savage (1 of 8,011)			
	Doink The Clown			
	Ultimate Edition Authentic Scaled Ring			
	Entrance Stage			
	Wrestlmania Ring Skirts			
	In Your House Ring Skirts			

ULTIMATE EDITION COLISEUM COLLECTION 2-PACKS		MIB	LOOSE	VALUE
2022	Hulk Hogan			
	Terry Funk			
2023	"Ravishing" Rick Rude			
	Jake "The Snake" Roberts			
	George "The Animal" Steele			
	"Rowdy" Roddy Piper			
2024	Bret "Hit Man" Hart (Standard Edtion – Blue Card)			
	Jim "The Anvil" Neidhart (Standard Edition – Blue Card)			
	Bret "Hit Man" Hart (Chase Edtion – Black Card)			
	Jim "The Anvil" Neidhart (Chase Edition – Black Card)			
	Ricky "The Dragon" Steamboat (Standard Edtion – Blue Card)			
	"Million Dollar Man" Ted Dibiase (Standard Edition – Blue Card)			
	Ricky "The Dragon" Steamboat (Chase Edtion – Black Card)			
	"Million Dollar Man" Ted Dibiase (Chase Edition – Black Card)			

MISCELLANEOUS SCALE & ARTICULATION

RETRO SERIES 1 (WALMART)	MOC	LOOSE	VALUE
Brock Lesnar			
John Cena ("Attitude Adustment")			
John Cena ("Attitude Adjustment")			
Kevin Owens			
Roman Reigns ("Superman Punch")			
Roman Reigns ("Super Punch")			
Ultimate Warrior			
The Undertaker			

RETRO SERIES 2 (WALMART)	MOC	LOOSE	VALUE
Kane			
Mankind			
Stone Cold Steve Austin			
Sting			
The Rock			
Triple H (1 Logo On Tights)			
Triple H (2 Logos On Tights)			

RETRO SERIES 3	MOC	LOOSE	VALUE
AJ Styles			
Dean Ambrose			
Goldberg			
Seth Rollins			

RETRO SERIES 4	MOC	LOOSE	VALUE
Finn Balor			
Kevin Owens			
Ric Flair			
Sami Zayn			

RETRO SERIES 5	MOC	LOOSE	VALUE
Big E			
Kofi Kingston			
Xavier Woods			
"Macho Man" Randy Savage (Arm Up)			
"Macho Man" Randy Savage (Arm Down)			

RETRO SERIES 6	MOC	LOOSE	VALUE
Bray Wyatt			
Daniel Bryan			
Shinsuke Nakamura			
Sting			

RETRO SERIES 7	MOC	LOOSE	VALUE
Chris Jericho			
Kurt Angle			
Shawn Michaels			
Sheamus			

RETRO SERIES 8	MOC	LOOSE	VALUE
Braun Strowman			
Iron Sheik			
Jeff Hardy			
Zack Ryder			

RETRO SERIES 9	MOC	LOOSE	VALUE
Goldust			
"Macho Man" Randy Savage			
Randy Orton			
Samoa Joe			

RETRO SERIES 10	MOC	LOOSE	VALUE
Diesel			
Elias			
Junkyard Dog			
"Woken" Matt Hardy			

RETRO SERIES 11 (MATTEL CREATIONS)	MOC	LOOSE	VALUE
"Cowboy" Bob Orton			
Mean Gene Okerlund			
Mr. T			
"Rowdy" Roddy Piper			

RETRO SERIES 12 (MATTEL CREATIONS)	MOC	LOOSE	VALUE
Bret "Hit Man" Hart			
Jim "The Anvil" Neidhart			
Jimmy Hart			
Nikolai Volkoff			

RETRO SERIES 13 (MATTEL CREATIONS)	MOC	LOOSE	VALUE
Doink The Clown			
Greg "The Hammer" Valentine			
Lex Luger			
Tugboat			

RETRO SERIES 14 (MATTEL CREATIONS)	MOC	LOOSE	VALUE
Jerry "The King" Lawler			
Paul Bearer			
The Undertaker			
Vader			

RETRO SERIES 15 (MATTEL CREATIONS)	MOC	LOOSE	VALUE
Big John Studd			
Hulk Hogan			
Muhammad Ali			
Wendi Richter			

RETRO SERIES 16 (MATTEL CREATIONS)	MOC	LOOSE	VALUE
Alundra Blayze			
British Bulldog			
Isaac Yankem			
Shawn Michaels			

RETRO SERIES 17 (MATTEL CREATIONS)	MOC	LOOSE	VALUE
Brother Love			

RETRO TAG TEAM 2-PACKS (RINGSIDE COLLECTIBLES)	MOC	LOOSE	VALUE
Scott Hall			
Kevin Nash			
"Hollywood" Hulk Hogan			
Syxx			

RETRO DX 2-PACKS (RINGSIDE COLLECTIBLES)	MOC	LOOSE	VALUE
Chyna			
Triple H			
Billy Gunn			
Road Dogg			

RETRO WRESTLING RINGS	MIB	LOOSE	VALUE
Official WWE Retro Ring			
Official Wrestlemania Retro Ring (Mattel Creations)			

MASTERS OF THE WWE UNIVERSE SERIES 1 (WALMART)	MOC	LOOSE	VALUE
Finn Balor			
Sting			
Triple H			
Ultimate Warrior			

MASTERS OF THE WWE UNIVERSE SERIES 2 (WALMART)	MOC	LOOSE	VALUE
Faker John Cena			
"Macho Man" Randy Savage			
Rey Mysterio			
Roman Reigns			

MASTERS OF THE WWE UNIVERSE SERIES 3 (WALMART)	MOC	LOOSE	VALUE
Braun Strowman			
The New Day (Big E Face Showing)			
The New Day (Kofi Kingston Face Showing)			
The New Day (Xavier Woods Face Showing)			
The Rock			
The Undertaker			

MASTERS OF THE WWE UNIVERSE SERIES 4 (WALMART)	MOC	LOOSE	VALUE
"The Fiend" Bray Wyatt			
Jake "The Snake" Roberts			
Mr. T			
Seth Rollins			

MASTERS OF THE WWE UNIVERSE SERIES 5 (WALMART)	MOC	LOOSE	VALUE
Becky Lynch			
"Macho Man" Randy Savage			
Ricky "The Dragon" Steamboat			
"Rowdy" Roddy Piper			

MASTERS OF THE WWE UNIVERSE SERIES 6 (WALMART)	MOC	LOOSE	VALUE
Goldberg			
Kane			
Stephanie McMahon			
Ultimate Warrior			

MASTERS OF THE WWE UNIVERSE SERIES 7 (WALMART)	MOC	LOOSE	VALUE
Andre The Giant			
Bret "Hitman" Hart			
Junkyard Dog			
Sgt. Slaughter			

MASTERS OF THE WWE UNIVERSE SERIES 8 (WALMART)	MOC	LOOSE	VALUE
Stone Cold Steve Austin			
Chyna			
Rey Mysterio			

MASTERS OF THE WWE UNIVERSE RINGS (WALMART)	MIB	LOOSE	VALUE
Grayskull Ring			
Grayskull Mania (w/ Triple H & John Cena)			
Rattlesnake Mountain (w/ Stone Cold Steve Austin & Hulk Hogan)			

SUPERSTARS

WWE SUPERSTARS SERIES 1 (WALMART)	MOC	LOOSE	VALUE
Bray Wyatt			
"Hollywood" Hulk Hogan			
Honky Tonk Man			
Ric Flair			

WWE SUPERSTARS SERIES 2 (WALMART)	MOC	LOOSE	VALUE
Kevin Nash			
Scott Hall			
Shawn Michaels			
Ultimate Warrior			

WWE SUPERSTARS SERIES 3 (WALMART)	MOC	LOOSE	VALUE
Mankind			
"Million Dollar Man" Ted Dibiase			
Papa Shango			
The Undertaker			

WWE SUPERSTARS SERIES 4 (WALMART)	MOC	LOOSE	VALUE
"Macho Man" Randy Savage			
Mr. T			
The Rock			
Typhoon			

WWE SUPERSTARS SERIES 5 (WALMART)		MOC	LOOSE	VALUE
	Earthquake			
	"Macho Man" Randy Savage			
	"Ravishing" Rick Rude			
	The Rock			

WWE SUPERSTARS SERIES 6 (WALMART)		MOC	LOOSE	VALUE
	Bam Bam Bigelow			
	Hulk Hogan (Red & Yellow)			
CHASE	Hulk Hogan (Blue & White)			
	Mr. Perfect			
	"Rowdy" Roddy Piper			

WWE SUPERSTARS SERIES 7 (WALMART)		MOC	LOOSE	VALUE
	Captain Lou Albano			
	Hulk Hogan (Red & Yellow)			
CHASE	Hulk Hogan (Blue & White)			
	"Rowdy" Roddy Piper			
	Vader			

WWE SUPERSTARS SERIES 8 (WALMART)		MOC	LOOSE	VALUE
	Andre The Giant			
	Doink The Clown			
	Hulk Hogan (Red Tights)			
CHASE	Hulk Hogan (Blue Tights)			

WWE SUPERSTARS SERIES 9 (WALMART)	MOC	LOOSE	VALUE
British Bulldog			
Kane			
Muhammad Ali			

WWE SUPERSTARS SERIES 10 (WALMART)	MOC	LOOSE	VALUE
Big Boss Man			
Kurt Angle			
Tatanka			

	WWE SUPERSTARS SERIES 11 (WALMART)	MOC	LOOSE	VALUE
	Brutus "The Barber" Beefcake			
	Razor Ramon (Blue Gear)			
CHASE	Razor Ramon (Purple Tights)			
	Rey Mysterio Jr.			

WWE SUPERSTARS SERIES 12 (WALMART)	MOC	LOOSE	VALUE

CREATE-A-WWE-SUPERSTAR SERIES 1	MIB	LOOSE	VALUE
Bray Wyatt			
Hulk Hogan			
John Cena			
Kane			
Randy Orton			
Sheamus			
Stone Cold Steve Austin			
The Rock			

CREATE-A-WWE-SUPERSTAR DELUXE SERIES 1		MIB	LOOSE	VALUE
Gladiator Set	Triple H			
Lucha Set	Rey Mysterio			
Martial Arts Set	Seth Rollins			
Rocker Set	Kane			
Special Ops Set	Roman Reigns			
Zombie Set	The Undertaker			

CREATE-A-WWE-SUPERSTAR 2-PACK	MIB	LOOSE	VALUE
John Cena			
Triple H			

CREATE-A-WWE-SUPERSTAR SERIES 2	MIB	LOOSE	VALUE
John Cena			
Goldust			
Rusev			
Ultimate Warrior			

CREATE-A-WWE-SUPERSTAR DELUXE SERIES 2		MIB	LOOSE	VALUE
Enforcer Set	Dean Ambrose			
Gladiator Set	Triple H			
Hip Hop Set	John Cena			
Shadow Vigilante Set	Sting			
Special Ops Set	Roman Reigns			

TOUGH TALKERS SERIES 1	MIB	LOOSE	VALUE
Bray Wyatt			
Dean Ambrose			
John Cena			
Kevin Owens			
Roman Reigns			
Seth Rollins			

TOUGH TALKERS SERIES 2	MIB	LOOSE	VALUE
Big E			
Brock Lesnar			
Dean Ambrose			
John Cena			
Kofi Kingston			
Xavier Woods			

TOUGH TALKERS 2-PACKS	MIB	LOOSE	VALUE
Brock Lesnar			
The Undertaker			
Stone Cold Steve Austin			
The Rock			
Roman Reigns			
Triple H			
Seth Rollins			
AJ Styles			

TOUGH TALKERS HALL OF FAME (TARGET)	MIB	LOOSE	VALUE
"Macho Man" Randy Savage			
Ric Flair			
"Rowdy" Roddy Piper			

TOUGH TALKERS: TOTAL TAG TEAM SERIES 1	MIB	LOOSE	VALUE
AJ Styles			
Big Cass			
Enzo Amore			
Finn Balor			
John Cena			
Randy Orton			
Sami Zayn			
Sting			
The Undertaker			
Xavier Woods			
Big E			
Kofi Kingston			
Kevin Owens			
Chris Jericho			

SOUND SLAMMERS SERIES 1	MIB	LOOSE	VALUE
Dean Ambrose			
John Cena			
Kevin Owens			
Roman Reigns			
Seth Rollins			

SOUND SLAMMERS SERIES 2	MIB	LOOSE	VALUE
AJ Styles			
Bobby Roode			
Finn Balor			
Kurt Angle			
The Miz			

SOUND SLAMMERS SERIES 3	MIB	LOOSE	VALUE
Bobby Roode			
Cesaro			
Finn Balor			
Seth Rollins			
"Woken" Matt Hardy			

SOUND SLAMMERS SERIES 4	MIB	LOOSE	VALUE
Randy Orton			
Roman Reigns			
Sheamus			
The Rock			

WREKKIN' 2019 ASSORTMENT	MIB	LOOSE	VALUE
AJ Styles			
John Cena			
Seth Rollins			
The Miz			
The Undertaker			
"Woken" Matt Hardy			

WREKKIN' 2020 ASSORTMENT	MIB	LOOSE	VALUE
Daniel Bryan			
Elias			
Finn Balor			
John Cena			
Kofi Kingston			
Randy Orton			
Rey Mysterio			
Ricochet			
Roman Reigns			
Seth Rollins			
The Miz			
The Rock			
Triple H			
The Undertaker			

WREKKIN' 2021 ASSORTMENT	MIB	LOOSE	VALUE
Drew McIntyre			
John Cena			
Randy Orton			
Roman Reigns			
Seth Rollins			
The Rock			
Triple H			
The Undertaker			

BEND 'N' BASH SERIES 1	MIB	LOOSE	VALUE
John Cena			
Rey Mysterio			
Roman Reigns			
The Rock			

BEND 'N' BASH SERIES 2	MIB	LOOSE	VALUE
Bobby Lashley			
Drew McIntyre			
Kofi Kingston			
The Undertaker			

BEND 'N' BASH SERIES 3	MIB	LOOSE	VALUE
Big E			
Damian Priest			
Rey Mysterio			
Seth Rollins			

BEND 'N' BASH DELUXE PACKS	MIB	LOOSE	VALUE
John Cena			
Roman Reigns			

POWER SLAMMERS SERIES 1	MIB	LOOSE	VALUE
John Cena (Green)			
Randy Orton			
Rey Mysterio (Yellow)			
Sheamus			

POWER SLAMMERS SERIES 2	MIB	LOOSE	VALUE
Alberto Del Rio			
Brodus Clay			
Kofi Kingston			
The Miz			
Zack Ryder			

POWER SLAMMERS SERIES 3	MIB	LOOSE	VALUE
Kane			
Santino Marella			
Sin Cara			
The Rock			

POWER SLAMMERS 2-PACKS SERIES 1	MIB	LOOSE	VALUE
John Cena			
Randy Orton			
Rey Mysterio (Black)			
Sheamus			

POWER SLAMMERS 2-PACKS SERIES 2	MIB	LOOSE	VALUE
CM Punk			
Kane			
John Cena (Blue)			
The Rock			

BRAWLIN' BUDDIES SERIES 1		MIB	LOOSE	VALUE
	John Cena (Camo)			
	Randy Orton			
	Rey Mysterio (Green)			
WALMART	Rey Mysterio (Red)			
	Sheamus			

BRAWLIN' BUDDIES SERIES 2	MIB	LOOSE	VALUE
Kofi Kingston			
Rey Mysterio (Blue)			
Zack Ryder			

BRAWLIN' BUDDIES 2-PACKS (TOYS 'R' US)		MIB	LOOSE	VALUE
BUDDIES	John Cena (Jorts)			
	Rey Mysterio (Green)			
CHAMPIONS	Ryback			
	John Cena			

CHAMPIONSHIP BRAWLIN' BUDDIES		MIB	LOOSE	VALUE
	Brodus Clay			
	John Cena			
TOYS 'R' US	Ryback			
	Sheamus			
	The Rock			

3-COUNT CRUSHERS	MIB	LOOSE	VALUE
John Cena			
Roman Reigns			
Seth Rollins			
The Rock			

12" 2013 ASSORTMENT	MIB	LOOSE	VALUE
Albertio Del Rio			
John Cena			
Kane			
Sheamus			
Sin Cara			

12" 2014 ASSORTMENT	MIB	LOOSE	VALUE
John Cena			
Kane			
Sheamus			

12" 2015 ASSORTMENT	MIB	LOOSE	VALUE
John Cena			
Sin Cara (Purple)			
Sin Cara (Yellow)			
The Rock			

12" 2017 ASSORTMENT	MIB	LOOSE	VALUE
Brock Lesnar			
Brock Lesnar (T-Shirt)			
Dean Ambrose			
Finn Balor			
Finn Balor (T-Shirt)			
John Cena (Blue Wrist Bands)			
John Cena (Orange Wrist Bands)			
John Cena (Red & Blue Wrist Bands)			
Kalisto			
Roman Reigns			
Seth Rollins			
Seth Rollins (T-Shirt)			
Sting			
Stone Cold Steve Austin			
The Rock			
The Rock (T-Shirt)			
Triple H			
Triple H (T-Shirt)			

TRUE MOVES SERIES 1	MIB	LOOSE	VALUE
AJ Styles			
Daniel Bryan			
Kalisto			
Kane			
Kevin Owens			
Kurt Angle			
Randy Orton			
Seth Rollins			

TRUE MOVES SERIES 2	MIB	LOOSE	VALUE
Bruan Strowman			
Bray Wyatt			
Cesaro			
Gran Metalik			
Kane			
Kevin Owens			
Randy Orton			
The Undertaker			

TRUE MOVES SERIES 3	MIB	LOOSE	VALUE
Jeff Hardy			
Rey Mysterio			

TRUE MOVES MAIN EVENT SET	MIB	LOOSE	VALUE
Kane			
The Undertaker			
John Cena			
Daniel Bryan			

WOMEN'S SUPERSTARS FASHIONS 12" DOLLS	MIB	LOOSE	VALUE
Alicia Fox			
Asuka			
Bayley			
Becky Lynch			
Carmella			
Charlotte Flair			
Eva Marie			
Lana			
Natalya			

WOMEN'S SUPERSTARS FASHIONS DELUXE 12" DOLLS	MIB	LOOSE	VALUE
Alexa Bliss			
Bayley			
Becky Lynch			
Brie Bella			
Charlotte Flair			
Naomi			
Natalya			
Nikki Bella			
Ronda Rousey			
Sasha Banks (Blue Dress)			
Sasha Banks (Green Dress)			

WOMEN'S SUPERSTARS FASHIONS 12" DOLLS MULTIPACKS		MIB	LOOSE	VALUE
5-PACK	Natalya			
	Becky Lynch			
	Sasha Banks			
	Brie Bella			
	Nikki Bella			
CANADA EXCLUSIVE 5-PACK	Becky Lynch			
	Charlotte Flair			
	Stephanie McMahon			
	Sasha Banks			
	Bayley			
SDCC 2017	Charlotte Flair			
	Sasha Banks			

WOMEN'S SUPERSTARS 6" ACTION FIGURES	MOC	LOOSE	VALUE
Alexa Bliss			
Brie Bella			
Becky Lynch			
Charlotte Flair			
Naomi			
Natalya			
Nikki Bella			

WOMEN'S SUPERSTARS MISCELLANEOUS RELEASES		MOC	LOOSE	VALUE
ULTIMATE FAN PACKS	Bayley			
	Bayley (w/ DVD)			
	Charlotte Flair			
	Sasha Banks			
	Sasha Banks (w/ DVD)			
TAG TEAM SUPERSTARS	Bayley			
	Becky Lynch			
	Sasha Banks			
PLAYSETS	Ultimate Entrance Playset (w/ Nikki Bella)			

2011 WWE RUMBLERS SINGLES ASSORTMENT	MOC	LOOSE	VALUE
Big Show			
CM Punk			
Edge			
Evan Bourne			
John Cena (Purple Wrist Bands, No Hat)			
John Cena (Purple Wrist Bands w/ Hat)			
John Cena (Orange Wrist Bands w/ Hat)			
John Morrison			
Kane			
Kofi Kingston			
Randy Orton			
Rey Mysterio (Black)			
Rey Mysterio (Blue)			
Rey Mysterio (Red)			
Sheamus			
The Miz			
Triple H			
The Undertaker			

2011 WWE RUMBLERS 2-PACK ASSORTMENT	MOC	LOOSE	VALUE
Alberto Del Rio			
Rey Mysterio (Black)			
Big Show			
Rey Mysterio (White)			
Big Show			
Triple H			
CM Punk			
R-Truth			
Drew McIntyre			
The Undertaker			
Edge			
Randy Orton			
Evan Bourne (Red Tights)			
John Morrison (Black Pants)			
Evan Bourne (Black Tights)			
The Miz (Blue Trunks)			
Goldust			
Kofi Kingston (Yellow Trunks)			
Hornswoggle			
John Cena (Purple Wrist Bands w/ Hat)			
Jack Swagger			
John Cena (Purple Wrist Bands, No Hat)			
John Cena (Orange Wrist Bands w/ Hat)			
Sheamus			
John Cena (Purple Wrist Bands w/ Hat)			
Wade Barrett			
Kane			
Rey Mysterio (Blue & Yellow)			
Kofi Kingston (Blue Trunks)			
Justin Gabriel			
Rey Mysterio (Red)			
John Morrison (Silver Pants)			
Santino Marella			
John Morrison (Black Pants, Red Boots)			
Sheamus			
Randy Orton			
The Great Khali			
Hornswoggle			
The Miz (Red Trunks)			
Kofi Kingston (Green Trunks)			
Triple H			
Shawn Michaels			
The Undertaker			
Mark Henry			

2011 WWE RUMBLERS MULTIPACKS		MOC	LOOSE	VALUE
3-PACKS (WALMART)	Kofi Kingston			
	Rey Mysterio			
	John Morrison			
	Sheamus			
	John Cena			
	Triple H			
BATTLE ROYAL 7-PACK (TOYS 'R' US)	CM Punk			
	Kofi Kingston			
	The Undertaker			
	John Cena			
	Triple H			
	JohnMorrison			
	Rey Mysterio			

2011 WWE RUMBLERS PLAYSETS	MOC	LOOSE	VALUE
Blast & Bash Battle Ring (w/ John Cena & Sheamus)			
Steel Cage (w/ Rey, Cena, Undertaker, Big Show, Triple H & Sheamus)			
Casket Match Playset (w/ The Undertaker)			
Entrance Blast Playset (w/ John Morrison)			
Ladder Match Playset (w/ John Morrison)			
Ringside Takedown Playset (w/ Randy Orton)			
Smack Attack Playset (w/ The Miz)			
Spinshot Ladder Playset (w/ Edge)			
Steel Cage (w/ Rey Mysterio)			
TitanTron Tower (w/ Evan Bourne)			
Rumblers Ring (w/ Rey Mysterio & Kane)			
Transforming Rumble Rig (w/ Rey Mysterio)			

2012 WWE RUMBLERS SINGLES ASSORTMENT	MOC	LOOSE	VALUE
Alberto Del Rio			
Big Show			
CM Punk			
John Cena (Navy Wrist Bands)			
John Cena (Red Wrist Bands)			
Kofi Kingston			
Randy Orton			
Rey Mysterio			
Sin Cara			
The Rock			
Triple H			
The Undertaker			
Wade Barrett			

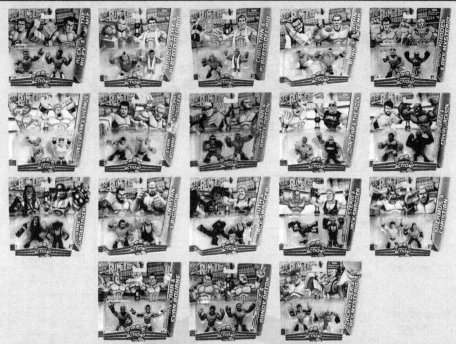

2012 WWE RUMBLERS 2-PACK ASSORTMENT	MOC	LOOSE	VALUE
Alex Riley			
The Miz			
Brodus Clay			
Alberto Del Rio			
Christian			
Alberto Del Rio			
CM Punk			
John Cena			
Cody Rhodes			
Rey Mysterio			
Daniel Bryan			
Sheamus			
Evan Bourne			
Dolph Ziggler			
John Cena (T-Shirt)			
Randy Orton			
John Cena (Red Hat)			
The Rock			
Justin Gabriel			
Exekiel Jackson			
Kane			
The Undertaker			
Mason Ryan			
Big Show			
Rey Mysterio (Gold & Silver)			
Jack Swagger			
R-Truth			
Jack Swagger			
Sheamus			
Christian			
Sin Cara			
Evan Bourne			
The Miz			
Randy Orton			
Zack Ryder			
Rey Mysterio			

2012 WWE RUMBLERS MISCELLANEOUS RELEASES		MIB	LOOSE	VALUE
BATTLE ROYAL 7-PACK	Big Show			
	The Miz			
	Randy Orton			
	John Cena			
	Rey Mysterio			
	Sheamus			
	Ezekiel Jackson			
APPTIVITY	CM Punk			
	John Cena			
	Mark Henry			
	Randy Orton			
	Rey Mysterio			
	Sheamus			
APPTIVITY 2-PACK	John Cena			
	Sin Cara			
APPTIVITY 3-PACK	Rey Mysterio			
	John Cena			
	Randy Orton			

2012 WWE RUMBLERS PLAYSETS	MIB	LOOSE	VALUE
Aerial Battle Playset (w/ Randy Orton)			
Attack Pack (w/ John Cena & The Miz)			
Attack Pack (w/ Rey Mysterio & R-Truth)			
Climb & Crash Playset (w/ Kofi Kingston)			
Flip-Out Ring Playset (w/ John Cena)			
Crash Cage Playset (w/ Kane)			
Crash Cage Playset (w/ Randy Orton)			
Ringing Entrance Playset (w/ Rey Mysterio)			
Slam Cam Playset (w/ Rey Mysterio)			
WWE Championship Playset (w/ Triple H)			
World Heavyweight Championship Playset (w/ Rey)			
World Heavyweight Championship Playset (w/ Orton)			
WWE Championship Playset (w/ John Cena)			
United States Championship Playset (w/ Kofi Kingston)			
Forklift Smashdown Playset (w/ John Cena)			
Launchin' Limo Playset (w/ Alberto Del Rio)			
Slambulance Playset (w/ Sheamus)			
Money In The Bank Playset (w/ The Miz)			
Rumblers Ring (w/ John Cena & The Miz)			
Rumblers Ring (w/ Alberto Del Rio & Rey Mysterio)			
Blastin' Breakdown Playset (w/ Alberto Del Rio & Cena)			
Ring Gift Set (w/ 10 Rumblers)			

2013 WWE RUMBLERS 2-PACK ASSORTMENT	MOC	LOOSE	VALUE
Antonio Cesaro			
Brodus Clay			
Big Show			
John Cena			
Booker T			
Cody Rhodes			
Brock Lesnar			
John Cena			
CM Punk			
Kane			
Hunico			
Rey Mysterio			
"Macho Man" Randy Savage			
CM Punk			
R-Truth			
The Miz			
Ryback			
Rey Mysterio			
Stone Cold Steve Austin			
The Rock			
Tensai			
Justin Gabriel			
The Rock			
Triple H			
Ultimate Warrior			
Sheamus			
Yoshi Tatsu			
Zack Ryder			

2013 WWE RUMBLERS MULTIPACKS		MIB	LOOSE	VALUE
ROYAL RUMBLE 7-PACK (TOYS 'R' US)	Kane			
	Big Show			
	Rey Mysterio			
	John Cena			
	Randy Orton			
	Kofi Kingston			
	Sheamus			

2013 WWE RUMBLERS RAMPAGE	MOC	LOOSE	VALUE
Brock Lesnar			
CM Punk			
John Cena (Power Punch)			
John Cena (Super Jump)			
Kane			
Kofi Kingston			
Randy Orton			
Rey Mysterio (Blue)			
Rey Mysterio (White)			
Sheamus			
Sin Cara (Red)			
Sin Cara (White)			
The Undertaker			
Zack Ryder			

2013 WWE RUMBLERS RAMPAGE PLAYSETS	MIB	LOOSE	VALUE
Crash Pack Playset (w/ John Cena)			
Crash Pack Playset (w/ Sheamus)			
Crash Cage Playset (w/ John Cena & The Rock)			
Ladder Battle Playset (w/ Randy Orton & Mark Henry)			
Scaffold Smash Playset (w/ The Miz & Kofi Kingston)			
Devastadium (w/ Rey Mysterio)			
Transforming Tour Bus (w/ The Rock)			

	WWE RUMBLERS EXCLUSIVES	MIB	LOOSE	VALUE
SDCC 2011	The Rock			
SDCC 2012	Rey Mysterio			
SDCC 2013	The Miz			
ROAD TO WM XXVIII	John Cena			
	The Rock			

SLAM CITY SERIES 1	MOC	LOOSE	VALUE
Alberto Del Rio			
Big Show			
Brock Lesnar			
John Cena			
Kane			
Rey Mysterio			

SLAM CITY SERIES 2	MOC	LOOSE	VALUE
Daniel Bryan			
Stone Cold Steve Austin			
The Undertaker			

SLAM CITY 2-PACKS SERIES 1	MOC	LOOSE	VALUE
CM Punk			
The Miz			
John Cena			
Dolph Ziggler			
Sheamus			
Wade Barrett			

SLAM CITY 2-PACKS SERIES 2	MOC	LOOSE	VALUE
Damien Sandow			
Alberto Del Rio			
Dolph Ziggler			
Randy Orton			
Brock Lesnar			
Mark Henry			

SLAM CITY 2-PACKS SERIES 3	MOC	LOOSE	VALUE
Randy Orton			
Santino Marella			
Sheamus			
Brock Lesnar			

SLAM CITY PLAYSETS & EXCLUSIVES		MIB	LOOSE	VALUE
4-PACK	Sheamus			
	Rey Mysterio			
	John Cena			
	Randy Orton			
PLAYSETS	Blast'N Smash Cart (w/ CM Punk)			
	Breakdown Assault Vault (w/ The Finisher)			
	Gorilla In The Cell Match (w/ Randy Orton & Gorilla)			
	Launch'N Crash Car (w/ John Cena)			
SDCC 2014	John Cena			

MIGHTY MINIS SERIES 1		MIB	LOOSE	VALUE
CHASE	Bret Hart (Blue)			
	Bret Hart (Pink)			
	Daniel Bryan			
	Dolph Ziggler			
	John Cena			
	Roman Reigns			
	Rusev			
	Seth Rollins			
	Ted Dibiase			
	The Undertaker			

MIGHTY MINIS SERIES 2		MIB	LOOSE	VALUE
	Brock Lesnar			
	Dean Ambrose			
	Goldust			
	John Cena			
	Kane			
	Stone Cold Steve Austin			
	The Rock			
	Triple H			
CHASE	Ultimate Warrior (White)			
	Ultimate Warrior (Orange)			

MIGHTY MINIS EXCLUSIVES & PLAYSETS		MIB	LOOSE	VALUE
RINGS	Portable Mini Ring (w/ Roman Reigns & Seth Rollins)			
	Portable Mini Ring (w/ Roman, Cena, HHH, Rock & Brock)			
EXCLUSIVES	Dean Ambrose (SDCC)			

BEAST MODE SERIES 1	MIB	LOOSE	VALUE
AJ Styles			
Becky Lynch			
Braun Strowman			
Daniel Bryan			
Finn Balor			
Roman Reigns			
The Rock			
Triple H			

BEAST MODE SERIES 2	MIB	LOOSE	VALUE
Becky Lynch			
Big E			
Bray Wyatt			
Kofi Kingston			
Seth Rollins			
The Rock			
The Undertaker			
Xavier Woods			

	MISCELLANEOUS MINI FIGURES	MIB	LOOSE	VALUE
MICRO SERIES 1	The Rock			
	John Cena			
	Finn Balor			
	Roman Reigns			
	AJ Styles			
MICRO SERIES 2	Braun Strowman			
	The Undertaker			
	The Rock			
	John Cena			
	AJ Styles			
FLEXTREMES	John Cena			
	The Rock			
	Roman Reigns			
	Finn Balor			

KNUCKLE CRUNCHERS SERIES 1	MIB	LOOSE	VALUE
John Cena			
Roman Reigns			
Seth Freakin' Rollins			
The Rock			

KNUCKLE CRUNCHERS SERIES 2	MIB	LOOSE	VALUE
Bobby Lashley			
Cody Rhodes			
Sheamus			
Stone Cold Steve Austin			

KNUCKLE CRUNCHERS SERIES 3	MIB	LOOSE	VALUE
AJ Styles			
Dominik Mysterio			
John Cena			
Rey Mysterio			

KNUCKLE CRUNCHERS RINGS & ACCESSORIES	MIB	LOOSE	VALUE
Rebound Ring w/ Brock Lesnar			

2010-2011 WRESTLING RINGS & PLAYSETS		MIB	LOOSE	VALUE
	ECW Superstar Ring			
TOYS 'R' US	Elimination Chamber			
	Elite Scale Ring			
	Raw Superstar Ring			
	Raw Superstar Ring (w/ John Cena & Big Show)			
	Ringside Battle Playset			
	Smackdown Superstar Ring			
K-MART	Steel Cage Match (w/ John Cena & Randy Orton)			
WALMART	Steel Cage Match (w/ John Cena & The Miz)			
K-MART	Tables, Ladders & Chairs Playset			
TOYS 'R' US	Wrestlemania Superstar Ring			

2012 WRESTLING RINGS & PLAYSETS		MIB	LOOSE	VALUE
K-MART	Backstage Brawl Playset			
TOYS 'R' US	Money In The Bank Playset (w/ Dolph Ziggler)			
K-MART	Raw Superstar Entrance Stage			
WALMART	Ringside Battle Playset (w/ John Cena & Alberto Del Rio)			
	Smackdown Superstar Ring			
	Steel Cage Accessory			
	Summerslam Superstar Ring			
K-MART	Survivor Series Superstar Ring			
	The Cell Playset			
K-MART	Tribute To The Troops Ring			
TOYS 'R' US	Wrestlemania Superstar Ring (w/ John Cena & The Rock)			
	Wrestlemania Superstar Ring (w/ Triple H & The Undertaker)			

2013-2014 WRESTLING RINGS & PLAYSETS		MIB	LOOSE	VALUE
	Behind The Scenes Brawl			
TOYS 'R' US	Money In The Bank Playset (w/ Seth Rollins)			
	Raw Superstar Ring			
TOYS 'R' US	Ringside Battle Playset (w/ Daniel Bryan)			
	Ringside Mayhem Accessory Set			
	Royal Rumble Superstar Ring			
	Smackdown Superstar Ring			
	Steel Cage Accessory			
	Summerslam Superstar Ring			
	The Cell Playset			
K-MART	Tornado Tag Team (w/ Goldust, Stardust, Mizdow & Miz)			
K-MART	Training Center Takedown			
	Ultimate Entrance Stage			
TOYS 'R' US	Wrestlemania Superstar Ring (w/ Brock Lesnar & Roman Reigns)			

	2015-2016 WRESTLING RINGS & PLAYSETS	MIB	LOOSE	VALUE
	WWE Crash Cage			
SMYTHS	Classic Steel Cage Playset (w/ Rick Rude & Ultimate Warrior)			
	Contract Chaos (w/ Finn Bálor)			
	Money In The Bank Playset (w/ Seth Rollins)			
	NXT Superstar Ring			
	Raw Superstar Ring			
SMYTHS	Ringside Battle Playset (w/ Kevin Owens)			
	Smackdown Superstar Ring			
SMYTHS	WWE Crash Cage (w/ Triple H)			

	2017-2018 WRESTLING RINGS & PLAYSETS	MIB	LOOSE	VALUE
	Contract Chaos (w/ AJ Styles)			
	Contract Chaos (w/ Sheamus)			
SMYTHS	Crash Cage (w/ AJ Styles)			
	Elimination Chamber (w/AJ Styles)			
	Money In The Bank (w/ Dean Ambrose)			
	NXT Ring			
TARGET	NXT Takeover Ring (w/ Finn Bálor)			
TOYS 'R' US	Ringside Mayhem			
	Raw Main Event Ring (w/ Goldberg)			
	Raw Ring 2017			
	Raw Ring 2018			
SMYTHS	Ringside Battle (w/ Finn Bálor)			
	Smackdown Main Event Ring (w/ Jinder Mahal)			
	Smackdown Live Ring			
TARGET	WCW Wing (w/ Dusty Rhodes)			
	Wrestlemania Ring			
TOYS 'R' US	Wrestlemania Superstar Ring (w/ The Rock & Triple H)			
TOYS 'R' US	Wrestlemania Superstar Ring (w/ John Cena & The Undertaker)			
	Wrestlemania 34 Ring (w/ Randy Orton)			
	WWE Live Ring			

	2019-2020 WRESTLING RINGS & PLAYSETS	MIB	LOOSE	VALUE
ARGOS	Contract Chaos (w/ John Cena)			
	Raw/Survivor Series Superstar Ring			
	Smackdown Live/Royal Rumble Superstar Ring			
	Wrestlemania/Summerslam Superstar Ring			
SMYTHS	Wrestlemania 36 Ring (w/ John Cena & Bray Wyatt)			

	2021-2023 WRESTLING RINGS & PLAYSETS	MIB	LOOSE	VALUE
	NXT Superstar Ring 2021			
	Raw Superstar Ring 2021			
	Smackdown Superstar Ring 2021			
	Wrestlemania Superstar Ring (w/ The Rock & John Cena)			
	Raw Superstar Ring 2022			
	Smackdown Superstar Ring 2022			
TARGET	WWE Legends Classic Ring			

WWE BLEACHER CREATURES 2013 ASSORTMENT	MIB	LOOSE	VALUE
CM Punk			
Daniel Bryan			
John Cena (Navy Shirt)			
Kane			
Ryback			
Sheamus			

WWE BLEACHER CREATURES 2014 ASSORTMENT		MIB	LOOSE	VALUE
WWESHOP EXCLUSIVES	Hulk Hogan			
	John Cena (Blue Hat)			
	Roman Reigns (Blue Outline)			
	Ultimate Warrior			

WWE BLEACHER CREATURES 2015 ASSORTMENT	MIB	LOOSE	VALUE
CM Punk			
John Cena (Green Hat)			
"Macho Man" Randy Savage (Big Stars)			
Randy Orton			

WWE BLEACHER CREATURES 2016 ASSORTMENT	MIB	LOOSE	VALUE
John Cena (Orange Shirt)			
Brock Lesnar			
Roman Reigns (Silver RR)			
The Rock (Just Bring It)			

	WWE BLEACHER CREATURES 2017 ASSORTMENT	MIB	LOOSE	VALUE
	AJ Styles (Red)			
	Bayley			
F.Y.E. EXCLUSIVE	Big E			
	Braun Strowman			
	Finn Balor (Demon)			
	John Cena (Blue Shirt)			
	Jeff Hardy			
	Kevin Owens			
F.Y.E. EXCLUSIVE	Kofi Kingston			
	Sasha Banks			
	Seth Rollins (White)			
	Shinsuke Nakamura			
	Stone Cold Steve Austin			
F.Y.E. EXCLUSIVE	Xavier Woods			

WWE BLEACHER CREATURES 2018 ASSORTMENT	MIB	LOOSE	VALUE
Alexa Bliss			
Asuka			
Big Cass			
Enzo Amore			
Finn Balor (Black Jacket)			
John Cena (Green Shirt & Hat)			
Ric Flair			
Ronda Rousey			
The Rock ($500 Shirt)			

WWE BLEACHER CREATURES 2019 ASSORTMENT	MIB	LOOSE	VALUE
AJ Styles (Blue)			
Becky Lynch			
Elias			
Finn Balor (Blue Jacket)			
"Macho Man" Randy Savage (Hat)			
Rey Mysterio			
Seth Rollins (Black Shirt)			

WWE BLEACHER CREATURES 2020 ASSORTMENT	MIB	LOOSE	VALUE
Adam Cole			
Bray Wyatt (Funhouse)			
Drew McIntyre			
"The Fiend" Bray Wyatt			
Kofi Kingston			
The Rock (Team Bring It)			
"Rowdy" Roddy Piper			
The Undertaker (Debut)			

WWE BLEACHER CREATURES 2021 ASSORTMENT		MIB	LOOSE	VALUE
MAIN LINE	Braun Strowman (Green Shirt)			
	Eddie Guerrero			
	Edge			
	Keith Lee			
	Otis			
	Randy Orton (Legend Killer)			
	Rhea Ripley			
	Triple H			
WALMART	Drew McIntyre (Talk Less T-Shirt)			
	"Macho Man" Randy Savage (Small Stars)			
	Roman Reigns (Wreck Everyone T-Shirt)			
	Stone Cold Steve Austin (Skull T-Shirt)			
	The Rock (Versace Shirt)			

WWE BLEACHER CREATURES 2022 ASSORTMENT	MIB	LOOSE	VALUE
Alexa Bliss (White Dress)			
Becky Lynch (Black Body Suit)			
Bianca Belair			
Bret Hart			
John Cena (UCME)			
Mr. T			
Riddle			
Sasha Banks			
Seth Freakin' Rollins			

WWE BLEACHER CREATURES 2023 ASSORTMENT	MIB	LOOSE	VALUE
Cody Rhodes (Entrance Gear)			
John Cena (Black Shirt)			

WWE BLEACHER CREATURES 2024 ASSORTMENT	MIB	LOOSE	VALUE
John Cena (Blue Shirt)			
LA Knight			
Roman Reigns (Tribal Chief)			

WWE KURICHA SERIES 1	MIB	LOOSE	VALUE
Becky Lynch			
"The Fiend" Bray Wyatt			
Hulk Hogan			
Rey Mysterio			
Roman Reigns			

WWE KURICHA SERIES 2	MIB	LOOSE	VALUE
Drew McIntyre			
John Cena			
"Macho Man" Randy Savage			
Seth Rollins			
The Rock			

WWE KURICHA SERIES 3	MIB	LOOSE	VALUE
Alexa Bliss			
Brock Lesnar			
Cody Rhodes			
Matt Riddle			
Randy Orton			
Roman Reigns (God Mode)			

WWE KURICHA SERIES 4	MIB	LOOSE	VALUE
Liv Morgan			
The Rock			
The Undertaker			

WWE KURICHA SERIES 5	MIB	LOOSE	VALUE
Bianca Bel Air			
Bray Wyatt			
John Cena			
Sami Zayn			
Stone Cold Steve Austin			

WWE KURICHA SERIES 6	MIB	LOOSE	VALUE
John Cena			
LA Knight			
Rhea Ripley			
Roman Reigns			

24" WWE BLEACHER BUDDIES SERIES 1	MIB	LOOSE	VALUE
Brock Lesnar			
Cody Rhodes			
Hulk Hogan			
John Cena			
Roman Reigns			
Stone Cold Steve Austin			
The Undertaker			

24" WWE BLEACHER BUDDIES SERIES 2	MIB	LOOSE	VALUE
Cody Rhodes (Suited)			
"Hollywood" Hulk Hogan			
John Cena (Blue Shirt)			
Roman Reigns (Tribal Chief)			
Seth Freakin' Rollins			
Ultimate Warrior			

WWE POP! VINYLS #01-10		MIB	LOOSE	VALUE
01	John Cena (Navy)			
01	John Cena (Orange)			
01	John Cena (Neon Green, WWEShop.com)			
01	John Cena (Blue, WWEShop.com)			
02	CM Punk			
02	CM Punk (Hot Topic)			
03	The Rock			
04	Sheamus			
05	Stone Cold Steve Austin			
05	Stone Cold Steve Austin (Gamestop)			
06	Rey Mysterio			
06	Rey Mysterio (7-Eleven)			
06	Rey Mysterio (2014 Conventions)			
07	Daniel Bryan			
07	Daniel Bryan (Hot Topic)			
07	Daniel Bryan (WWEShop.com)			
08	The Undertaker			
09	Triple H			
10	"Macho Man" Randy Savage			
10	"Macho Man" Randy Savage (FYE)			
10	"Macho Man" Randy Savage (WWEShop.com)			

WWE POP! VINYLS #11-20		MIB	LOOSE	VALUE
11	Hulk Hogan			
11	Hulk Hogan (WWEShop.com)			
11	"Hollywood" Hulk Hogan (2K15)			
12	AJ Lee (WWEShop.com)			
13	Brock Lesnar (Walmart)			
14	Brie Bella			
15	Nikki Bella			
16	Paige			
17	"Nature Boy" Ric Flair			
18	"Rowdy" Roddy Piper			
19	Sting			
19	Wolfpac Sting (Gamestop)			
20	Ultimate Warrior			

	WWE POP! VINYLS #21-30	MIB	LOOSE	VALUE
21	Andre The Giant			
22	Dolph Ziggler		UNRELEASED	
23	Roman Reigns (5 O'Clock Shadow)			
23	Roman Reigns (No 5 O'Clock Shadow)			
24	Seth Rollins			
24	Seth Rollins (FYE)			
25	Bret Hart			
26	Eva Marie			
27	Kevin Owens			
28	Bray Wyatt			
29	Big E			
30	Xavier Woods			

	WWE POP! VINYLS #31-40	MIB	LOOSE	VALUE
31	Kofi Kingston			
32	"The Heartbreak Kid" Shawn Michaels (Walgreens)			
33	Kane (Walgreens)			
34	Finn Balor			
34	Finn Balor (Chase)			
35	Mick Foley			
36	Goldberg			
37	AJ Styles			
38	"The Demon" Finn Balor (FYE)			
39	Bayley (Toys 'R' Us)			
40	Chris Jericho			
40	Chris Jericho (FYE)			

	WWE POP! VINYLS #41-50	MIB	LOOSE	VALUE
41	"Million Dollar Man" Ted Dibiase			
41	"Million Dollar Man" Ted Dibiase (Chase)			
42	Sasha Banks			
43	Iron Sheik			
43	Iron Sheik (Chase)			
44	Zack Ryder (2017 New York Comic Con Sticker)			
44	Zack Ryder (2017 Fall Convetion Sticker)			
44	Zack Ryder (Funko HQ, 1 of 500)			
45	Shinsuke Nakamura (Toys 'R' Us)			
46	The Rock			
46	The Rock (Chase)			
46	The Rock (Smackdown Live 25th Anniversary)			
47	Razor Ramon			
47	Razor Ramon (Chase)			
47	Razor Ramon (Gamestop)			
48	Bruan Strowman			
49	Alexa Bliss			
50	Shawn Michaels			

	WWE POP! VINYLS #51-60	MIB	LOOSE	VALUE
51	Jake "The Snake" Roberts			
51	Jake "The Snake" Roberts (Chase)			
52	Triple H			
52	Triple H (Chase)			
53	Mr. McMahon			
53	Mr. McMahon (Chase)			
54	Sgt. Slaughter			
55	Kurt Angle			
56	Asuka (2018 SDCC)			
56	Asuka (Target)			
56	Asuka (Walmart)			
57	Ric Flair (2K19)			
58	Ronda Rousey			
59	John Cena (Amazon Sticker)			
59	John Cena (WWEShop.com Sticker)			
60	Randy Orton			

	WWE POP! VINYLS #61-70	MIB	LOOSE	VALUE
61	Batista			
62	Charlotte Flair			
62	Charlotte Flair (Footlocker Sticker)			
62	Charlotte Flair (WWEShop.com)			
63	Ric Flair			
64	Andre The Giant (Walmart)			
65	Becky Lynch			
66	Trish Stratus			
66	Trish Stratus (Diamond Collection)			
67	Elias			
68	Bret "Hit Man" Hart			
69	The Undertaker			
69	The Undertaker (Amazon)			
70	Becky Lynch (Amazon)			

	WWE POP! VINYLS #71-80	MIB	LOOSE	VALUE
71	Hulk Hogan (Walmart)			
72	The Miz			
73	"Mean" Gene Okerlund			
74	Diesel			
74	Kevin Nash (Chase)			
75	Naomi			
75	Naomi (Chase)			
76	John Cena			
77	"The Fiend" Bray Wyatt (Amazon)			
78	The Rock			
79	"Macho Man" Randy Savage			
79	"Macho Man" Randy Savage (Gamestop)			
80	Mr. T			

	WWE POP! VINYLS #81-90	MIB	LOOSE	VALUE
81	The Undertaker (Amazon)			
82	Ric Flair (Gamestop)			
83	"Macho Man" Randy Savage (Walmart)			
84	Stone Cold Steve Austin			
85	Chyna			
86	Edge			
87	Drew McIntyre			
88	Otis			
89	Stone Cold Steve Austin (7-Eleven)			
90	Eddie Guerrero (Gamestop)			

	WWE POP! VINYLS #91-100	MIB	LOOSE	VALUE
91	The Rock (Entertainment Earth)			
92	Xavier Woods (Target)			
93	Rey Mysterio			
93	Rey Mysterio (Amazon)			
94	Angelo Dawkins			
95	Montez Ford			
96	Asuka			
97	Jerry Lawler			
98	Roman Reigns (Amazon)			
99	Triple H (Gamestop)			
100	The Fiend – Holiday (Walmart)			

	WWE POP! VINYLS #101-110	MIB	LOOSE	VALUE
101	Shawn Michael (Gamestop)			
-	The Rock – Stylized (Walmart)			
102	Becky Lynch (Target Con)			
103	Mankind (Gamestop)			
104	Alexa Bliss w/ Lilly (Walmart)			
105	Cactus Jack (Gamestop)			
106	Undertaker In Coffin (Gamestop)			
107	Alexa Bliss			
107	Alexa Bliss (Chase)			
108	Bianca Belair			
109	Dude Love			
110	Brock Lesnar (Amazon)			

	WWE POP! VINYLS #111-120	MIB	LOOSE	VALUE
111	Roman Reigns (Walmart – White Shirt)			
112	"Macho King" Randy Savage (Entertainment Earth)			
113	Paul Heyman (Gamestop)			
114	Dusty Rhodes			
115	Riddle			
116	Randy Orton			
117	Rob Van Dam (Gamestop)			
118	Finn Balor (Amazon)			
119	Bam Bam Bigelow (Walmart)			
120	Rocky Maivia			
120	Rocky Maivia (eBay)			

	WWE POP! VINYLS #121-130	MIB	LOOSE	VALUE
121	Ricky "The Dragon" Steamboat			
122	Rhea Ripley			
123	"The American Nightmare" Cody Rhodes (Walmart)			
124	"Million Dollar Man" Ted Dibiase (Gamestop)			
124	"Million Dollar Man" Ted Dibiase (Gamestop - Chase)			
125				
126	British Bulldog			
127	Beth Phoenix			
127	Beth Phoenix (Chase)			
128	King Booker			
129	Liv Morgan (Walmart)			
130	Liv Morgan			

	WWE POP! VINYLS #131-140	MIB	LOOSE	VALUE
131	Roman Reigns			
132				
133				
134	Johnny Knoxville (2023 SDCC)			
135	Big Boss Man (Gamestop)			
136	John Cena			
137	The Rock			
138	Vader			
139	Triple H (Skull King)			
140	"Ravishing" Rick Rude			

	WWE POP! VINYLS #141-150	MIB	LOOSE	VALUE
141				
142	Ultimate Warrior (Gamestop)			
143	Kane (Fanatics – 1 of 5,000)			
144	Undertaker			
145	Braun Strowman			
146	Kurt Angle			
147	"Rowdy" Roddy Piper			
148	Shotzi			
149	Hulk Hogan			
150	Rikishi (Target)			

	WWE POP! VINYLS #151-160	MIB	LOOSE	VALUE
151	The Hurricane (Target)			
152	"The American Nightmare" Cody Rhodes			
153	Sami Zayn (Funko Shop)			
154	Drew McIntyre			
155	Eddie Guerrero			
156	The Undertaker			
157	Umaga (Fanatics)			
158	Seth Rollins			
159	Lex Luger			
160	Zelina Vega			

	WWE POP! VINYLS #161-170	MIB	LOOSE	VALUE
161	Razor Ramon			
162	Mr. America			
163	Dominik Mysterio			
164				
165				
166				
167				
168	The Rock "Final Boss"			
169				
170				

WWE POP! VINYL MULTIPACKS 2015-2016		MIB	LOOSE	VALUE
BELLA TWINS	Brie Bella (Red, Live Event Exclusive)			
	Nikki Bella (Red, Live Event Exclusive)			
BELLA TWINS	Brie Bella (Black, WWEShop.com)			
	Nikki Bella (Black, WWEShop.com)			
NEW DAY	Big E (Toys 'R' Us)			
	Xavier Woods (Toys 'R' Us)			
	Kofi Kingston (Toys 'R' Us)			

WWE POP! VINYLS MULTIPACKS 2017-2018		MIB	LOOSE	VALUE
ENZO & CASS	Enzo Amore (Walgreens)			
	Big Cass (Walgreens)			
NEW DAY	Big E (FYE)			
	Xavier Woods (FYE)			
	Kofi Kingston (FYE)			
STING & LUGER	Sting (FYE)			
	Lex Luger (FYE)			
MONEY, INC.	Ted Dibiase (Walgreens)			
	I.R.S. (Walgreens)			
HARDY BOYZ	Jeff Hardy			
	Matt Hardy			

WWE POP! VINYL MULTIPACKS 2019-2021		MIB	LOOSE	VALUE
FLAIRS	Ric Flair (WWEShop.com)			
	Charlotte Flair (WWEShop.com)			
HULK & T	Hulk Hogan (Amazon)			
	Mr. T (Amazon)			
AUSTIN VS. ROCK	Stone Cold Steve Austin (w/ Raw Ring)			
	The Rock (w/ Raw Ring)			
ROCK & SOCK	The Rock (Walmart)			
	Mankind (Walmart)			

	WWE POP! VINYL MULTIPACKS 2022	MIB	LOOSE	VALUE
WM XXVIII	John Cena (w/ WM XXVIII Ring)			
	The Rock (w/ WM XXVIII Ring)			
DX	Triple H (Walmart)			
	Shawn Michaels (Walmart)			
WM IX	The Undertaker			
	Paul Bearer			
NWO	"Hollywood" Hulk Hogan (Walmart)			
	Scott Hall (Walmart)			
	Kevin Nash (Walmart)			

	WWE POP! VINYL MULTIPACKS 2023	MIB	LOOSE	VALUE
WM XII	Shawn Michaels (w/ WM XII Ring)			
	Bret "Hit Man" Hart (w/ WM XII Ring)			
WM III	Hulk Hogan (w/ WM III Ring)			
	Andre The Giant (w/ WM III Ring)			
WM 30	Brock Lesnar			
	The Undertaker			
WM 34	Triple H			
	Ronda Rousey			
SUMMER SLAM 2002	Triple H			
	Shawn Michaels			
USOS	Jey Uso			
	Jimmy Uso			

	WWE POP! VINYL MULTIPACKS 2024	MIB	LOOSE	VALUE
CHAMPS TARGET)	Edge			
	Kane			
WM VI (FANATICS)	Hulk Hogan			
	Ultimate Warrior			
USOS (FANATICS)	Jey Uso			
	Jimmy Uso			
HOGAN & THE OUSIDERS	Hulk Hogan			
	Scott Hall			
	Kevin Nash			

	WWE POP! VINYLS RIDES	MIB	LOOSE	VALUE
284	Eddie Guerrero (w/ Low Rider)			
122	Stone Cold Steve Austin (w/ Ice Machine)			

	WWE POP! MAGAZINE COVERS	MIB	LOOSE	VALUE
01	Hulk Hogan (Wrestlemania)			
02	Mr. T (Wrestlemania)			
03	Andre The Giant (Wrestlemania III)			
04	Hulk Hogan (Wrestlemania III)			
01	Hulk Hogan (Sports Illustrated)			

	WWE DELUXE POP! MOMENTS	MIB	LOOSE	VALUE
05	The Rock / Stone Cold Steve Austin / Hulk Hogan – WMXXX Toast			

	WWE FREDDY FUNKO POP! VINYLS	MIB	LOOSE	VALUE
34	Fred Rules (2015 SDCC, 1 of 500)			
34	Funkomania (2015 SDCC, 1 of 500)			
34	Battle Damage Funkomania (2015 SDCC, 1 of 500)			
52	Freddy Funko As Sting (2016 SDCC, 1 of 500)			
SE	Freddy Funko as "Macho Man" Randy Savage (2022 SDCC, 1 of 2,000)			
SE	Freddy Funko as Stone Cold Steve Austin (2023 Camp, 1 of 3,000)			

WWE BITTY POP!		MIB	LOOSE	VALUE
68	Bret "Hit Man" Hart			
50	Shawn Michaels			
73	"Mean" Gene Okerlund			
114	Dusty Rhodes			
97	Jerry "The King" Lawler			
121	Ricky "The Dragon" Steamboat			
47	Razor Ramon			
74	Diesel			
93	Rey Mysterio			
61	Batista			
126	British Bulldog			
69	The Undertaker			
11	Hulk Hogan	1/6		
52	Triple H	1/6		
84	Stone Cold Steve Austin	1/3		
46	The Rock	1/3		

WWE VINYL SODA FIGURES		MIC	LOOSE	VALUE
1 OF 15,000	Stone Cold Steve Austin			
1 OF 2,500	Stone Cold Steve Austin (Chase)			

WWE POCKET POP! 14 DAY COUNTDOWN CALENDAR	MIB	LOOSE	VALUE
Bret "Hit Man" Hart			
Chyna			
Hulk Hogan			
Jerry "The King" Lawler			
Kevin Nash			
"Macho Man" Randy Savage			
"Mean" Gene Okerlund			
Rey Mysterio			
The Rock			
Shawn Michaels			
Stone Cold Steve Austin			
Triple H			
Trish Stratus			
The Undertaker			

	WWE MYSTERY MINIS SERIES 1	MIB	LOOSE	VALUE
	Andre The Giant			
	Brie Bella			
	Daniel Bryan			
	George "The Animal" Steele			
	Hulk Hogan			
	Iron Sheik			
	John Cena			
	Nikki Bella			
	Ric Flair			
	The Rock			
	Ultimate Warrior			
	The Undertaker			
WALMART EXCLUSIVES	"Hacksaw" Jim Duggan			
	"Macho Man" Randy Savage			
	"Rowdy" Roddy Piper			

	WWE MYSTERY MINIS SERIES 2	MIB	LOOSE	VALUE
	Bret Hart			
	Brock Lesnar			
	Dusty Rhodes			
	Goldust			
	John Cena			
	Kevin Nash			
	"Million Dollar Man" Ted Dibiase			
	Randy Orton			
	Roman Reigns			
	Seth Rollins			
	Sting			
	Stone Cold Steve Austin			
TARGET EXCLUSIVES	Jake "The Snake" Roberts			
	Razor Ramon			
	Sgt. Slaughter			

	WWE PINT SIZE HEROES	MIB	LOOSE	VALUE
	Andre The Giant			
	Big E			
	Bray Wyatt			
	Brock Lesnar			
	Enzo Amore			
	John Cena			
	Kevin Owens			
	Kofi Kingston			
	"Macho Man" Randy Savage			
	Nikki Bella			
	Roman Reigns			
	Sasha Banks			
	Seth Rollins			
	Ultimate Warrior			
	The Undertaker			
	Xavier Woods			
TOYS 'R' US EXCLUSIVES	Finn Balor			
	Ric Flair			
	Stone Cold Steve Austin			
T-SHIRT BUNDLE	Ultimate Warrior			

	WWE 31" GIANT SIZE ACTION FIGURES	MIB	LOOSE	VALUE
2014	John Cena (Navy)			
	The Rock			
	John Cena (Red)			
2015	Daniel Bryan			
	"Hollywood" Hulk Hogan			
	Hulk Hogan			
	John Cena (Blue)			
2016	Brock Lesnar			
	John Cena (Green & Orange)			
	Seth Rollins			

	WWE MICRO MANIAX	MOC	LOOSE	VALUE
SERIES 1	Alexa Bliss			
	Braun Strowman			
	Daniel Bryan			
	Finn Balor			
	John Cena			
	"Macho Man" Randy Savage			
	Roman Reigns			
	Ronda Rousey			
PLAYSETS	Battle Game On Ring			

STACKDOWN

WWE STACKDOWN UNIVERSE STARTER SETS SERIES 1		MIB	LOOSE	VALUE
SCHOOL OF HARD KNOCKS	Damien Sandow			
HIGH FLYIN'	Sin Cara			
LADDER MATCH	Kofi Kingston			
COBRA CAGE	Santino Marella			
UNDERTAKERS ENTRANCE	The Undertaker			

WWE STACKDOWN UNIVERSE DELUXE SETS SERIES 1		MIB	LOOSE	VALUE
STACKDOWN RING	John Cena			
	The Miz			
	Referee			
TRAIN & RUMBLE PLAYSET	Rey Mysterio			
	Sheamus			
THE WYATT FAMILY	Luke Harper			
	Bray Wyatt			
	Erick Rowan			
WRESTLEMANIA XXX RING SET	John Cena			
	Randy Orton			
	Triple H			
	Referee			
WRESTLEMANIA XXX ENTRANCE SET	Daniel Bryan			
	John Cena			
	Batista			

WWE STACKDOWN UNIVERSE STARTER SETS SERIES 2		MIB	LOOSE	VALUE
FUNKASAURUS	Brodus Clay			
ZIG ZAG CYCLE	Dolph Ziggler			
SPRINGBOARD SPLASH	Rey Mysterio			
BROGUE KICK	Sheamus			
VIPER PIT	Randy Orton			

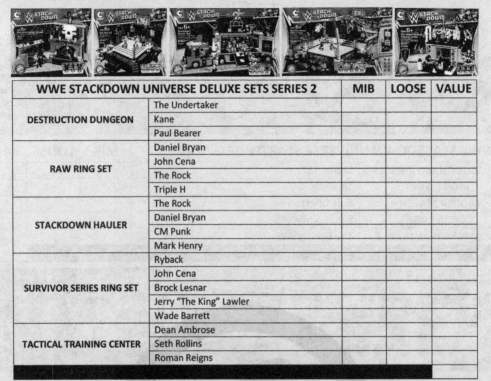

WWE STACKDOWN UNIVERSE DELUXE SETS SERIES 2		MIB	LOOSE	VALUE
DESTRUCTION DUNGEON	The Undertaker			
	Kane			
	Paul Bearer			
RAW RING SET	Daniel Bryan			
	John Cena			
	The Rock			
	Triple H			
STACKDOWN HAULER	The Rock			
	Daniel Bryan			
	CM Punk			
	Mark Henry			
SURVIVOR SERIES RING SET	Ryback			
	John Cena			
	Brock Lesnar			
	Jerry "The King" Lawler			
	Wade Barrett			
TACTICAL TRAINING CENTER	Dean Ambrose			
	Seth Rollins			
	Roman Reigns			

WWE STACKDOWN UNIVERSE STARTER SETS SERIES 3		MIB	LOOSE	VALUE
SWAMP HOUSE	Bray Wyatt			
LADDER MATCH	Dolph Ziggler			
WEIGHT ROOM	Big E			
BROGUE KICK	Sheamus			
VIPER PIT	Randy Orton			

WWE STACKDOWN UNIVERSE DELUXE SETS SERIES 3		MIB	LOOSE	VALUE
AUSTIN VS. McMAHON	Stone Cold Steve Austin			
	Mr. McMahon			
DANIEL BRYAN VS. TRIPLE H	Daniel Bryan			
	Triple H			
THE RHODES BROTHERS	Goldust			
	Stardust			
THE USOS	Jimmy Uso			
	Jey Uso			
BROCK'S ENTRANCE	Brock Lesnar			
	The Undertaker			
	Paul Heyman			
THE SHIELD SWAT TRUCK	Dean Ambrose			
	Seth Rollins			
	Roman Reigns			

WWE STACKDOWN UNIVERSE STARTER SETS SERIES 4		MIB	LOOSE	VALUE
LADDER MATCH	Bad News Barrett			
TABLE MATCH	Batista			
WEIGHT ROOM	Rusev			

WWE STACKDOWN UNIVERSE DELUXE SETS SERIES 4		MIB	LOOSE	VALUE
HOGAN VS. SAVAGE	Hulk Hogan			
	"Macho Man" Randy Savage			
CENA VS. ROCK	John Cena			
	The Rock			
HARPER & ROWAN	Luke Harper			
	Erick Rowan			
THE ROAD WARRIORS	Animal			
	Hawk			
JOHN CENA'S ENTRANCE	John Cena			
	Randy Orton			
	Nikki Bella			

WWE STACKDOWN UNIVERSE DELUXE SETS SERIES 5		MIB	LOOSE	VALUE
SMACHDOWN RING	Roman Reigns			
	Seth Rollins			
	Ultimate Warrior			

WWE STACKDOWN UNIVERSE ROYAL RUMBLE SET	MIB	LOOSE	VALUE
Roman Reigns			
Rusev			
Daniel Bryan			
Dean Ambrose			
Dolph Ziggler			
The Boogeyman			
Stardust			
Kane			
R-Truth			
Cesaro			
Bray Wyatt			

WWE STACKDOWN UNIVERSE 3-PACKS		MOC	LOOSE	VALUE
WWE LEGENDS	Andre The Giant			
	Ultimate Warrior			
	Hulk Hogan			
SHIELD	Dean Ambrose			
	Seth Rollins			
	Kane			
BEAST VS. BIG DOG	Roman Reigns			
	Brock Lesnar			
	Big Show			
WRESTLEMANIA	Roman Reigns			
	Brock Lesnar			
	Daniel Bryan			
NWO	Kevin Nash			
	"Hollywood" Hulk Hogan			
	Scott Hall			

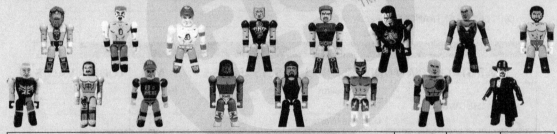

WWE STACKDOWN UNIVERSE BLING BAGS		MIB	LOOSE	VALUE
	Brock Lesnar			
	Daniel Bryan			
WALGREEN'S	Jake "The Snake" Roberts			
	John Cena (Blue)			
	John Cena (Red Shirt & Hat)			
WALGREEN'S	John Cena (Red Hat)			
	Kofi Kingston			
	Randy Orton			
	Roman Reigns			
	Sheamus			
	Sin Cara			
WALGREEN'S	Sting (Walgreen's)			
	The Rock (Trunks)			
WALGREEN'S	The Rock (Red Tank)			
	The Undertaker			
	Wade Barrett			

WWE SOFUBI FIGHTING ACTION FIGURES (2014-2015)		MIB	LOOSE	VALUE
2014	Hulk Hogan (Yellow Trunks)			
	Ultimate Warrior (Green Trunks)			
2015	Road Warrior Animal (Red)			
	Road Warrior Hawk (Red)			
	Road Warrior Animal (Blue)			
	Road Warrior Hawk (Blue)			
	Road Warrior Animal (AWA)			
	Road Warrior Hawk (AWA)			
	"Hollywood" Hulk Hogan			
	Sting (Orange Tights)			
	Ultimate Warrior (Orange Trunks)			

WWE SOFUBI FIGHTING ACTION FIGURES (2016-2017)		MIB	LOOSE	VALUE
2016	Andre The Giant (Black Strap)			
	Andre The Giant (Blue Trunks, Long Hair)			
	Andre The Giant (Blue Trunks, Afro)			
	Sting (USA)			
	Sting (Crow)			
	Undertaker (w/ Hat)			
	Vader (Black Singlet)			
	Vader (Red Vader Time Singlet)			
2017	Andre The Giant (Red Trunks, Red Boots)			
	Andre The Giant (Yellow Trunks)			
	Sting (NWO Wolfpac)			

WWE SOFUBI FIGHTING ACTION FIGURES (2018-2023)		MIB	LOOSE	VALUE
2018	Giant Machine			
2021	Andre The Giant (Red Trunks, Green Boots)			
	Mr. T (Wrestlemania I)			
	Mr. T (Wrestlemania II)			
	Ultimate Warrior (White Trunks)			
2022	Hulk Hogan (Ichiban)			
	Hulk Machine			
	Mr. America			
	Vader (Black Vader Time Singlet)			
2023	Davey Boy Smith			

WWE BE@RBRICKS		100%	400%	MOC	LOOSE	VALUE
2015	Hulkamania Logo					
	NWO Logo					
	The Undertaker					
2019, 2023	AJ Styles					
	Shinsuke Nakamura					

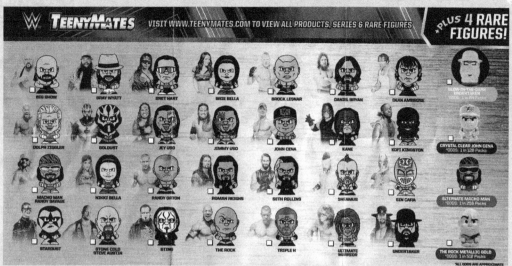

	WWE TEENYMATES SERIES 1 (2015)	MIB	LOOSE	VALUE
	Big Show			
	Bray Wyatt			
	Bret "Hitman" Hart			
	Brie Bella			
	Brock Lesnar			
	Daniel Bryan			
	Dean Ambrose			
	Dolph Ziggler			
	Goldust			
	Jey Uso			
	Jimmy Uso			
	John Cena			
1:128	John Cena (Clear)			
	Kane			
	Kofi Kingston			
	"Macho Man" Randy Savage (Orange)			
1:256	"Macho Man" Randy Savage (Purple)			
	Nikki Bella			
	Randy Orton			
	Roman Reigns			
	Seth Rollins			
	Sheamus			
	Sin Cara			
	Stardust			
	Sting			
	Stone Cold Steve Austin			
	The Rock			
1:512	The Rock (Gold)			
	Triple H			
	Ultimate Warrior			
	The Undertaker			
1:64	The Undertaker (Glow In The Dark)			

	WWE TEENYMATES SERIES 2 (2016)	MIB	LOOSE	VALUE
	AJ Styles			
	Andre The Giant			
	Becky Lynch			
	Big E			
	Bray Wyatt			
	Brock Lesnar			
	Chris Jericho			
	Dean Ambrose			
	Finn Bálor			
1:56	Finn Bálor (Glow In The Dark)			
	Jake "The Snake" Roberts			
	John Cena			
1:128	John Cena (Blue Ice)			
	Kane			
	Kevin Owens			
	Kofi Kingston			
	"Macho Man" Randy Savage			
	Mankind			
	Ric Flair (Pink)			
1:256	Ric Flair (Blue)			
	Roman Reigns			
	"Rowdy" Roddy Piper			
	Sasha Banks			
	Seth Rollins			
1:32	Sgt. Slaughter			
	Shawn Michaels			
	Sting			
	The Rock			
	Triple H			
	Ultimate Warrior			
1:512	Ultimate Warrior (Gold)			
	Xavier Woods			

WWE/TMNT NINJA SUPERSTARS SERIES 1		MIB	LOOSE	VALUE
DONATELLO	The Undertaker			
LEONARDO	John Cena			
MICHELANGELO	"Macho Man" Randy Savage			
RAPHAEL	Sting			

WWE/TMNT NINJA SUPERSTARS SERIES 2		MIB	LOOSE	VALUE
DONATELLO	Ultimate Warrior			
LEONARDO	Finn Balor			
MICHELANGELO	"Rowdy" Roddy Piper			
RAPHAEL	The Rock			

S.H.Figuarts

S.H. FIGUARTS WWE SUPERSTAR SERIES	MIB	LOOSE	VALUE
Stone Cold Steve Austin			
The Rock			
Triple H			
The Undertaker			
Kane			

2016 WWE ASIA EXCLUSIVE ACTION FIGURES		MIB	LOOSE	VALUE
CARDED	John Cena			
	Roman Reigns			
	Dean Ambrose			
	Kalisto			
BOXED	John Cena			
	The Rock			
	The Undertaker			
	Kalisto			
MISC.	WWE Arena Playset			
	WWE World Heavyweight Championship w/ John Cena			

WWE SUPERSTAR BUDDIES		MIB	LOOSE	VALUE
BOXED	AJ Styles			
	John Cena			
	The Rock			
BAGGED (RINGSIDE COLLECTIBLES)	Finn Balor			
	Jeff Hardy			
	Matt Hardy			

WWE DISCOUNT STORE SUPERSTARS		MOC	LOOSE	VALUE
SERIES 1 (GENERIC CARD)	The Undertaker			
	John Cena (Blue Shoes)			
	Brock Lesnar			
	Roman Reigns (Silver Chest Logo)			
SERIES 1 (PHOTO CARD)	The Undertaker			
	John Cena (Black Shoes)			
	Brock Lesnar			
	Roman Reigns (Gold Chest Logo)			

WWE M.U.S.C.L.E. 3-PACKS		MOC	LOOSE	VALUE
SET 1	"Hacksaw" Jim Duggan			
	Sgt. Slaughter			
	Ted Dibiase			
SET 2	Iron Sheik			
	Ric Flair			
	"Mean" Gene Okerlund			
SET 3	Junkyard Dog			
	Jake "The Snake" Roberts			
	Ultimate Warrior			
SET 4	"Rowdy" Roddy Piper			
	Andre The Giant			
	"Macho Man" Randy Savage			

WWE METALS	2.5"	4"	6"	MIB	LOOSE	VALUE
AJ Styles		■	■			
Brock Lesnar		■	■			
Charlotte		■	■			
Finn Balor (Red)		■	■			
Finn Balor (White)		■	■			
John Cena		■	■			
John Cena (Loot Crate)		■	■			
Kevin Owens		■	■			
Paige		■	■			
Sami Zayn		■	■			
Sasha Banks		■	■			
Seth Rollins		■	■			
The Rock		■	■			
The Rock (Loot Crate)		■	■			
Triple H		■	■			

	WWE NANO METALFIGS SERIES 1	MOC	LOOSE	VALUE
W1	John Cena			
W2	Triple H			
W3	The Rock			
W4	Roman Reigns			
W5	Charlotte Flair			
W6	Bayley			
W7	Sami Zayn			
W8	Chris Jericho			
W9	Dean Ambrose			
W10	"Macho Man" Randy Savage			
W11	Sting			
W12	The Undertaker			

	WWE NANO METALFIGS SERIES 2	MOC	LOOSE	VALUE
W13	AJ Styles			
W14	Kevin Owens			
W15	Seth Rollins			
W16	Finn Balor			
W17	Sasha Banks			
W18	Brock Lesnar			
W19	Becky Lynch			
W20	Kalisto			
W21	Bray Wyatt			
W22	Nikki Bella			
W23	"Rowdy" Roddy Piper			
W24	Ultimate Warrior			

	WWE NANO METALFIGS BOX SET EXCLUSIVES	MIB	LOOSE	VALUE
SERIES 2 20-PACK EXCLUSIVES	Stone Cold Steve Austin			
	Alexa Bliss			
	Asuka			
	Braun Strowman			
	Bret "Hit Man" Hart			
	The Miz			
	Kofi Kingston			
	Randy Orton			
	Samoa Joe			
	Seth Rollins (White)			
	Shawn Michaels			

WWE DIE CAST FIGURES & VEHICLES	MIB	LOOSE	VALUE
"Macho Man" Randy Savage & 1973 Ford Bronco			

WWE SLAM STARS SERIES 1		MIB	LOOSE	VALUE
01.01	Stone Cold Steve Austin			
01.02	Triple H			
01.03	The Undertaker			
01.04	The Rock			

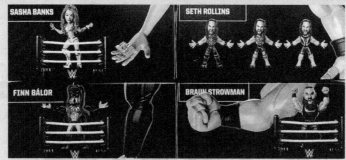

WWE SLAM STARS SERIES 2		MIB	LOOSE	VALUE
02.01	Sasha Banks (Pink Hair)			
02.02	Finn Balor			
02.03	Seth Rollins (Black & Green)			
02.03	Seth Rollins (Gray & Black)			
02.03	Seth Rollins (Black & Gold)			
02.04	Braun Strowman			

WWE SLAM STARS SERIES 3		MIB	LOOSE	VALUE
03.01	Alexa Bliss			
03.02	Ultimate Warrior			
03.03	AJ Styles			
03.04	Chris Jericho			
S.E.	Seth Rollins (White & Gold)			
S.E.	Sasha Banks (Blue Hair)			

ACTION VINYLS

WWE ACTION VINYLS SERIES 1		MIB	LOOSE	VALUE
1/12	AJ Styles			
2/12	Brock Lesnar			
1/12	"The Demon" Finn Balor (Red)			
1/96	"The Demon" Finn Balor (White)			
1/96	Finn Balor			
2/12	John Cena			
1/12	"Macho Man" Randy Savage (Purple)			
1/48	"Macho Man" Randy Savage (USA)			
ONLY 2 MADE	"Macho Man" Randy Savage (Gold)			
CLUB 28	Referee			
CLUB 28	Referee (Glow In The Dark)			
2/12	Roman Reigns			
1/48	Sasha Banks			
1/12	Shinsuke Nakamura (Red)			
1/24	Shinsuke Nakamura (Black)			
1/24	Sting			
1/12	The Undertaker			
	RAW Ring			

WWE ACTION VINYLS SERIES 2 (WALMART)		MIB	LOOSE	VALUE
2/12	AJ Styles			
2/12	Brock Lesnar			
2/12	John Cena			
CLUB 28	Referee			
2/12	Roman Reigns			
1/96	Sting (Wolfpac)			
2/12	Ultimate Warrior			
1/48	Ultimate Warrior (White)			
2/12	The Undertaker			
	Wrestlemania Ring			

WWE ACTION VINYLS SERIES 3 (TARGET)		MIB	LOOSE	VALUE
1/48	AJ Styles (Red)			
2/8	Brock Lesnar			
2/8	John Cena			
CLUB 28	Referee (Club 28)			
2/8	Roman Reigns			
2/8	"Rowdy" Roddy Piper (White)			
1/96	"Rowdy" Roddy Piper (Black)			
ONLY 1 MADE	"Rowdy" Roddy Piper (Gold)			
	Smackdown Live! Ring			

WWE ACTION VINYLS SERIES 4	MIB	LOOSE	VALUE
Andre The Giant			
Hulk Hogan (w/ Shirt)			
Hulk Hogan (w/o Shirt)			
Ric Flair			
Stone Cold Steve Austin (Silver Vest Text)			
Stone Cold Steve Austin (Gold Vest Text)			
The Rock			
The Rock (Red Outline On Trunks)			
The Rock (Bald)			
The Rock (Team Bring It)			

WWE ACTION VINYLS SDCC EXCLUSIVES		MIB	LOOSE	VALUE
	John Cena (Translucent)			
	John Cena (Translucent Blue)			
	John Cena (Translucent Green)			
1 OF 150	Andre The Giant (Chrome - 1 of 150)			
1 OF 150	Hulk Hogan (Hulk Rules - 1 of 150)			
1 OF 150	Ric Flair (Pink Robe - 1 of 150)			
1 OF 150	Stone Cold Steve Austin (Bronze Deco -1 of 150)			
1 OF 150	The Rock (Bronze Deco - 1 of 150)			

WWE ACTION VINYLS 2-PACKS		MIB	LOOSE	VALUE
PACK 1	AJ Styles			
	Shinsuke Nakamura			
PACK 2	Brock Lesnar			
	Roman Reigns			
PACK 3	John Cena			
	The Undertaker			

GARBAGE PAIL KIDS X WWE		MIB	LOOSE	VALUE
GIGANTIC ANDRE	Andre The Giant			
SAVAGE RANDY	"Macho Man" Randy Savage			
SEETHING STEVE	Stone Cold Steve Austin			
UNRAVELED WARRIOR	Ultimate Warrior			

WWE CHEEBEES	MIB	LOOSE	VALUE
"The Fiend" Bray Wyatt			
Hulk Hogan			
John Cena			
Roman Reigns			
Seth Rollins			

WWE 16D COLLECTION		MIB	LOOSE	VALUE
PVC 003	Shinsuke Nakamura			
PVC 004	Andre The Giant			
PVC 011	Asuka (Empress Mask)			
PVC 011	Asuka (Green Mask)			
PVC 018	Hulk Hogan			
PVC 018	"Hollywood" Hulk Hogan			
PVC 021	The Rock			

COLLECTOR'S BOX 3" VINYL FIGURES		MIB	LOOSE	VALUE
WYATT GYM	Muscle Man			
	Huskus The Pig Boy			
FUNHOUSE HOLIDAY	Abby The Witch			
	Ramblin' Rabbit			
THE FIEND BOX	Bray Wyatt			
	The Fiend			
MERCY THE BUZZARD	Mercy The Buzzard			
	The Boss			
WARRIOR BOX	Ultimate Warrior			
PIPER BOX	"Rowdy" Roddy Piper			
AUSTIN BOX	Stone Cold Steve Austin			
SAVAGE BOX	"Macho Man" Randy Savage			
TAKER BOX	The Undertaker			
	Paul Bearer			
EDDIE BOX	Eddie Guerrero			
RAZOR BOX	Razor Ramon			
EDGE BOX	Edge			
FOLEY BOX	Mankind			
NWO 25TH BOX	Scott Hall			
	Kevin Nash			

WWE LITTLE PEOPLE COLLECTOR SERIES BOX SET	MIB	LOOSE	VALUE
Ultimate Warrior			
"Macho Man" Randy Savage			

WWE SQUISH 'UMS	MIB	LOOSE	VALUE
John Cena			
Randy Orton			
Triple H			
Roman Reigns			
Seth Rollins			
Ronda Rousey			
Stone Cold Steve Austin			
Ultimate Warrior			

WWE COLLECTIBLE VINYL MINIS	MIB	LOOSE	VALUE
AJ Styles			
Alexa Bliss			
Andre The Giant			
Charlotte Flair			
John Cena			
Ric Flair			
Roman Reigns			
Ronda Rousey			
Sasha Banks			
Shawn Michaels			
The Rock			
Triple H			
Ultimate Warrior			
The Undertaker			

WWE OOSHIES SERIES 1	MIB	LOOSE	VALUE
AJ Styles			
Brie Bella			
Golden John Cena			
John Cena			
The Rock			

WWE STRETCH WRESTLERS		MOC	LOOSE	VALUE
SERIES 1	AJ Styles			
	Finn Balor			
	Roman Reigns			
	John Cena			
SERIES 2	AJ Styles			
	Finn Balor			
	Roman Reigns			
	John Cena			
BOX SET	Roman Reigns			
	John Cena			
	Finn Balor			

WWE GIANT STRETCH WRESTLERS		MIB	LOOSE	VALUE
SERIES 1	AJ Styles (Blue)			
	AJ Styles (Black)			
	Roman Reigns			

WWE SMASH BRAWLERS		MIB	LOOSE	VALUE
SERIES 1	Finn Bálor			
	Seth Rollins			
BATTLE GAME SET	AJ Styles			
	John Cena			

WWE BLITZ BRAWLERS	MIB	LOOSE	VALUE
AJ Styles			
John Cena			

WWE COLLECTIBLE MINIS	STAMPER	TOPPER	KEYCHAIN	MIB	LOOSE	VALUE
AJ Styles						
Alexa Bliss						
Bayley						
Becky Lynch						
Braun Strowman						
Bray Wyatt						
Daniel Bryan						
Finn Balor						
Jeff Hardy						
John Cena						
Kofi Kingston						
Rey Mysterio						
The Rock						
Roman Reigns						
Seth Rollins						
Shinsuka Nakamura						
Ultimate Warrior						
The Undertaker						

WWE WUBBLE RUMBLERS	MIB	LOOSE	VALUE
Roman Reigns			
Daniel Bryan			
The Undertaker			
Randy Orton			
Stone Cold Steve Austin			
Big E			

WWE SUPERSTARS BEND-EMS SERIES 1	MOC	LOOSE	VALUE
John Cena			
Rey Mysterio			
Roman Reigns			
Seth Rollins			

WWE LEGENDS BEND-EMS SERIES 1	MOC	LOOSE	VALUE
Hulk Hogan			
The Rock			
Stone Cold Steve Austin			
The Undertaker			

	WWE BEND-EMS MULTIPACKS	MIB	LOOSE	VALUE
MAIN EVENT ICONS 6-PACK	Bruno Sammartino			
	Charlotte Flair			
	Hulk Hogan			
	John Cena			
	The Rock			
	Roman Reigns			

SOFUBI PRO-WRESTLING SERIES 4	MOC	LOOSE	VALUE
Hulk Hogan (Yellow Trunks)			
Hulk Hogan (Ichiban)			

MISCELLANEOUS FIGURES, UNAFFILIATED RELEASES & INDEPENDENT BRANDS

LEGENDS OF PROFESSIONAL WRESTLING 2016 ASSORTMENT		MOC	LOOSE	VALUE
	The Blue Meanie			
	Jim Cornette (Red Blazer)			
VARIANT	Jim Cornette (Green Blazer)			
	New Jack			
	PJ Polaco			

LEGENDS OF PROFESSIONAL WRESTLING 2017 ASSORTMENT		MOC	LOOSE	VALUE
	Jerry Lynn			
	Shane Douglas			
	Mikey Whipwreck (Blue)			
VARIANT	Mikey Whipwreck (Pink)			
	Juventud Guerrera			

LEGENDS OF PROFESSIONAL WRESTLING 2018 ASSORTMENT		MOC	LOOSE	VALUE
	The Demon			
1 OF 200	The Demon (Spooky Empire Edition)			
	Konnan			

LEGENDS OF PROFESSIONAL WRESTLING 2020 ASSORTMENT		MOC	LOOSE	VALUE
	Chris Candido			
1 OF 100	Chris Candido			
	Francine			
1 OF 100	Francine			
	Scott Norton			
1 OF 100	Scott Norton			
	Vince Russo			
1 OF 100	Vince Russo			

LEGENDS OF PROFESSIONAL WRESTLING 2021 ASSORTMENT		MOC	LOOSE	VALUE
	Alex Wright			
VARIANT	Mikey Whipwreck (Bloody)			
VARIANT	New Jack (Bloody)			
1 OF 300	Jim Cornette (Commentator Playset)			

LEGENDS OF PROFESSIONAL WRESTLING 2022 ASSORTMENT		MOC	LOOSE	VALUE
VARIANT	Jim Cornette (Bloody)			
VARIANT	Jim Cornette (Christmas)			
VARIANT	Jim Cornette (Fuschia)			
VARIANT	Jim Cornette (Pink)			
VARIANT	The Demon (Black Hair, Silver Tights)			
VARIANT	The Blue Meanie (Blue Shirt)			
	The Sandman			
1 OF 300	The Sandman (w/ Belt & Barbed Wire)			
	Nova			

LEGENDS OF PROFESSIONAL WRESTLING 2023 ASSORTMENT	MOC	LOOSE	VALUE
Brad Armstrong			
Louie Spicolli			
Mr. Hughes			
Savio Vega			
Tom Prichard			

LEGENDS OF PROFESSIONAL WRESTLING 2024 ASSORTMENT	MOC	LOOSE	VALUE
Bobby Eaton			
Dennis Condrey			
Stan Lane			

MIDNIGHT EXPRESS 40TH ANNIVERSARY 4-PACK (2023)	MOC	LOOSE	VALUE
"Loverboy" Dennia Condrey			
"Beautiful" Bobby Eaton			
Jim Cornette			
"Sweet" Stan Lane			

LEGENDS OF PROFESSIONAL WRESTLING TAG TEAM PACKS		MOC	LOOSE	VALUE
HEAVENLY BODIES	"Doctor" Tom Prichard			
	"Sweet" Stan Lane			
MIDNIGHT EXPRESS	"Loverboy" Dennis Condrey			
	"Beautiful" Bobby Eaton			
MIDNIGHT EXPRESS	"Sweet" Stan Lane			
	"Beautiful" Bobby Eaton			

RISING STARS OF WRESTLING 2016 ASSORTMENT		MOC	LOOSE	VALUE
	AJ Styles (Red)			
VARIANT	AJ Styles (Blue)			
	Matt Jackson			
	Nick Jackson			

RISING STARS OF WRESTLING 2017 ASSORTMENT		MOC	LOOSE	VALUE
	Amber Gallows			
	Brian Cage			
	Brian Myers (Orange)			
VARIANT	Brian Myers (Blue)			
	Cliff Compton			
	Colt Cabana (White Detailing On Singlet)			
VARIANT	Colt Cabana (Red Detailing On Singlet)			
	Doc Gallows (Unpainted)			
VARIANT	Doc Gallows (Painted)			
	Kenny Omega			
VARIANT	Kenny Omega (Alternate Gear)			
	Sami Callihan			
	Tama Tonga (Painted)			
VARIANT	Tama Tonga (Unpainted)			

RISING STARS OF WRESTLING 2018 ASSORTMENT		MOC	LOOSE	VALUE
	Bull James			
	Chris Hero (Blue)			
VARIANT	Chris Hero (White)			
	Chuck Taylor (White Stripe)			
VARIANT	Chuck Taylor (Pink Stripe)			
	Homicide			
	Ivelisse			
	Jeff Cobb			
	Joey Ryan			
	Rocky Romero			
	Sonjay Dutt			
	Taya			
	Trent?			
	Trevor Lee			

RISING STARS OF WRESTLING 2020 ASSORTMENT		MOC	LOOSE	VALUE
	Flip Gordon			
	Joey Janela			
1 OF 100	Joey Janela			
	Shane Strickland			
1 OF 100	Shane Strickland			

RISING STARS OF WRESTLING 2021 ASSORTMENT		MOC	LOOSE	VALUE
	Chase Owens			
	Eli Drake			
	Ethan Page			

RISING STARS OF WRESTLING 2022 ASSORTMENT		MOC	LOOSE	VALUE
	Brian Pillman Jr.			
	David Finlay			
VARIANT	Ivelisse			
	Jay White			
	Jimmy Jacobs (Ring Gear)			
VARIANT	Jimmy Jacobs (Drag)			
	Juice Robinson			
	Rosemary			
1 OF 100	Ethan Page (V-Log Special Edition)			

	HULK HOGAN ACTION FIGURES	MIB	LOOSE	VALUE
RINGSIDE EXCLUSIVES	Hollywood Hogan (Black Box)			
	Hollywood Hogan (Red Box)			
	Hulk Hogan (Red Shirt, Long Tights)			
	Hulk Hogan (Yellow Shirt, Long Tights)			
	Hulk Hogan (Red Shirt, White Trunks)			
	Hulk Hogan (White Shirt, Blue Trunks)			
	Hulk Hogan (Yellow Shirt, Yellow Trunks)			
1:6 SCALE	Hollywood Hulk Hogan			
	Hulk Hogan (Hulkamania)			
1:4 SCALE	Hulk Hogan (Hulkamania)			

MICRO BRAWLERS

2017 PRO WRESTLING CRATE EXCLUSIVE MICRO BRAWLERS		MIB	LOOSE	VALUE
MARCH	Colt Cabana			
APRIL	Matt Jackson			
MAY	Nick Jackson			
JUNE	Taz			
JULY	"Villain" Marty Scurll			
AUGUST	Big Van Vader			
SEPTEMBER	Kenny Omega			
OCTOBER	Joey Ryan			
NOVEMBER	Penta El Zero M			
DECEMBER	CM Punk			

2017-2020 LIMITED EDITION MICRO BRAWLERS		MOC	LOOSE	VALUE
	Colt Cabana (White Elbow Pad)			
1 OF 350	Kevin Nash			
1 OF 150	Kurt Angle			
1 OF 250	Swoggle (Zombie)			
	Swoggle (Famous Wrestling Midget Shirt)			
	Vickie Guerrero			

2018 PRO WRESTLING CRATE EXCLUSIVE MICRO BRAWLERS		MIB	LOOSE	VALUE
JANUARY	Cody			
FEBRUARY	Road Warrior Animal			
MARCH	Andre The Giant			
APRIL	"Hangman" Adam Page			
MAY	Road Warrior Hawk			
JUNE	Candice Lerae			
JULY	Tetsuya Naito			
AUGUST	Tama Tonga			
SEPTEMBER	Zack Sabre Jr.			
OCTOBER	Papa Shango			
NOVEMBER	Eddie Guerrero			
DECEMBER	Kazuchika Okada			

2018 MICRO BRAWLERS SERIES 1	MIB	LOOSE	VALUE
Jay Briscoe			
Mark Briscoe			
British Bulldog			
Brooklyn Brawler			
Burnard The Business Bear			
Cheeseburger			
Chris Hero			
Cody			
Dalton Castle			
Jay Lethal			
Jay White			
Kenny Omega			
Marty Scurll			
Ricky "The Dragon" Steamboat			
"Rowdy" Roddy Piper			
Rosemary			
Sami Callihan			
Swoggle			
Tenille Dashwood			
Vickie Guerrero			
Matt Jackson			
Nick Jackson			

2019 PRO WRESTLING CRATE EXCLUSIVE MICRO BRAWLERS		MIB	LOOSE	VALUE
JANUARY	Rey Fenix			
FEBRUARY	Kota Ibushi			
MARCH	Jim Ross			
APRIL	Ultimate Warrior			
MAY	MJF			
JUNE	"Macho King" Randy Savage			
JULY	Raven			
AUGUST	Jeff Cobb			
SEPTEMBER	Ax			
OCTOBER	Smash			
NOVEMBER	Brutus "The Barber" Beefcake			
DECEMBER	Bruiser Brody			

2019 MICRO BRAWLERS SERIES 2	MIB	LOOSE	VALUE
"Badd Ass" Billy Gunn			
"Mrs. Nightmare" Brandi Rhodes			
Bushi			
Christopher Daniels			
Evil			
Flip Gordon			
Frankie Kazarian			
Hiromu Takahashi			
Joey Ryan			
Sanada			
Scorpio Sky			
Tetsuya Naito			
X-Pac			

2019 MICRO BRAWLERS SERIES 3	MIB	LOOSE	VALUE
The Blue Meanie			
Brian Cage			
Chelsea Green			
Colt Cabana			
Hiroshi Tanahashi			
Johnny Gimmick Name			
King Kong Bundy			
Mandy Leon			
Marty Scurll (2-Up)			
Masa			

2019 MICRO BRAWLERS SERIES 4	MIB	LOOSE	VALUE
Bandido			
"The Flambouyant" Juice Robinson			
Matt Taven			
TK O'Ryan			
Vinny Marseglia			
Penta El Zero M			
Hawk			
Animal			
Rush			
"Big Poppa Pump" Scott Steiner			
Taiji Ishimori			
Tomohiro Ishii			

2020 PRO WRESTLING CRATE EXCLUSIVE MICRO BRAWLERS		MIB	LOOSE	VALUE
JANUARY	Bret "The Hitman" Hart			
FEBRUARY	Kamala			
MARCH	El Generico			
APRIL	"Hacksaw" Jim Duggan			
MAY	Matt Cardona (S.T.O.M.P. In Paradise)			
JUNE	Brian Myers (S.T.O.M.P. In Paradise)			
JULY	Tommy Dreamer			
AUGUST	Honky Tonk Man			
SEPTEMBER	Chris Hero			
OCTOBER	The Boogeyman			
NOVEMBER	Koko B. Ware			
DECEMBER	Tatanka			

2020 MICRO BRAWLERS SERIES 5	MIB	LOOSE	VALUE
Arn Anderson			
Bad Luck Fale			
Chase Owens			
Dustin Rhodes			
Kazuchika Okada (Gold)			
Terry Funk			

2020 MICRO BRAWLERS SERIES 6	MIB	LOOSE	VALUE
Brody King			
Ian Riccaboni			
PCO			
Rhino			
Taya Valkyrie			
Tessa Blanchard			

2021 HARDCORE EDITION MICRO BRAWLER COLLECTION		MOC	LOOSE	VALUE
	Rob Van Dam			
1 OF 100	Rob Van Dam (Chase)			
	Sabu			
	The Sandman			

2021 PRO WRESTLING CRATE EXCLUSIVE MICRO BRAWLERS		MOC	LOOSE	VALUE
JANUARY	Jake "The Snake" Roberts			
	Jake "The Snake" Roberts (Chase - 1 of 250)			
FEBRUARY	Owen Hart			
	Owen Hart (Chase – 1 of 250)			
MARCH	Kevin Nash			
	Kevin Nash (Chase – 1 of 250)			
APRIL	Tanga Loa			
	Tanga Loa (Chase – 1 of 250)			
MAY	The Iron Sheik			
	The Iron Sheik (Chase – 1 of 250)			
JUNE	Bully Ray			
	Bully Ray (Chase – 1 of 250)			
JULY	"Flyin'" Brian Pillman			
	"Flyin'" Brian Pillman (Chase – 1 of 250)			
AUGUST	Lex Luger			
	Lex Luger (Chase – 1 of 250)			
SEPTEMBER	Adam Bomb			
	Adam Bomb (Chase – 1 of 250)			
OCTOBER	Shane Helms			
	Shane Helms (Chase – 1 of 250)			
NOVEMBER	Virgil			
	Virgil (Chase – 1 of 250)			
DECEMBER	Glacier			
	Glacier (Chase – 1 of 250)			

2021 MACHO MAN MICRO BRAWLER COLLECTION	MOC	LOOSE	VALUE
"Macho Man" Randy Savage (Classic Orange)			
"Macho Man" Randy Savage (Lime Green)			
"Macho Man" Randy Savage (Classic Pink)			
"Macho Man" Randy Savage (Mega)			
"Macho Man" Randy Savage (Black & White)			
"Macho Man" Randy Savage (USA)			
"Macho Man" Randy Savage (Stars & Stripes)			

2021 LIMITED EDITION MICRO BRAWLERS		MOC	LOOSE	VALUE
	Danhausen (w/ Cape)			
	Jordynne Grace			
	Big Van Vader (Mastadon)			
1 OF 350	Brian Knobbs (Nasty Boys)			
	Dragon Lee			
	Dynamite Kid			
1 OF 300	Francine			
1 OF 300	Frank The Clown			
1 OF 350	Jerry Sags (Nasty Boys)			
	Jonathan Gresham			
	Loose Cannon Brian Pillman			
	Luna Vachon			
1 OF 100	Luna Vachon (Chase)			
	Mortis			
	New Jack			
1 OF 250	Owen Hart			
	Owen Hart (Japan Tour)			
EXPO LUCHA	Psychosis			
	Terry Funk (Bloody)			
1 OF 150	The Iron Sheik			
1 OF 150	Barracuda Mailbox Bomber (Staff Edition)			
1 OF 150	Marvelous Matt Knicks (Staff Edition)			
	Tenille Dashwood (Teal Suit)			

2022 JOHNNY GARGANO MICRO BRAWLER COLLECTION	MOC	LOOSE	VALUE
Johnny Gargano (Stark)			
Johnny Gargano (Logan)			
Johnny Gargano (Kasady)			

2022 TALK N' SHOP-A-MANIA MICRO BRAWLER COLLECTION	MOC	LOOSE	VALUE
Sex Ferguson			
Chad 2 Badd			
Chico El Luchador			

2022 RIC FLAIR MICRO BRAWLER COLLECTION		MOC	LOOSE	VALUE
	Ric Flair (Red Robe)			
	Ric Flair (Interview)			
1 OF 100	Ric Flair (Space Mountain Chase)			
	Ric Flair (Blue Robe)			
	Ric Flair (Bloody)			
	Ric Flair (Purple Robe)			

2022 PRO WRESTLING CRATE EXCLUSIVE MICRO BRAWLERS		MOC	LOOSE	VALUE
JANUARY	I.R.S.			
	I.R.S. (Chase)			
FEBRUARY	Konnan			
	Konnan (Chase)			
MARCH	Chris Candido			
	Chris Candido (Chase)			
APRIL	The 1-2-3 Kid			
	The 1-2-3 Kid (Chase)			
MAY	The Shockmaster			
	The Shockmaster (Chase)			
JUNE	One Man Gang			
	One Man Gang (Chase)			
JULY	Awesome Kong			
	Awesome Kong (Chase)			
AUGUST	King Harley Race			
	King Harley Race (Chase)			
SEPTEMBER	Ric Flair			
	Ric Flair (Chase)			
OCTOBER	Frankenhousen			
	Frankenhausen (Chase)			
NOVEMBER	Jeff Jarrett			
	Jeff Jarrett (Chase)			
DECEMBER	Ultimo Dragon			
	Ultimo Dragon (Chase)			

2022 LIMITED EDITION MICRO BRAWLERS		MOC	LOOSE	VALUE
	Abdullah The Butcher			
1 OF 100	Abdullah The Butcher (Chase)			
	Andre The Giant (Retro)			
	Bret Hart (Hart Foundation)			
1 OF 100	Bret Hart (Hart Foundation Chase)			
	British Bulldog (Hart Foundation)			
1 OF 300	Bushwhacker Butch			
1 OF 300	Bushwhacker Luke			
1 OF 200	Cassie Lee (The Iinspiration)			
1 OF 250	Custom Cabana (WhatNot Exclusive)			
	Danhausen (Sommarhausen)			
1 OF 100	Danhausen (Sommarhausen Chase)			
1 OF 250	Delirious			
	Don West			
	Hana Kimura			
1 OF 200	Jessie McKay (The Iinspiration)			
1 OF 300	Josh Mathews			
	Nick Gage (All Star Edition)			
1 OF 250	Rachael Ellering			
	Rosemary			
	Scott Hall (Red Drips)			
1 OF 100	Scott Hall (White Drips Chase)			
1 OF 250	Warlord			

2023 LIMITED EDITION BRAWLER BUDDIES		MIB	LOOSE	VALUE
1 OF 75	Colt Cabana			
1 OF 300	Danhausen			
1 OF 250	"Macho Man" Randy Savage (Orange Trunks)			
	"Macho Man" Randy Savage (Pink Trunks)			
1 OF 250	Owen Hart			
1 OF 250	Ric Flair (Bloody)			
7"	Ric Flair (Promo)			
1 OF 250	Vader			

2023 PRO WRESTLING CRATE EXCLUSIVE MICRO BRAWLERS		MOC	LOOSE	VALUE
JANUARY	Shane Douglas			
	Shane Douglas (Chase)			
FEBRUARY	Ricky "The Dragon" Steamboat			
	Ricky "The Dragon" Steamboat (Chase)			
MARCH	Akeem			
	Akeem (Chase)			
APRIL	Greg "The Hammer" Valentine			
	Greg "The Hammer Valentine" (Chase)			
MAY	Matt Sydal			
	Matt Sydal			
JUNE	Hayabusa			
	Hayabusa (Chase)			
JULY	Scott Hall			
	Scott Hall (Chase)			
AUGUST	Skinner			
	Skinner (Chase)			
SEPTEMBER	The Berzerker			
	The Berzerker (Chase)			
OCTOBER	Gangrel			
	Gangrel (Chase)			
NOVEMBER	Big John Studd			
	Big John Studd (Chase)			
DECEMBER	Santahausen			
	Santahausen (Chase)			
	Santahausen (Ultra Chase)			

2023 LIMITED EDITION MICRO BRAWLERS		MOC	LOOSE	VALUE
	Bobby "The Brain" Heenan			
1 OF 100	Bobby "The Brain" Heenan (Chase)			
	Eddie Guerrero (Black Tiger II)			
	Mercedes Mone			
	William Regal			
1 OF 100	William Regal (Chase)			
	(AJ) Swoggle			
1 OF 50	(AJ) Swoggle (Chase)			
	Danhausen w/ Cape (Color Variant)			
	Frankenhausen (Glow In The Dark)			
	Meng			
	Katsuyori Shibata			
1 OF 400	Shark Boy			
	Will Ospreay			
	Jack Spade (Heels)			
	Breeze			
	Breeze (Chase)			
	Diamond Dallas Page (Retro)			
	Dusty Rhodes (Son of a Plumber)			
1 OF 100	Dusty Rhodes (Bloody Chase)			
	Scotty Goldman (Whatnot Exclusive)			
	Lou Lou La Duchesse De Riere			
	CM Punk (Retro)			
	Shawn Spears			
1 OF 100	Shawn Spears (Chase)			

2024 LIMITED EDITION MICRO BRAWLERS		MOC	LOOSE	VALUE
	Abraham Lincoln			
	Kurt Angle (Meme Machine)			
1 OF 500	Amazing Red			
	Jordynne Grace (Hard To Kill 2023)			
	Chris Jericho (Five Alive Edition)			
	Chavo Guerrero Jr.			
	Freelance Jack			
1 OF 300	Honky Tonk Man			
1 OF 300	Blue Meanie			
1 OF 500	Demolition Ax (w/ Mask)			
1 OF 500	Demolition Smash (w/ Mask)			
1 OF 300	Steph De Lander			

2024 PRO WRESTLING CRATE EXCLUSIVE MICRO BRAWLERS		MOC	LOOSE	VALUE
JANUARY	King Haku			
	King Haku (Chase)			
MARCH	David Arquette			
	David Arquette (Chase)			
	RJ City			
	RJ City (Chase)			
MAY	Ricky Morton			
	Ricky Morton (Chase)			
	Robert Gibson			
	Robert Gibson (Chase)			
JULY				
SEPTEMBER				
NOVEMBER				

ULTIMATE WRESTLING ACTION FIGURES		MIB	LOOSE	VALUE
ANDRE THE GIANT	Andre The Giant (Brown Entrance Vest)			
	Andre The Giant (1971 IWA World Series)			
	Andre The Giant (Yellow Trunks)			
	Andre The Giant (1987 Black Strap)			
TALK N' SHOP	Doc Gallows (Camo Jumpsuit)			
	Karl Anderson (Trunks)			

REACTION FIGURES		MOC	LOOSE	VALUE
ANDRE THE GIANT	Andre The Giant (Brown Entrance Vest)			
	Andre The Giant (Singlet)			

WRESTLING SUPERSTARS TAG TEAM	MIB	LOOSE	VALUE
Matt Jackson			
Nick Jackson			

MEGO 8" LEGENDS		MOC	LOOSE	VALUE
SERIES 1	Andre The Giant			

Pro Wrestling LOOT

BRIAN PILLMAN JR. — **JOEY RYAN** — **JUVENTUD GUERRERA** — **KAMALA** — **RODRIGUEZ**

WRESTLING SUPERSTARS BY PRO WRESTLING LOOT	MIB	LOOSE	VALUE
Brian Pillman Jr.			
Joey Ryan			
Juventud Guerrera			
Kamala			
Rodriguez			

2020 PINT SIZE ALL STARS BY PRO WRESTLING LOOT		MOC	LOOSE	VALUE
JUNE	Brian Pillman Jr.			
JULY	Ricky Morton			
	Ricky Morton (Blue Chase – 1 of 50)			
AUGUST	TJP			
	TJP (Blue Chase – 1 of 50)			
SEPTEMBER	Bobby Eaton			
	Bobby Earon (Gold Chase – 1 of 25)			
OCTOBER	Robert "Ego" Anthony			
	Robert "Ego" Anthony (Blue Chase – 1 of 50)			
	Robert "Ego" Anthony (Gold Chase – 1 of 25)			
NOVEMBER	Barry Horowitz			
DECEMBER	Paul London			
	Paul London (Blue Chase – 1 of 50)			
	Paul London (Gold Chase – 1 of 25)			

2021 PINT SIZE ALL STARS BY PRO WRESTLING LOOT		MOC	LOOSE	VALUE
JANUARY	Lisa Marie Varon			
	Lisa Marie Varon (Blue Chase – 1 of 50)			
	Lisa Marie Varon (Gold Chase – 1 of 25)			
FEBRUARY	Bobby Fulton			
	Bobby Fulton (Blue Chase – 1 of 100)			
MARCH	Harley Race			
	Harley Race (Blue Chase – 1 of 50)			
	Harley Race (Gold Chase – 1 of 25)			
APRIL	Sabu			
	Sabu (Purple Chase – 1 of 50)			
	Sabu (Red Chase – 1 of 25)			
MAY	Nick Gage (Black MDK Shirt)			
	Nick Gage (Red MDK Shirt)			
	Nick Gage (Black GCW Shirt)			
	Nick Gage (Red GCW Shirt)			
JUNE	Scott Lost			
	Scott Lost (Pink Chase – 1 of 100)			
	Scott Lost (Yellow Chase – 1 of 100)			
JULY	2 Cold Scorpio			
	2 Cold Scorpio (Red Chase – 1 of 100)			
AUGUST	Ethan Page			
SEPTEMBER	Tommy Rich			
	Tommy Rich (Blue Chase)			
DECEMBER	Ricky Morton			
	Robert Gibson			

2022 PINT SIZE ALL STARS BY PRO WRESTLING LOOT		MIB	LOOSE	VALUE
	Gene Okerlund (Blue Jacket)			
CHASE	Gene Okerlund (White Jacket)			
	George South (Red Jacket)			
CHASE	George South (Blue Jacket)			
PG-13	JC Ice			
	Wolfie D			
	Jimmy Rave (Blue Pants)			
CHASE	Jimmy Rave (White Pants)			
	Robert Ego Anthony (Red & Blue Tights)			
CHASE	Robert Ego Anthony (Purple & Yellow Tights)			
	Superstar Bill Dundee (White Suit)			
CHASE	Superstar Bill Dundee (Purple Suit)			

2023 PINT SIZE ALL STARS BY PRO WRESTLING LOOT	MIB	LOOSE	VALUE
Bushwhacker Luke			
Jordan Oliver			

	SOFUBI PRO WRESTLING SERIES 2	MOC	LOOSE	VALUE
	Bruiser Brody			
1 OF 220	Bruiser Brody (Silver Variant)			
	Bull Nakano			
	Dynamite Kid			
1 OF 220	Dynamite Kid (Red & Yellow Variant)			
	Terry Funk (Red Trunks)			
1 OF 110	Terry Funk (Bloody Variant)			
	Road Warrior Animal			
	Road Warrior Hawk			
	Genichiro Tenryu			
	Giant Baba			
	Davey Boy Smith			
	Atsushi Onita (White & Blue)			

SOFUBI PRO WRESTLING SERIES 3	MOC	LOOSE	VALUE
Terry Funk (Blue Tights)			
Atsushi Onita (Black Jacket)			
Tiger Mask			
Aja Kong			
The Great Sasuke			
The Destroyer			
JONAH			

SOFUBI PRO WRESTLING SERIES 5	MOC	LOOSE	VALUE
Takagi Shingo			

	SOFUBI PRO WRESTLING EXCLUSIVES	MOC	LOOSE	VALUE
20TH ANNIVERSARY MEMORIAL	Giant Baba (Blue Trunks)			
	Giant Baba (Green Trunks)			
	Giant Baba (Purple Trunks)			

WRESTLING MEGASTARS SERIES 1		MOC	LOOSE	VALUE
MIND OF THE MEANIE	Nick Aldis			
	The Blue Meanie			
	Josh Shernoff			
	Bull Nakano			
	Hayabusa			
1 OF 500	"All Ego" Ethan Page (Red Trunks)			
	The Dynamite Kid			

WRESTLING MEGASTARS SERIES 1 VARIANTS			MOC	LOOSE	VALUE
	1 OF 100	Nick Aldis (Gold)			
WRESTLING TRADER	1 OF 100	Nick Aldis (Black Tights)			
JB TOYS	1 OF 100	Nick Aldis (Blue Tights)			
FIGURE COLLECTIONS	1 OF 100	Nick Aldis (Crockett Cup 2019)			
		Hayabusa (Blue)			
FITE TV		Josh Shernoff			
UK VARIANT		The Dynamite Kid (Red & Blue Attire)			
		"All Ego" Ethan Page (Black Trunks)			

WRESTLING MEGASTARS SERIES 2		MOC	LOOSE	VALUE
	Adam Bomb			
VARIANT	Adam Bomb (Radioactive)			
	Giant Haystacks (Blue)			
VARIANT	Giant Haystacks (Brown)			
	Big Daddy			
FC TOYS	Gangrel			
	Gangrel (Bloody)			
	Luna Vachon			
	Big Stevie Cool			
	The Blue Meanie			
	The Blue Meanie (Painted Beard)			
	Hollywood Nova			
	King Haku			
	Tanga Loa			

WRESTLING MEGASTARS SERIES 3		MOC	LOOSE	VALUE
	Atsushi Onita			
	Bobby "The Brain" Heenan (Red Jacket)			
1 OF 1250	Bobby "The Brain" Heenan (Black Jacket)			
	Boris Zhukov			
	Eddie Guerrero			
FC TOYS	Swoggle			

WRESTLING MEGASTARS SERIES 4	MOC	LOOSE	VALUE
"Dr. Death" Steve Williams			
Vader			

WRESTLING MEGASTARS SINGLE DROPS		MOC	LOOSE	VALUE
STANDARD CARD	Al Snow			
HEAD ART CARD	Al Snow			
AL ART CARD	Al Snow			
	Greg "The Hammer" Valentine			
DELUXE	Diamond Dallas Page			

WRESTLING MEGASTARS TAG TEAM 2-PACKS		MOC	LOOSE	VALUE
DEMOLITION	Ax			
	Smash			
POWERS OF PAIN	Warlord			
	Barbarian			
BRITISH BULLDOGS	Davey Boy Smith			
	Dynamite Kid			

	OFFICIAL ALL KNIGHTERS PRODUCT	MOC	LOOSE	VALUE
1 OF 100	Joey Knight (Purple)			
	Joey Knight (Green)			
	Joey Knight (Pink)			
1 OF 100	Joey Knight (Blue – Legion of Hasbro)			
1 OF 100	Joey Knight (Orange – Monday Night Quiz)			
1 OF 100	Joey Knight (Light Blue – 3POA Podcast)			
1 OF 100	Joey Knight (Black – Rock & Roll Collectibles)			
1 OF 100	Joey Knight (JWO)			

	OFFICIAL PREMIER WRESTLING	MOC	LOOSE	VALUE
1 OF 40	Josh Shernoff (Blue)			
1 OF 50	Josh Shernoff (Last Match)			
1 OF 50	Josh Shernoff (Premier)			
1 OF 50	Josh Shernoff (Showcase '22)			
1 OF 50	Josh Shernoff (Showcase '23)			

	UNCENSORED COLLECTION SERIES 1	MIB	LOOSE	VALUE
	Dynamite Kid (White Tights)			
CHASE	Dynamite Kid (White & Blue Tights)			
	Sabu			

	WRESTLE DUDEZ SERIES 1	MIB	LOOSE	VALUE
01	Demolition Ax			
02	Demolition Smash			

WRESTLING'S HEELS & FACES SERIES 1	MOC	LOOSE	VALUE
Brian Myers			
Matt Cardona			
Dino Bravo			
Sabu			
Earl Hebner			

WRESTLING'S HEELS & FACES SERIES 2	MOC	LOOSE	VALUE
Andre The Giant (Blue Strap)			
Bruiser Brody			
Kevin Sullivan			
King Kong Bundy			
Nick Gage			
Raven			

WRESTLING'S HEELS & FACES SERIES 3	MOC	LOOSE	VALUE
Hercules Hernandez			
Jack Tunney			
One Man Gang			
Paul Roma			
Slick			

WRESTLING'S HEELS & FACES SERIES 4	MOC	LOOSE	VALUE
Abdullah The Butcher			
Bad News Allen			
Mike Awesome			
Ric Flair			
Yoshihiro Tajiri			

WRESTLING'S HEELS & FACES 2-PACKS		MOC	LOOSE	VALUE
GCW HOMECOMING 2021	Matt Cardona			
	Nick Gage			
PUBLIC ENEMY	Johnny Grunge			
	Rocco Rock			

WRESTLING'S HEELS & FACES: SAVAGE LEGACY COLLECTION	MOC	LOOSE	VALUE
"Macho Man" Randy Savage			

WRESTLING'S HEELS & FACES SINGLE DROPS		MOC	LOOSE	VALUE
SDCC 2021	Jeff Jarrett			
BLACK FRIDAY 2021	Danhausen			
	Danhausen Accessory Pack			
NYCC 2022	Sabu (Purple Pants)			
SDCC 2023	Mike "Booger" Shaw			
NYCC 2023	Todd Pettengill (1 of 1,500)			
	"Smart" Mark Sterling (1 of 1,200 – Red Tie)			
	"Smart" Mark Sterling (1 of 500 – Purple Tie)			
BLACK FRIDAY 2023	Andre The Giant (Black Strap)			
	Johnny Gargano (Red Card)			
	Johnny Gargano (Blue Card)			
WRESTLECON 2024	Slick (1 of 1,250 – Grey Suit)			
	CM Punk			
	Larry			
SDCC 2024	Chris Candido (1 of 2,000)			
	Big Bully Busick (1 of 1,250)			

WRESTLING'S HEELS & FACES 6" SERIES 1	MIB	LOOSE	VALUE
Brian Pillman			
Jeff Jarrett			
King Kong Bundy			
Abdullah The Butcher			

	BONE CRUSHING WRESTLER SERIES 1	MOC	LOOSE	VALUE
	The Blue Meanie (Meanie Shirt)			
VARIANT	The Blue Meanie (BWO Shirt)			
	Bryan Clark (Black & Orange Singlet)			
VARIANT	Bryan Clark (Blue & Yellow Singlet)			
	Duane Gill			
	Ultimo Dragon (Green Tights)			
	Sonny Onoo (Green Suit)			
1 OF 500	Ultimo Dragon (Pink Tights)			
1 OF 500	Sonny Onoo (Yellow Suit)			
1 OF 100	Ultimo Dragon (Blue Tights)			
1 OF 100	Sonny Onoo (Black Suit)			
	"Macho Man" Randy Savage (Pink & Black)			
1 OF 200	"Macho Man" Randy Savage (Black & White)			

	BONE CRUSHING WRESTLERS RINGSIDE COLLECTION	MOC	LOOSE	VALUE
	"Sinister Minister" Father James Mitchell (Red Suit)			
1 OF 150	"Sinister Minister" Father James Mitchell (Purple Suit)			
1 OF 150	"Sinister Minister" Father James Mitchell (Black Suit)			

	WRESTLE-SOMETHING WRESTLERS SERIES 1	MOC	LOOSE	VALUE
	Chelsea Green (Blue Gear)			
1 OF 400	Chelsea Green (Major Players Gear)			
1 OF 500	Colt Cabana (Black & White Singlet)			
1 OF 500	Colt Cabana (Black & Orange Singlet)			
1 OF 500	Colt Cabana (Red Singlet)			
	Effy (Pink Jacket)			
1 OF 500	Effy (Purple Jacket)			
	Headbanger Mosh (Headbangers Shirt)			
	Headbanger Thrasher (Headbangers Shirt)			
1 OF 250	Headbanger Mosh (Figure Shirt)			
1 OF 250	Headbanger Thrasher (Figure Shirt)			
	Mike Chioda			
	Mike Chioda (Retro Carding)			
	Vlad The Superfan			

POWERTOWN ULTRAS SERIES 1		MIB	LOOSE	VALUE
#01	Verne Gagne			
#02	Lou Thesz			
#03	Magnum T.A.			
#04	Kerry Von Erich			
#05	Stan Hansen			
#06	Bruiser Brody			

POWERTOWN ULTRAS SERIES 2	MIB	LOOSE	VALUE
Dory Funk Jr.			
Jack Brisco			
Junkyard Dog			
Kamala			
Madusa			
Wahoo McDaniel			

POWERTOWN ULTRAS DIAMOND COLLECTION		MIB	LOOSE	VALUE
1 OF 2,000	Kerry Von Erich			

REMCO POWERTOWN ALL-STAR WRESTLERS SERIES 1	MOC	LOOSE	VALUE
Bobo Brazil			
"Hacksaw" Jim Duggan			
Nick Bockwinkel			
The Missing Link			
Tito Santana			
Tully Blanchard			
Magnum TA			
Ricky Morton			
Robert Gibson			

RINGMASTERS WAVE 1	MOC	LOOSE	VALUE
"The French Angel" Maurice Tillet			
JONAH			
Larry Zybszko			
Roadblock			

RINGMASTERS WAVE 1 EXCLUSIVES			MOC	LOOSE	VALUE
ASYLUM STORE (USA)	1 OF 150	JONAH (Red & Black Flames)			
ROCK & ROLL (UK)	1 OF 150	JONAH (Grey Flames)			
RUSH (USA)	1 OF 150	JONAH (Grey On Grey)			
ASYLUM STORE (USA)	1 OF 150	Larry Zybszko (Red Trunks)			
ROCK & ROLL (UK)	1 OF 150	Larry Zybszko (Red & White Trunks)			
ASYLUM STORE (USA)	1 OF 150	Roadblock (Road Closed Singlet)			
ROCK & ROLL (UK)	1 OF 150	Roadblock (Red & White Singlet)			

RINGMASTERS WAVE 2	MOC	LOOSE	VALUE
Chris Harris			
James Storm			
Joel Gertner			
Mil Muertes			

RINGMASTERS SINGLE DROPS	MOC	LOOSE	VALUE
Chris Van Vliet (Blue Suit)			
Chris Van Vliet (Black Suit)			

	FIG HEEL RETRO ACTION FIGURES	MIB	LOOSE	VALUE
	Fig Heel (Biz Logo)			
1 OF 5	Fig Heel (OG Logo)			

ASYLUM ALL-STARS SERIES 1	MIB	LOOSE	VALUE
Buff Bagwell			
Earl Hebner (Blue Shirt)			
Earl Hebner (Striped Shirt)			
Road Warrior Animal			
Road Warrior Hawk			
Scott Norton			

ASYLUM ALL-STARS SERIES 2	MIB	LOOSE	VALUE
Black Tiger			
Eddie Guerrero			
Karate Man			
"Mr. 1derful" Paul Orndorff			
Sgt. Slaughter			
Tatanka			

	GRAPPLERS AND GIMMICKS SERIES 1	MOC	LOOSE	VALUE
	"Smoke Train" Charles Wright F.K.A. The Godfather			
1 OF 100	"Smoke Train" Charles Wright F.K.A. The Godfather (SDCC)			
	Tony Norris F.K.A. Ahmed Johnson			

GRAPPLERS AND GIMMICKS SERIES 2	MOC	LOOSE	VALUE
Nelson Fraszier F.K.A. Mabel			
Bobby Horne F.K.A. Mo			

GRAPPLERS AND GIMMICKS SERIES 3	MOC	LOOSE	VALUE
Mark Canterbury F.K.A. Henry O. Godwin			
Dennia Knight F.K.A. Phineas I. Godwin			
Tio Savio F.K.A. Savio Vega			

GRAPPLERS AND GIMMICKS SERIES 4	MOC	LOOSE	VALUE
Mike Droese F.K.A. Duke "The Dumpster" Droese			
Greg Girard F.K.A. Oscar			
Carlos Colon Jr. F.K.A. Carlito			

	GRAPPLERS AND GIMMICKS 2-PACKS	MOC	LOOSE	VALUE
1 OF 1,000	British Bulldog			
	Diana Hart Smith			
THE CANADIANS	Pierre Carl Ouellet			
	Jacques Rougeau			
THE ROUGEAUS	Jacques Rougeau			
	Raymond Rougeau			
NEW ROCKERS	Marty Jannetty			
	Leif Cassidy			

GRAPPLERS AND GIMMICKS LIMITED EDITION RELEASES		MOC	LOOSE	VALUE
1 OF 100	"Smoke Train" Charles Wright F.K.A. The Godfather (SDCC)			
1 OF 150	Nelson Frazier Jr. F.K.A. Mabel (NYCC)			
	Bobby Horne F.K.A. Mo (NYCC)			
1 OF 700	King Nelson F.K.A. King Mabel			
1 OF 700	Nelson Frazier Jr. F.K.A. Mabel			
	Bobby Horne F.K.A. Mo			
1 OF 500	Bob Cardona			
1 OF 300	Marc Mero (Black Trunks)			
1 OF 300	Marc Mero (Yellow Trunks)			

GRAPPLERS AND GIMMICKS SINGLE DROPS	MOC	LOOSE	VALUE
Al Snow			
Aldo Motoya			
British Bulldog (1994 Bikers)			
British Bulldog (Bull Dog Trunks)			
British Bulldog (1997 Union Jack Trunks)			
Dan Spivey F.K.A. Waylon Mercy			
Harvey Whippleman			
James W. Ware F.K.A. Koko B. Ware			
Lord Alfred Hayes			
Lord Alfred Hayes (Black Suit)			
"Macho Man" Randy Savage (Hat & Jacket)			
"Macho Man" Randy Savage (1992 Edition)			
Marc Mero (Red Trunks)			
Ray Rougeau			
Sean Mooney			
Sean Mooney (Black Suit)			
Sean Morley F.K.A. Val Venis			
Tony Anthony F.K.A. TL Hopper			
Uncle Tony			

GRAPPLERS AND GIMMICKS REGIUM SERIES	MOC	LOOSE	VALUE
Al Snow			
Gangrel			
Kurt Fuller			
Tony Norris			

	KAYFABE HEROES SERIES 1	MOC	LOOSE	VALUE
1 OF 350	Mike "Mantaur" Halac (Variant A)			
1 OF 350	Mike "Mantaur" Halac (Variant B)			
1 OF 10	Mike "Mantaur" Halac (Testshot)			
1 OF 5	Mike "Mantaur" Halac (Prototype)			
	Komet Kid (Variant A)			
	Komet Kid (Variant B)			
1 OF 250	PN News (Variant A)			
1 OF 250	PN News (Variant B)			
	Yoshi Tatsu (Variant A)			
	Yoshi Tatsu (Variant B)			
	Yoshi Tatsu (Asia Exclusive)			
	Yoshi Tatsu (Merch Table Exclusive)			

KAYFABE HEROES SERIES 2	MOC	LOOSE	VALUE
Conquistador No. 1			
Conquistador No. 2			
Rene Dupree			
Sylvain Grenier			
Taka Michinoku			
TJP			

KAYFABE HEROES SERIES 3	MOC	LOOSE	VALUE
Laredo Kid			
Ox Baker			
Sam Adonis			
Samuray Del Sol			
The Great Kabuki			

MAT MANIACS SERIES 1	MOC	LOOSE	VALUE
Road Warrior Animal			
Road Warrior Hawk			
Rick Steiner			
Scott Steiner			

MEET THE AUTHOR

Fig Heel is a self-proclaimed Professional Wrestler Collector, Author, TikToker, YouTuber and overall content creator with over 130,000 social media followers. With over 32 years of collecting under his belt, Fig Heel has amassed over 10,000 pieces from all decades and eras of wrestling as well as a vast knowledge on the hobby.

In 2023, Fig Heel teamed up with WWE Superstar Xavier Woods to compete in Wheel of Fortune's Tournament of Champions for Wrestlemania week. Soon after, he accomplished a lifetime goal of releasing his own action figure and now hosts The Case Fresh Podcast alongside Fig Vault.

Other works include The Unreleased Wrestling Figure Coloring Book series and The Ultimate Wrestling Figure Checklist series which is an Amazon.com number 1 Bestseller! When not figure hunting and adding to his collection, he enjoys bodybuilding, graphic design and spending time with family and friends.

FOLLOW FIG HEEL ON SOCIAL MEDIA @FIGHEEL

MEET THE PHOTOGRAPHER

Matthew Goldberg is a photographer, videographer, brand ambassador, avid wrestling action figure collector and former collectibles columnist for WrestleZone.com, just to name a few.

Matt has created animated videos for World Wrestling Entertainment, Inc. and was the former studio photographer for All Elite Wrestling's Jazwares action figure and toy line. He is also the founder of Wrestling Figure News Source (@WrestleFigNews) on Twitter and his work was recently featured in the May 2023 issue of Pro Wrestling Illustrated as well.

You may have seen his work over the years featured by Mattel, Ringside Collectibles, TNA Impact, Jakks Pacific and many other worldwide brands!. When not producing content for brands and entertainment companies, he likes to produce imagery and videos on his social media pages.

FOLLOW MATTHEW ON SOCIAL MEDIA @MBG1211

Made in the USA
Monee, IL
16 March 2025